LITERARY CRITICISM
IN AMERICA

The American Heritage Series
OSKAR PIEST, FOUNDER

The American Heritage Series

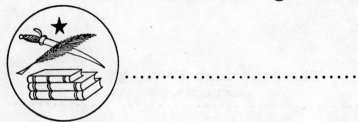

LITERARY
CRITICISM
IN AMERICA

Edited, with an Introduction, by
ALBERT D. VAN NOSTRAND

Associate Professor of English, Brown University

· ·

The American Heritage Series

published by

THE BOBBS-MERRILL COMPANY, INC.
A Subsidiary of Howard W. Sams & Co., Inc.
Publishers • Indianapolis • New York • Kansas City

ACKNOWLEDGMENTS

"The What and How in Art" is reprinted from William Dean Howells' *Literature and Life* by permission of William White Howells.

"Tradition and the Individual Talent" is from *Selected Essays 1917-1932* by T. S. Eliot, copyright, 1932, by Harcourt, Brace and Company, Inc., and reprinted with their permission.

"The Critical Process" is reprinted from *A Mencken Chrestomathy* by H. L. Mencken, by permission of Alfred A. Knopf, Inc. Copyright 1922, 1949 by Alfred A. Knopf, Inc.

"The Critic and American Life" is reprinted from Irving Babbitt's *On Being Creative,* copyright 1932 by Houghton Mifflin Company.

"Poets Without Laurels" is reprinted from *The World's Body* by John Crowe Ransom (copyright 1938 by Charles Scribner's Sons) with the permission of the publishers.

"The Figure a Poem Makes" is reprinted from *Complete Poems of Robert Frost.* Copyright, 1930, 1949, by Henry Holt and Company, Inc. Copyright, 1936, 1948, by Robert Frost. By permission of the publishers.

"Philoctetes: The Wound and the Bow" is reprinted from Edmund Wilson's *The Wound and the Bow* by permission of the author.

"Language as Gesture," copyright, 1943, by Richard P. Blackmur, is reprinted from his volume *Language as Gesture: Essays in Poetry,* by permission of Harcourt, Brace and Company, Inc.

CONTENTS
....

Introduction: The American Accent in Criticism   vii

LITERARY CRITICISM IN AMERICA

THE AMERICAN ACCENT
IN CRITICISM

Grant that the significance of any body of literature depends on its relevance to the rest of literature, past and present. Then consider a more particular proposition: that any national literature probably represents a characteristic way of thinking, and has, therefore, if you listen, a characteristic way of sounding—an accent. The accent of this literature probably represents several definable emphases of philosophy or ideology, and the conventions of rendering them. It is some characteristic way in a group of writers of turning a local instance to general significance. After reading and hearing a great deal of this literature you begin to recognize the accent, which explains, now and then, the sound of a line of poetry, the tone in which a character represents himself, or the manner of conveying a fashionable attitude. Delivering a lecture on "Americanism in Literature" in 1844, William Gilmore Simms began with a pause. The phrase, "American literature," was pale, he thought, with scarcely the special meaning he wanted. Rather, "Americanism is the right word," he said; "it indicates the becoming object of our aim: . . . to put Americanism in our letters." Simms's meticulous preoccupation with his subject suggests there is an American accent. His lecture was an essay at literary criticism, where characteristic attitudes are most likely to be heard, for criticism is a reliable shorthand of the whole literature.

Although its limits cannot easily be defined, literary criticism is the discipline of appraising the status and structure of particular works within a tradition of writing. The process of appraisal goes something like this paradigm: collecting precedents, acknowledging or justifying them as principles or criteria of performance, and measuring, by these principles, the work at hand. But the paradigm oversimplifies, for literary standards exist at any time about as precisely as standards of morality or worship exist. The process of criticism, moreover, continuously involves discernment. Dryden's summoning the works of Ovid and Chaucer, for instance, or Eliot's the works of Milton—each to explain his own writings—are themselves acts of discernment.

Literary criticism responds to certain conventions which make its shape and dimensions bewilderingly vague. It is a contingent discipline, depending primarily on those prior structures, imaginative writings, which it appraises and amplifies. The criteria by which criticism measures these works, furthermore, are not necessarily literary. Fashioning a context for fruitful appraisal, criticism has drawn on anthropology, linguistics, semantics, law, psychology and psychoanalysis, biology, mathematics, and philosophy, as well as history and biography. Even the estimates to be made vary in kind, and literary criticism countenances differing emphases: aesthetics, literary theory, social and ethical theory, and the criticism of literary criticism. That Aristotle, Lessing, Whitman, and Vachel Lindsay all wrote literary criticism suggests a certain range of the subject.

With all its enabling and qualifying conventions, literary criticism in America is like criticism in any other national literature. And, as in any other criticism, its native qualities reflect emphases in the whole literature. American writing began in the mature tradition of English literature, and, by the end of the eighteenth century, responded to ideas and forms of expression in Germany, France, and Spain. Domestication was a complicated process, involving both the imitation and repudiation of inherited literary forms and ideas. But almost from the time of drafting the Constitution, American writing began to change the European legacies. Several historical facts— more properly, the combination of these facts—conditioned this process of domestication. One was the political fact of independence. Another was the economic fact of commercial book production. And a third was the acute consciousness of the doctrine of a utilitarian literature.

Political independence bred a self-consciousness of autonomy
and a conviction that the nation was set apart from all others,
not only politically and economically, but philosophically and
culturally as well. This self-conscious independence has remained. The immediate preoccupation was with a literary tradition—or the lack of one; and the attempt to codify a national
literature and the concern for borrowing, imitation, and originality are still matters of critical concern. This vexing need for
a national literature found expression in a kind of syllogism:
the glories of the ancient world and the mother country have
prevailed by means of a dedicated literature: America has
achieved comparable beginnings: our accomplishments, therefore, will prevail by means of a literature similarly dedicated.
But there were minority reports, like the statement of Walter
Channing, in 1815, that we could have no literature so long as
we shared the language of a country so totally unlike ours. He
invited his readers to consider the futility of attempting
the majesty of the Mississippi in language made for the
Thames. And contemporaries of this critic, like the garrulous
novelist, John Neal, believed that a native literature could
grow only out of authentic accounts of speech and manners in
the new republic. Like Bryant, Poe, and Howells, Neal complained of the supremacy of European literary fashions and
the initiation of conventionalities, in fiction, which had nothing to do with life at home. Neal's doctrine of exploiting the
national scene for a native literature precisely complemented
the tariff of 1816, the rechartering of the national bank, and
Henry Clay's "American System" of exploiting and marketing
the nation's material resources.

There are even political analogies in nineteenth-century
America for the process by which partisan views about literature were apotheosized into a more or less official literary theory. The *Federalist* papers, in 1787-1788, for instance, were
public and partisan, but several years later, when Hamilton
was Secretary of the Treasury, his reports on credit, banking,
and manufactures were not only public but official. Similarly,
Richard Henry Lee's convictions in his pamphlets opposing

the Constitution largely accounted for the Bill of Rights—after he became a United States senator. In literary affairs, publication in the *North American Review,* and later in the *Democratic Review* and the *Whig Review,* constituted public authority; and the criticism in these journals about the responsibilities of the critic, about the primacy of the audience, and about a native literature hardened into an official *ars criteria.*

Documenting the native scene in a responsible way remained one of the canons of critical judgment throughout the nineteenth century, and most of the literary theories of realism, after the Civil War, reflect this preoccupation. Like the poor, the charge of poverty is always with us. A hundred years after Walter Channing, Theodore Dreiser mourned the lack of any literature endemic to this materially wealthy country. The urgency of building or domesticating a literature even caused Longfellow to turn aside from the narrative of his novel, *Kavanagh* (1849), and to interpolate a discourse in which his spokesman countered chauvinism by proposing a natural—and therefore universal—rather than a merely national literature. But Longfellow's judgment was ahead of the times.

The parochial concern over borrowing and imitation, in America, promptly involved itself with the concepts of originality and of tradition, which have always been in the public domain of criticism. William Cullen Bryant's notion of the history of poetry as an incremental process anticipated by nearly a hundred years T. S. Eliot's statement of the pastness of the present and the timeliness of the past. According to Eliot, conformity to traditional, recognizable human experiences is much the same, for a writer, as individuality. Poe understood this apparent contradiction when he argued that Hawthorne's monotone was merely self-repetition, not to be mistaken for that originality which reanimates the old truths. On this point, as on most, Henry Thoreau started from scratch, waiving the supposed values of writing in consultation with predecessors. Thoreau's insistence on the firsthand experience, which Emerson made so explicit, finds a faithful response in Theodore Dreiser's "Life, Art and America" (1917), a lamentation over our secondhand literature. "Personally," wrote Dreiser, "my quarrel is with America's quarrel with original thought." Nearly everywhere you search in contemporary American writing you will discover a self-conscious awareness of original composition. Listen to Robert Frost following "The Figure a Poem Makes," or to Ernest Hemingway's Nobel Prize speech: "The writer should always try for something that has never been done or that others have tried and failed . . . . It is because we have had such great writers in the past that a writer is driven far out past where he can go, out where no one can help him."

A second fact which shaped writing in the new nation was economic. By the end of the eighteenth century in Europe, the means were at hand to produce large quantities of books. Inexpensive books widely distributed is an old idea among publishers, but it was unachievable until production methods and material could help produce machine-made paper, mechanical typesetters, and large capacity presses. Most of the basic inventions, and many of the improvements for mechanical book production were put to use in America by 1800. From the beginning, therefore—and the timing is important—from the beginning, a national literature in America has been involved with and influenced by the imperious commercial process of manufacture and distribution.

Samuel Miller, a Presbyterian clergyman, set down a careful account of this development in his two-volume history of science and the liberal arts, *A Brief Retrospect of the Eighteenth Century* (1803), reporting that more books had been printed during the past century than during the whole time preceding it since the invention of movable type. Never has the world abounded with such a profusion of literary works, he wrote; but, more significantly, authorship for the first time has become a trade. Multitudes of writers toil, "not for the promotion of science, nor even with a governing view to advance their own reputation, but for the market." "Swarms of *book-makers by profession*" have arisen, inquiring "not whether the subjects which they undertook to discuss stood in need of further investigation; or whether they were able to do them more ample justice than their predecessors; but whether *more books* might not be palmed upon the public, and made a source of emolument to the authors." This grave statement sounds curiously contemporary. It sounds, in fact, like the dark hints of commercialism which occasionally appear in *Publishers' Weekly,* the book industry's trade magazine.

Large distribution meant more than new readers; it meant that a popular book could create a significant demand for other books like it. Moreover, the lack of copyright controls, not established internationally until 1891, made it cheaper for a printer in America to pirate British writing than to pay American authors. In these facts John Neal discovered the reason for widespread imitation in America of certain literary fashions. To judge by our novel-writers, play-makers, and poets, Neal said, life in America is lived according to the conventionalities of third-rate English novels. And he distinguished, among contemporary writings, between the merchandise and the genuine art.

Two assumptions of most American literary criticism are that art and merchandise are mutually exclusive, and that one is genuine and the other spurious. Parts of Thoreau's early journals make this arbitrary distinction, and set about exposing the merchandise. "All that are printed and bound are not books," he charged; "they do not necessarily belong to letters, but are oftener to be ranked with the other luxuries and appendages of civilized life." Paper is cheap, he wrote, and there is a kind of craftsmanship by which books are cunningly compiled. And then he got to the point: there was something organized about this. "Books are for the most part wilfully and hastily written, as parts of a system, to supply a want real or imagined." The distinction between the true poet, in tune with the infinite, and the poetaster cultivating fashionable techniques is part of the romantic critical canon, another instance of which is Frank Norris' *The Responsibilities of the Novelist* (1903), but the notion of commodity trespassing on art is not exclusively romantic. Even Irving Babbitt has attributed to merchandising the success of what the book trade calls realistic fiction: "The reputation of certain books one might mention may be regarded as a triumph of 'creative' advertising. What has been created is a mirage of masterpieces where no masterpieces are."

Notwithstanding this commonplace distinction between two kinds of literature, most American criticism has stopped short of speculating on the consequences of clergyman Miller's statement that the "SPIRIT OF TRADE" has led men to write primarily "in accommodation to the *public taste,* however depraved, with a view to the most *advantageous sale."* Aside from James T. Farrell's anguish in *The Fate of Writing in America* (1946) over the limitations imposed on art by notoriety, and aside from Poe's acknowledgment of the response of audiences to the literary experience—his last review of Hawthorne's tales, for instance—American critics have generally withheld themselves from the problem of literary popularity. William Dean Howells, alone, has made a frontal assault on the subject. His noteworthy essay, "The Man of Letters as a Man of Business" (1893), analyzes the effects of commercial subsidy, and in a half-dozen other essays he makes some significant judgments. He admits the primacy of audiences, the limitations of their verdicts, and success that can be had for pandering to them. Then, having given away so much, he takes a brave and difficult position, insisting that the significant work of art must not only have fulfilled itself, but that it must also win the moral, personal, and partial-seeing public to its side. Howells regrets the artist who "gets so far away from the general, so far within himself or within a little circle of amateurs, that his highest and best work awakens no response in the multitude." Significantly, the commercial process is as much involved in Poe's judgment on Hawthorne, in Neal's judgment on contemporary fiction, in Farrell's on notoriety, or in Norris' on the artist in society as it is in Howells'. That the business of writing involves both art and commodity appears to be more characteristically American than otherwise.

These literary consequences we have been talking about

have grown not only from certain political and economic facts but as well from a self-conscious conviction that imaginative writing must be utilitarian, that it must primarily serve some calculable and purposive mission. Omnipresent in the literature, this proposition has no single legator. British neoclassicism is one source of influence; and New England Puritanism another, less obvious and more lasting. Contemporary critics have not precisely agreed on the consequential qualities of Puritanism. H. L. Mencken understood the movement in terms of a perverse and narrow morality; Van Wyck Brooks has considered it a spiritual balm for the characteristically American acquisitive instinct; John Crowe Ransom sees in it an organized effort for the technical perfection of parts, to the detriment of the whole experience. But all agree that Puritanism, whatever it was, has significantly influenced literary history in America.

Puritan doctrine clearly provided for the writer's function: to help conduct the search for self-enlightenment, that is, for the symptoms of divine grace or wrath in one's daily living; and the urgency of his mission is everywhere evident in the diaries and personal narratives of the Puritans, in their poems, their sermons, and their histories. The need to justify one's desire to improve produced a change from orthodox Calvinism to the doctrine of salvation by works, which persisted through four generations of Congregationalists. This strong ethical sense throve in Unitarianism, according to which sin is a matter of morality and salvation a matter of character. Irving Babbitt saw this development as the growth of a formidable and frightening humanitarianism. Almost from the beginning, certainly, the American mind has canonized the Arminian heresy, and there is evidence everywhere in the literature of this determination to make the writing serve some ideology or philosophy or ethic. The convictions of Franklin, of Longfellow, and of Sinclair, as disparate as they could be, were all nevertheless concerned with immediate and practical consequences.

The most sustained and explicit statement of the moral

function of literature, in American criticism, has come from a group of academic critics in the 1930s, anticipated by William Crary Brownell and led by Babbitt and Paul Elmer More. These spokesmen formulated a theory of literature and criticism called the New Humanism, committed to demonstrating that the values of literature are primarily moral values. The New Humanist assumed a dualistic view of experience and tended to associate all phenomena with moral absolutes. He postulated a realm of being—uniquely human—compassing the natural and supernatural; and he asserted, ironically, that the method of discovering this realm lay in the intuition, which could symbolically convey moral knowledge. The correlative of this moral awareness was the form of a piece of writing, although the New Humanist tended to judge literature by what it does rather than by what it is. These concepts he argued on the assumption of the critic's responsibility to enforce his ideas on the literary experience. The New Humanism subsided after a brief, noisy episode with its critics. It was hopelessly eclectic and full of logical contradictions and word-mongering. But its influences have been underrated, and the movement appears now to have been less an isolated eruption of literary theory than an explicit overstatement of this continuing characteristic—a utilitarian view of literature.

The New Humanists called for new standards of morality and art, and were greeted with standards other than they had anticipated. One response to contemporary experience was Marxist criticism, an insistent judgment of imaginative writing based on a view of the class struggle abstracted from that writing. James T. Farrell's *A Note on Literary Criticism* (1936) attacks the abuse of this principle of judgment, as practiced by Granville Hicks, Michael Gold, Isidor Schneider, Clifford Odets, and others. Farrell pointed out that Karl Marx had understood the value of the aesthetic qualities of art, but that in order to combat Kantian idealism, Marx had had to overstate his case for "functional" and "objective" art, and ought not to be so slavishly interpreted. Distinguishing between art and propaganda, both valid, Farrell saw no reason why a strike bulletin, for instance, should obviate the values of *Paradise Lost*. The kind of Marxist criticism Farrell prescribed was more nearly achieved by T. K. Whipple, a socialist on the order of Edward Bellamy. Whipple's ideal of a co-operative society committed him to applaud a functional literature. Appraising Jack London's literary achievement, for instance, Whipple wrote: "As pure literature it is small—but perhaps literature had better not be too pure." Marxist criticism, in short, represents a range of attitudes. But whatever its quarrels with other systems of ideas, however intolerable it was to the New Humanist, Marxist criticism is one more symptom of the stamina, in America, of a utilitarian view of literature.

Neither Marxist criticism nor the New Humanism had yet arrived when Van Wyck Brooks, in *America's Coming-of-Age* (1914), lamented the "conscious moral purpose" of so much American writing: "Since the day of Emerson's address on 'The American Scholar,'" he wrote, "the whole of American literature has had the semblance of one vast, all-embracing baccalaureate sermon, addressed to the private virtues of young men." And Brooks's quarrel with the consequences of this "shining deluge of righteousness" is the substance of much of his literary criticism. But Brooks notwithstanding, Emerson's theory, at least, countenanced a kind of moral beauty, whose parts are mutual causes and organically one—something like the Greek *sophrosynē*. Henry James and John Crowe Ransom have more or less subscribed to this identity, since each assigns to art the responsibility of representing nothing less than the whole experience. And on this premise, more than any other, the contemporary movement known as the New Criticism has found its way.

Coined by Joel Spingarn and defined by Ransom, the term New Criticism represents a specific philosophy of criticism. The work of art is itself an experience. The critic's appraisal must not contaminate an understanding of the experience by moral, social, historical, or other irrelevant material. In his own vocabulary, the New Critic considers admission of the history of ideas or its bearing on a poem either "fallacious" or "heretical." The business of criticism must be to inspect the complexities of the work and the architectural relationship between the parts and the whole experience which is the artifact. The form of a work is the proper subject for appraisal, but not as a symptom for moral awareness—as the New Humanism would have it. Rather, form is the whole meaning of a literary structure.

This understanding is a refinement of assumptions drawn from surprisingly disparate sources in American criticism. Attention to the internal elements of a poem or a novel, the hypothesis that the efficacy of a work is in its "expression," and that the business of criticism is not the writer's material but what he makes of it had been variously anticipated by Bryant, by Emerson and Poe, by James and Santayana and Howells, and by Garland and Norris. There were others; in fact, a primer of this kind of appraisal is Brander Matthews' "An Apology for Technic." All these spokesmen have to some degree been aware of two matters: the psychological process of transforming actual experience into art; and the properties of language. Bryant's inventories of the faculties which beget and receive poetry, Emerson's and Whitman's concept of symbolic language, Poe's hierarchy of art forms leading to beauty, and Santayana's understanding of the affinities of language and the poet's fortuitous dream, his argument that form necessarily disintegrates actuality, and his understanding—like Robert Frost's—that sound is the reality of the symbol, all testify to this simultaneous awareness of the properties of language and the process of building with these properties. The development from Walter Channing's morose prophecy to R. P. Blackmur's "Language as Gesture" scarcely needs comment.

These are some of the definable characteristics of American literary criticism. But despite definition there remains an atonal quality about the American accent. The roll call of critics in America offers no conclusively representative man: no Pope, no Johnson, no Coleridge or Arnold, who has spoken authoritatively for an age or codified the convictions of a great many people. However compelling his dicta, the American critic has tended to speak for himself. Eclecticism does not build a culture, although he has been eclectic in a perverse way: borrowing to qualify or demolish, criticizing criticism, and sticking at first assumptions—the true morality, the validity of inherited ideas, the artist in society, and the essence of originality—from the likes of which grow theories of literature. In all this he tends, each time, to begin again. This independence of thought reflects a parochialism in the whole literature, a habit of dissent about as old as the Puritan colony at Massachusetts Bay, which Thomas Hooker abandoned after two years, and from which Roger Williams and, later, Anne Hutchinson were expelled within five years of their arrivals. None of these dissenters agreed with one another, except in their distrust of orthodoxy. This parochialism somehow fits the self-conscious American manner, with a literature bent on a mission, and with the political fact which shaped its national beginnings: the fact of a new republic, and the abrupt awareness of both the privilege and the responsibility of redefining ideas, institutions, and perhaps even the way of the world.

ALBERT D. VAN NOSTRAND

LITERARY CRITICISM
IN AMERICA

WALTER CHANNING

Anonymously published, September 1815, in the third number of William Tudor's new literary magazine, the *North American Review,* this essay offers a useful comment on the literary scene in America, scarcely forty years after the fact of political independence. Its author was a layman in literary criticism. He was Walter Channing (1786-1876), born in Newport, Rhode Island, brother of William Ellery Channing and of Edward Tyrrell Channing, who later edited the *North American Review.*

Walter Channing's professional interests were broad. He was the first professor of obstetrics and of medical jurisprudence at the Harvard Medical School, and for twenty-eight years its acting dean. He was one of the founders of the Boston Lying-In Hospital, and coeditor of a medical journal. His enthusiasms were apparently countless. A member of the American Academy of Arts and Sciences, he published a volume of poems (1851), biographies of four of his medical colleagues, and two volumes of observations of medicine in Europe. An ardent Unitarian, he was a temperance reformer, a pacifist, and an educationalist. The concern of this decidedly nonprofessional critic for a national literature suggests the growing awareness of this problem in the young republic.

ESSAY ON AMERICAN LANGUAGE AND LITERATURE

"So multiplied are the connexions existing between nation and nation in modern times, that intellectual originality may justly be regarded as one of the greatest phenomena in nature."—*Lond. Quart. Review, Oct. 1814*

THE remark which stands at the head of this article comes with peculiar force from the work which contains it. It has, with the writer of the following pages, unqualified belief. He has only regretted that the authors of that work have not always written under the influence of so liberal a sentiment. They might have found in its truth some good reasons for the barrenness of American Literature.

National literature seems to be the product, the legitimate product, of a national language. Literary peculiarities and even literary originality being, the one little more than peculiarities of language, the other the result of that uncontrolled exercise of mind which a slavery to a common tongue almost necessarily prevents. If then we are now asked, why is this country deficient in literature? I would answer, in the first place, because it possesses the same language with a nation totally unlike it in almost every relation; and in the second, delights more in the acquisition of foreign literature than in a laborious independent exertion of its own intellectual powers.

Unhappily, so enslaving are these influences, that it is hardly to be hoped that we shall ever make our language conform to our situation, our intellectual vigor and originality. But is it true that a nation of real spirit and character will forever consent to copy, even though it does not get rid of the language it inherited? Would not what we have already accomplished in literature be thought well for a young people, if we wrote in our *own* tongue? Is it not the fact that when we write we are regarded as Englishmen, and are required to do as well as if we lived in England?—With these inquiries we have at present no concern; our object is rather the causes why we have done no more.

The remotest germs of literature are the native peculiarities of the country in which it is to spring. These are diversified beyond all estimation by the climate and the various other circumstances which produce them.—Next to these are the social institutions into which the various tribes of intellectual beings resolve themselves for certain specific objects. Then follow the relations which issue from these, which constitute the moral, religious, and political states, together with all the other various objects of history. All the circumstances now mentioned as the elements of literature are essentially peculiar to every nation. And we accordingly find states, even bordering on each other and the subjects at times of the same government, exhibiting striking peculiarities in their literary character. It will not refute this remark to point to a celebrated modern poet of Scotland and ask how he has done so much with a language similar to that, nay, the same with that, of a sister kingdom. Mr. Scott has given us a mere translation of his national dialect, and has most happily rendered native beauties of idiom, and even national peculiarities, by another language. But his works do not form the smallest part of the Scotch literature. We look for that in the verses of Allan Ramsay, and in the far sweeter ones of Robert Burns. These authors are essentially original. They not only give us manners, which are but practical, intellectual operations, but give them to us in the language that was made for them, and which only can give them their true form and pressure.

It will be easy to show the importance of a peculiar language to the rise and progress of literature in a country. In the first place, every nation has a strong attachment to its language. This enters into the sum total of its patriotism. Its language is valued because it is the vehicle of the intellectual state of a country to all others. It is cultivated, that the character it may be the means of establishing may be exalted. Above all other reasons, it is loved because it is peculiar, gives a peculiar national character, and preserves the intellectual labors of man. Unfortunately for this country, language in itself can never have these attractions and this importance. The language in which we speak and write is the vernacular tongue of a nation which thinks it corrupted on every other lip but its own;—of a nation which has limited its perfection by pronouncing it already perfect;—of a nation whose natural, political, religious, and literary relations and peculiarities are totally unlike our own.

The whole external character of our country is totally unlike that of England. Our descriptions, of course, which must, if we ever have a poetry, be made in the language of another country, can never be distinctive. They can never possess the peculiar claims which those of native individuality teem with; which are more beautiful to a foreigner, because he is willing, in reading them, to heighten the beauties of an obscure passage by lending it the aid of his own imagination. How tame will his language sound who would describe Niagara in language fitted for the falls at London bridge,* or attempt the majesty of the Mississippi in that which was made for the Thames? It is not meant to be even hinted that the English language is incapable of all that language can do; but that peculiarities of country, especially the great distinctive characteristic ones, and manners likewise, can be perfectly rendered only by the language which they themselves have given use to. I mean a peculiar language.

If there be nothing peculiar in the language of a country, if it be strictly the same with that of a nation very distant from it, to say the least;—if it be a country, or rather *nation of ease,*† if I may so say, a receptacle in the first place of men who had in view by emigration anything but a literary speculation, their descendants will have nothing less at heart than the cultivation of their language, and other nations will hardly look to them for literary originality.—The peculiarities of character of his ancestors will more or less tincture the descendant, and if they depended on others for their language, he will be very willing to look to the same source for his literature. If he should presume to write, however, and endeavor to convey the sentiments and emotions which peculiar circumstances have given birth to in his heart, if he should attempt the still harder task of description, how incapable would foreigners to his country and his home be to judge of the truth of his feelings or descriptions; and though in his own countrymen the language might excite kindred feelings, to his transatlantic brethren how little would there be in his

---

* These are specified because they are the only falls the author recollects to have seen in *England*. [Channing's note.]

† This allusion may not be perfectly familiar to every reader in this country. In Great Britain, as the parishes increase, so that the original parish church will not contain all the parishoners, new chapels are erected, connected with the original parish church, and these are called *chapels of ease*. [Channing's note.]

labors to admire, but the *American language and the American literature?*

In matters of science, and especially in those of the fine arts, the new country may even excel the old. By the pursuit of the first, they improve their physical condition, and original genius may find in the labors of his own pencil a language which all nations understand, and which none has been daring enough to monopolize as the peculiar vehicle of its own genius. In science, and more especially in the fine arts, America has done its part for the world. If I loved their excellence in these pursuits half as much as Englishmen, or rather English reviewers, despise our literary attainments, I would pay a passing compliment to the venerable President of the Academy, and hunt for a sentence of eulogy for the memory of Dr. Franklin.

In nothing, perhaps, can we so little pride ourselves on account of our ancestry as for its entails on our literature. And in the Babel of the revolution, which gave us a different moral and political existence, it is for our literature most heartily to be lamented that we had not found a confusion of tongues. We might to this day have wanted a grammar and a dictionary; but our descendants would have made for themselves a literature. Any man at all conversant with other languages besides his own is perpetually sensible how much the foreign literature depends upon its language. We even read most familiar thoughts as if they were new. New words, to us, give the old sentiment a new form and spirit. And, I have little doubt, few have read the pleasures of memory, as contained in the Italian of Maffei in his *Merope,* without pronouncing it original, though he had read the same things before, as well, perhaps better, sung by another poet.

The importance of a national language to the rise and progress of the literature of a country can be argued from all we know of every nation which has pretended to originality. All will be found to have attached so much consequence to their own language as to have despised most heartily, or carelessly regarded, all others but their own. Thus the French, in their best days, slighted the Augustan age of England, and even now regard her best literary productions with but slight admiration. It is also of great importance for a nation to possess and cherish peculiarities. These result from situation, from mind, or rather from the circumstances which most powerfully affect the mind. The institutions of government, &c. in the first instance borrow their peculiarities from the character of the people, and from the government these are transferred to the people; a peculiarity of feeling is thus found at last to result from the government and other various institutions of the country. Unfortunately for this country, there is no national character, unless its absence constitute one: all acknowledge the wisdom which framed its constitution, but how few have been willing to permit its influence over their characters? Their biases have all been foreign. How unlike is this to what exists in other countries? The smaller as well as the largest states of Europe have regarded all others with a jealousy which has bound them immovably to their national peculiarities. Hence all that we know of them is original. Hence their literary eminence. Now if the Germans had caught the foppery of France, and the language of England; if they had ever adopted the government of the one, and the mode of religion of the other, we should not have been dazzled with the splendid obscurity of their metaphysics, much less overwhelmed with the power of their drama, or enchanted with their sentimentality. The German government and the German established faith gave rise to remarkable character, and their language could alone embody it. The genuine patriotism which the political institutions of this country might have produced, and even with the aid of the English language might have lent its aid to the rise of literature among us, has been lost in a servile dependence on foreign politicians for political creeds, and the liberality with which nature has ornamented our native scenery has been unnoticed in a love for the mere descriptions of foreign poetry. That we are not destitute of the materials for the poet may be gained from what Mr. Campbell has done with them. His Gertrude only affords us the mournful reflection of regret that a foreigner can do as much with all that is peculiar now left us as one of our own countrymen, and that he has done more than we have any good reason to expect from them.

There is something peculiarly opposed to literary originality in the colonial existence which was unfortunately so long the condition in America. This is mentioned incidentally under the head of the importance of a peculiar language to national literature. This circumstance precluded the possibility of our possessing such a language. All that can be expected from such a colony, made up of all sorts of materials, speaking not only the dialects of the original language but the different languages of the three different nations from which it sprung, is to preserve a purity in one of them. It must first choose one, then guard it from even the least corruption to which it would be remarkably liable. It must be forever jealous to prevent and put down that adaptation of new terms for new objects, and especially for the new ideas, that different scenes and new relations might give rise to. It must wait for all improvements from abroad, acquire a literary tone from the mother country, and, like the civil jurisprudence of India, should it be as original in literature as that may be in crime, it must wait for a decision on its merits, or demerits, from the higher authorities of London. Farther, as a colony, it would never be supposed capable of altering or improving its literature, any more than its political or religious systems. When did England look to the West Indies for anything but its sugars, or to Canada for anything but its furs?

If it should happen that a mind of superior capability should find its birth in such a country, the very character of such a mind would drive it from home. It might not find time in its greater operations of thought to preserve the perfection of its language, and it would dread the contamination of an ill-educated and strictly economical association. Such minds were phenomena in the American colonies, and the possibility of this occurrence was never admitted: hence the agents of government, and the leaders at the bar, &c. like the institu-

tions themselves, were all transatlantic. The growth of prejudice was the natural production of the country, and in due
time this flourished into revolution and independence.

Farther, so far are we from possessing a literature that men
of some considerable poetical merit, men who have cultivated
their talents, have shrunk from American publication and
sought in another region for the patrons of genius. This country has a literature notwithstanding all that has been said in
this paper to the contrary. But it is not the least indebted for
it to the labor of its colonies. I now refer to the oral literature
of its aborigines.

In their original language we have names of places and
things which are but feebly rendered by our own, I should
say by the English. Their words of description are either derived from incidents, and of which they are famed to convey
their very most exact ideas, or are so formed as to convey their
signification in their sounds; and although so ridiculous in the
English dress as to be a new cause for English satire and merri-
ment, are in themselves the very language for poetry, for they
are made only for expression, and their objects are the very
element for poetry.

The language of the Indian is no less peculiar than his
manners. With him as with all other beings, language is but
the expression of manner. It was made to express his emotions
during his observance of nature, and these emotions were
taught him at a school in which the master was nature and a
most unsophisticated heart the scholar. Hence it is as bold as
his own unshackled conceptions, and as rapid as his own step.
It is now as rich as the soil on which he was nurtured, and
ornamented with every blossom that blows in his path. It is
now elevated and soaring, for his image is the eagle, and now
precipitous and hoarse as the cataract among whose mists he
is descanting. In the oral literature of the Indian, even when
rendered in a language enfeebled by excessive cultivation,
everyone has found genuine originality. Its beauties are most
of them to be traced to its peculiarities. We are delighted with
what appears its haughty independence, although we feel con-

scious at the same time it has never been submitted by its authors to the test of comparison. They have not advanced far enough in the diplomacy of letters to hazard a competition with neighboring tribes. They are most perfectly contented with their language and, if it may be so called, their literary condition. That this remark is correct I will hazard the following anecdote. A Lancastrian school was established in one of the English provinces in this country, whose benevolent object it was to improve the intellectual condition of the neighboring Indians. One Indian submitted for a few hours to the task of being taught writing. His rude efforts were applauded, and he was asked if he would return to the school the next day. His answer is remarkable, and highly characteristic. "How much will you pay me for coming?" This anecdote is not introduced with a view to show that the Indian was fearful of the debilitating effects of an English education on his *national literature,* but to show with what perfect contentment he reposed in the knowledge of that which was peculiarly his own. The length to which this discussion has already extended compels the writer to bring it to a close; and this without entering more fully than has already been done on what was considered the second cause of the barrenness of American literature, viz., the dependence of Americans on English literature, and their consequent negligence of the exertion of their own intellectual powers.

JOHN NEAL

John Neal (1793-1876) was a Quaker, born in Maine, where he spent most of his life. He was also a novelist, editor, critic, poet, real-estate promoter, historian, and student of law and language, whose literary career began with his first novel in 1817 and lasted for more than fifty years. His reputation as a novelist and a man of letters, which rivaled Cooper's, grew quickly after Neal's journey to England, in 1824, and his publication in *Blackwood's Magazine* of a series of papers on American political and literary personalities. He returned to New York and then to Portland, Maine, where, in 1829, he became editor of the literary periodical, *Yankee,* and for the rest of his life pursued his several careers.

Randolph (1823) is an epistolary novel marked by sentimentality and intrigue. Neal's description of another of his novels in the course of this fiction very nearly fits *Randolph:* "It would seem rather a vehicle for the peculiar and daring opinions of the author, than any connected and intentional development of a preconceived design. It is a great void, peopled with phantoms." Interpolated in *Randolph,* and comprising a quarter of its length, are a half-dozen letters from its hero, Edward Molton, to George Stafford, a correspondent in England. In this one-way correspondence, Edward Molton speaks for the garrulous John Neal, who was fond of larding his critical opinions with teasing conjectures—his early novels were published anonymously—about Neal's own writing.

The letter from which the present selection is reprinted is a discussion of the literary situation in America in 1823 and, in detail, of the novels of Charles Brockden Brown, James Fenimore Cooper, and, of course, John Neal.

Neal characteristically assumed that the attempt of the novelist is—or ought to be—naturalness, toward the illusion of reality. This need for naturalness, for authenticity, Neal was forever talking about; and, in this respect, his preface to the novel, *The Down-Easters, &c. &c. &c.* (1833) faithfully represents his opinions of a native literature.

FROM RANDOLPH

O UR NOVELISTS—You have frequently spoken of them, with emphasis. We have no such thing with us.—I know not why it is; but the trade of novel writing has been of late, as if by common consent, relinquished by men of genius and power, to women and children; and if, now and then, a tolerable affair comes out, like these late Scotch novels, all the world seems to run mad after it.—It is surely not well considered, this thing. Is it, Stafford? There is no class of literature which may be made to have, nay, which *has* in reality, such an influence—upon society;—and if a man who had the strength and vividness of a dramatist and a poet were called upon to reflect and to choose that mode of writing which would be most likely, if he were truly powerful, to give him the widest theater for a display of that power, it is my deliberate opinion that he would choose a *novel;*—and yet, in whose hands do we find this body of our literature?—In the feeble of heart—and the faint of spirit—the gossipping and childish. Now and then, it is true, a Godwin will break the seals and invoke the genii to ascend; but it is with an uncertain aim, and as if he were not proud of the office. So, too, there is a Maturin—he might do well; but he is haunted by the spirit of Byron and the devil himself at the same time. Such men are out of their element—novels might be made, yet, full of distinctness; full of reality, yet carrying the marvelous in every page.

But in our country, there is everything to discourage a novelist—nothing to incite him. The very name of having written a novel—although the wise and reflecting acknowledge that no literature has such an influence upon our language and manners—none such fascination—for, in its witchery, it surpasses the stage—and is read, secretly, by them that read nothing else—and them that are not permitted to visit the theater—and none so wants to be purged and purified—yet the

without any emotion, has been dug up and embalmed abroad —and lo, we have to go to another people even yet to understand who or what he was. We call him great, not because we have read him—not because he *was* great; but because foreign Reviewers have called him so.—Oh, we are a base and treacherous people—base to the reputation of our fathers; and treacherous to the inheritance of our children. We suffer all men to dictate to us—in that empire where God never meant man to be dictated to—in the empire of genius.

PREFACE TO THE DOWN-EASTERS

IF THE language and general behavior of those whom a traveler meets with in journeying over this country now should improve as much and alter as much in proportion during the next fifty years as they have within the last fifteen or twenty, there will be hardly a vestige left of our strongest and sharpest peculiarities. Our grandchildren—perhaps our children—may know as little of their immediate progenitors in the familiar business of life, of their speech, dress and general deportment, as we know in this day of research and prying curiosity about the fireside feelings, the everyday habits, and the real *spoken* language of our primitive fathers.

And what price would be too much to pay now, by any hearty lover of his country or of his country's literature, for a dialogue of their day, faithfully reported from their lips?—not imagined and put together in the closet; taken down word for word from the mouth of the *talker*—not soberly and thoughtfully prepared by a learned or popular author from a glossary and a grammar; a rough sketch if you will, but trustworthy and characteristic, and all alive with individuality—not a language that nobody on earth ever talked or thought of talking, although everybody of any pretension may have *written* it all his life long; nor such as may be found every day of the year in some quiet, sleepy, good-for-nothing book, made up to order from Dr. Blair, Allison on Taste, or the British Classics hashed over?

Tell me not that faithful representations of native character, which are neither intended for example nor offered for imitation, are of no use. They *are* of use. They bring strangers acquainted with what we are most anxious to conceal—*the truth;* and what is more, they bring us acquainted with ourselves, with our own peculiarities and our own faults.

Were I to say that, after hundreds and hundreds of volumes have been written purporting to describe the New Englander, there are but two upon the face of the earth (one a novel and the other a play) containing so much as one single phrase of *pure Yankee,* the reader would be astonished. And yet I should say no more than the simple truth. Let him go into the largest of our circulating libraries tomorrow, and tumble over a cart load of storybooks and novels, English or Scotch, native or otherwise; for the Yankee, like the Indian of our country, has been tried by every whippersnapper in literature, and by not a few distinguished writers of England, Scotland, France, Germany, and the United States; one day in a story, another in a poem; here in a play and there in a history—and for every phrase of pure New-England speech he meets with, I will undertake to find a lump of pure gold in the sweepings of the first poorhouse I come to, or to fish up a pearl from the first puddle of dirty water I find.

To judge by our novel-writers, play-makers and poets, with here and there a partial exception, rather by accident than otherwise, we have cottages and skylarks in our country; pheasants and nightingales, first families, youth of a "gentle blood," and a virtuous *peasantry;* moss-grown churches, curfews and ivy-mantled towers; with a plenty of hardhearted fathers, runaway matches—to nobody knows whom, for nobody knows what; unfaithful wives, cruel stepmothers, treacherous brothers—anything and everything, in short, which goes to the groundwork of a third-rate English or Scotch novel, and nothing—absolutely nothing—whereby a stranger would be able to distinguish an *American* story from any other, or to obtain a glimpse of our peculiar institutions or of the state of society here, if I except a short story or two by Flint—or myself—in our baby-house annuals—here and there a passage of Miss [S]edgwick, a portion of Paulding's rough, honest and powerful, though sometimes rather ill-natured portraitures, the earlier efforts of Cooper—and, I wish I might say, of Brown and Irving, but even *they* are not examples: their books are not American, though they themselves are.

Are these things to continue? I hope not. I believe not. Something I have attempted here; and more I *may* attempt hereafter, should I have time for pursuing the experiment and preparing the way for a change; but the chief work and the glory thereof must be left to others; to the younger and the more enthusiastic, with a longer life before them.

Is the language here put into the mouth of the New Englander that which is heard in real life? Are the manners here ascribed to him characteristic? Then, however peculiar and however absurd they may appear, they ought to be portrayed; nay—the more absurd and the more peculiar, so much the more do they deserve to be portrayed; and so much the better will it be, not only for my book, but for the New Englander himself. At first, he may deny the truth of the portrait—I have known such a thing to occur—I have known people refuse to believe their own ears. Do you doubt this?—Try the experiment for yourself. Do me the favor to stop the first man you hear talking, no matter where; and you will never persuade him that the transcript of his speech you hold in your hand is a faithful copy. Ten to one, he flies in a passion with you; but if you can persuade him to go home quietly, and watch his next-door neighbor for a day or two, you will be astonished at the difference in his manner when you meet again. But who would believe it! he will say. Everybody about me *talks* one language, and *writes* another.

The first step toward improvement is having our faults made visible to ourselves—and to others.

But perhaps it may be said that I do *not* give a faithful

picture. To which I answer—perhaps I *do*. And if I do not, how easy to expose me.

And if the picture *is* faithful, I am betraying my country. Be it so. If she is only to be upheld by untruth; if to speak the truth is to betray her—I shall do my best to betray her, now and forever—here and hereafter—whenever and wherever I may think it for her advantage.

WILLIAM CULLEN BRYANT

William Cullen Bryant (1794-1878), editor, poet, lawyer, and abolitionist, was born in Cummington, Massachusetts, son of a country physician, and was buried from a Unitarian church in Roslyn, Long Island. Educated partly in the rural district schools of western Massachusetts and partly by tutors, he trained for the bar and practiced in Massachusetts from 1815 to 1825. His reputation as a poet began with the publication of "Thanatopsis" in the *North American Review* in 1817, six years after he had written the poem; and his literary stature grew rapidly. He published an edition of poems (1821), and, while still practicing law, he agreed to furnish the *United States Literary Gazette* a hundred lines of poetry a month. In 1825 he became coeditor of the *New York Review and Athenaeum Magazine,* then assistant editor and finally editor and part owner of the New York *Evening Post.* The *Post* was a vigorous force in the Democratic party until Bryant's abolitionism allied the paper with the new Republican party in 1856. His editorial career effectively limited his literary energies, and the 1832 edition of his poems represents substantially his canon of poetry, although he later translated the *Iliad* and the *Odyssey* and published a half-dozen or more titles of his own. The standard editions of his works are: Parke Godwin, *The Poetical Works of William Cullen Bryant* (2 vols., 1883); and Parke Godwin, *Prose Writings of William Cullen Bryant* (2 vols., 1884).

"On Originality and Imitation" is the last of four lectures on poetry Bryant delivered to the New York Athenaeum, in 1825, at about the time he became coeditor of the *New York Review and Athenaeum Magazine.* The lectures "On the Nature of Poetry," "The Value and Uses of Poetry," "The Relation of Poetry to Time and Place," and "On Originality and Imitation," were first published in *The Prose Writings of William Cullen Bryant* by Bryant's editor and son-in-law, Parke Godwin, who wrote: "Among his papers these lectures were found, and though apparently no more than sketches, which he doubtless filled up in his oral delivery of them, they are yet full and consecutive enough to furnish us valuable information as to his views of the elementary principles of his art."

ON ORIGINALITY AND IMITATION

I PROPOSE in this lecture to say a few words on the true use and value of imitation in poetry. I mean not what is technically called the imitation of nature, but the studying and copying of models of poetic composition. There is hardly any praise of which writers in the present age, particularly writers in verse, are more ambitious than that of originality. This ambition is a laudable one, for a captivating originality is everything in the art. Whether it consists in presenting familiar things in a new and striking yet natural light, or in revealing secrets of emotion and thought which have lain undetected from the birth of literature, it is one of the most abundant and sure sources of poetic delight. It strikes us with the same sort of feeling as the finding of some beautiful spot in our familiar walks which we had never observed before, or the exhibition of some virtue in the character of a friend which we were ignorant that he possessed. It is of itself a material addition to the literary riches of the country in which it is produced; and it impresses something of its character upon that literature, which lasts as long as the productions in which it is contained are read and remembered.

Nor does it lose its peculiar charm with the lapse of time, for there is an enduring freshness and vividness in its pictures of nature, of action and emotion, that fade not with years. The poetry of Shakespeare, for instance, maintains its original power over the mind, and no more loses its living beauty by the lapse of ages than the universe grows dim and deformed in the sight of men.

It is not at all strange that a quality of so much importance to the poet should be sought after with great ardor, and that, in the zeal of pursuit, mistakes should sometimes be made as to that characteristic of it which alone is really valuable. Poets have often been willing to purchase the praise of it at the sacrifice of what is better. They have been led, by their own overeagerness to attain it, into puerile conceits, into extravagant vagaries of imagination, into overstrained exaggerations of passion, into mawkish and childish simplicity. It has given birth to outrages upon moral principle, upon decency, upon common sense; it has produced, in short, irregularities and affectations of every kind. The grandiloquous nonsense of euphuism, which threatened to overlay and smother English literature in its very cradle, the laborious wit of the metaphysical poets, who were contemporaries of Milton, the puling effeminacy of the cockney school, which has found no small favor at the present day—are all children of this fruitful parent.

It seems to me that all these errors arise from not paying sufficient attention to the consideration that poetry is an art; that, like all other arts, it is founded upon a series of experiments—experiments, in this instance, made upon the imagination and the feelings of mankind; that a great deal of its effect depends upon the degree of success with which a sagacious and strong mind seizes and applies the skill of others, and that to slight the experiences of our predecessors on this subject is a pretty certain way to go wrong. For, if we consider the matter a little more narrowly, we shall find that the most original of poets is not without very great obligations to his predecessors and his contemporaries. The art of poetry is not perfected in a day. It is brought to excellence, by slow degrees, from the first rude and imperfect attempts at versification to the finished productions of its greatest masters. The gorgeousness of poetic imagery, the curious felicities of poetic language, the music of poetic numbers, the spells of words that act like magic on the heart, are not created by one poet in any language, in any country. An innumerable multitude of sentiments, of illustrations, of impassioned forms of expression, of harmonious combinations of words, both fixed in books and floating in conversation, must previously exist either in the vernacular language of the poet or in some other which he has studied, and whose beauties and riches he seeks to transplant into his own, before he can produce any work which is destined to live.

Genius, therefore, with all its pride in its own strength, is but a dependent quality and cannot put forth its whole powers nor claim all its honors without an amount of aid from the talents and labors of others which it is difficult to calculate. In those fortunate circumstances which permit its most perfect exercise, it takes, it is true, a pre-eminent station; but, after all, it is elevated upon the shoulders of its fellows. It may create something in literature, but it does not create all, great as its merit may be. What it does is infinitely less than what is done for it; the new treasures it finds are far less in value than the old of which it makes use. There is no warrant for the notion, maintained by some, that the first poets in any language were great poets, or that, whatever their rank, they did not learn their art from the great poets in other languages. It might as well be expected that a self-taught architect would arise in a country whose inhabitants live in caves, and, without models or instruction, raise the majestic Parthenon and pile up St. Peter's into the clouds.

That there were poets in the English language before Chaucer, some of whom were not unworthy to be his predecessors, is attested by extant monuments of their verse; and, if there had not been, he might have learned his art from the polished poets of Italy, whom he studied and loved. Italy had versifiers before Dante, and, if they were not his masters, he at least found masters in the harmonious poets of a kindred dialect, the Provençal. In the Provençal language, the earliest of the cultivated tongues of modern Europe, there arose no great poet. The reason was that their literature had scarcely been brought to that degree of perfection which produces the finest specimens of poetry when the hour of its decline had come. It possessed, it is true, authors innumerable, revivers of the same art, enrichers of the same idiom, and polishers of the same system of versification, yet they never looked for models out of their own literature; they did not study the remains of ancient poetry to avail themselves of its riches; they confined themselves to such improvements and enlargements of the art as were made among themselves; and therefore their progress, though wonderful for the circumstances in which they were placed, was yet limited in comparison with that of those nations who have had access to the treasures they neglected.

In Roman literature there were poets before Lucretius, who is thought to have carried the poetry of the Latins to its highest measure of perfection; before even Ennius, who boasted of having introduced the melody of the hexameter into Latin verse. But Ennius and Lucretius and Horace and Virgil, and all the Roman poets, were, moreover, disciples of the Greeks, and sought to transfuse the spirit of the Grecian literature into their domestic tongue. Of the Greeks we discover no instructors. The oldest of their poems which we possess, the writings of Homer, are also among the most perfect. Yet we should forget all reverence for probability were we to suppose that the art of poetry was born with him. The inferior and more mechanical parts of it must have been the fruit of long and zealous cultivation; centuries must have elapsed, and thousands of trials must have been made, before the musical and various hexameter could have been brought to the perfection in which we find it in his works. His poems themselves are full of allusions to a long antiquity of poetry. All the early traditions of Greece are sprinkled with the names of its minstrels, and the heroic fables of that country are probably, in a great measure, the work of these primitive bards. Orpheus, whose verse recalled the dead, Sinus and Musæus, whom Virgil, the disciple of Homer, seats in that elysium where he forgets to place his master, are examples of a sort of immortality conferred on mere names in literature, the dim but venerable shadows of the fathers of poetry, whose works have been lost for thousands of years. These were undoubtedly the ancient bards from whose compositions Homer kindled his imagination, and, catching a double portion of their spirit, emulated and surpassed them.

At the present day, however, a writer of poems writes in a

language which preceding poets have polished, refined, and filled with forcible, graceful, and musical expressions. He is not only taught by them to overcome the difficulties of rhythmical construction, but he is shown, as it were, the secrets of the mechanism by which he moves the mind of his reader; he is shown ways of kindling the imagination and of interesting the passions which his own sagacity might never have discovered; his mind is filled with the beauty of their sentiments, and their enthusiasm is breathed into his soul. He owes much, also, to his contemporaries as well as to those who have gone before him. He reads their works, and whatever excellence he beholds in them inspires him with a strong desire to rival it—stronger, perhaps, than that excited by the writings of his predecessors; for such is our reverence for the dead that we are willing to concede to them that superiority which we are anxious to snatch from the living. Even if he should refuse to read the writings of his brethren, he cannot escape the action of their minds on his own. He necessarily comes to partake somewhat of the character of their genius, which is impressed not only on all contemporary literature, but even on the daily thoughts of those with whom he associates. In short, his mind is in a great degree formed by the labors of others; he walks in a path which they have made smooth and plain, and is supported by their strength. Whoever would entirely disclaim imitation, and aspire to the praises of complete originality, should be altogether ignorant of any poetry written by others, and of all those aids which the cultivation of poetry has lent to prose. Deprive an author of these advantages, and what sort of poetry does anyone imagine that he would produce? I dare say it would be sufficiently original, but who will affirm that it could be read?

The poet must do precisely what is done by the mathematician, who takes up his science where his predecessors have left it, and pushes its limits as much farther, and makes as many new applications of its principles, as he can. He must found himself on the excellence already attained in his art, and if, in addition to this, he delights us with new modes of sublimity, of beauty, and of human emotion, he deserves the praise of originality, and of genius. If he has nothing of all this, he is entitled to no other honor than belongs to him who keeps alive the practice of a delightful and beautiful art.

This very necessity, however, of a certain degree of dependence upon models in poetry has at some periods led into an opposite fault, to the inordinate desire of originality. The student, instead of copying nature with the aid of knowledge derived from these models, has been induced to make them the original from which the copy was to be drawn. He has been led to take an imperfect work—and all human works are imperfect—as the standard of perfection, and to dwell upon it with such reverence that he comes to see beauties where no beauties are, and excellence in place of positive defects. Thus the study of poetry, which should encourage the free and unlimited aspirations of the mind after all that is noble and beautiful, has been perverted into a contrivance to chill and repress them. It has seduced its admirers from an admiration of the works of God to an idolatry for the works of men; it has carried them from living and inexhaustible sources of poetic inspiration to drink at comparatively scanty and impure channels; it has made them to linger by the side of these instead of using them as guides to ascend to their original fountain.

It is of high importance, then, to inquire what are the proper limits of poetic imitation, or, in other words, by what means the examples and labors of others may be made use of in strengthening, and prevented from enfeebling, the native vigor of genius. No better rule has been given for this purpose than to take no particular poem nor poet, nor class of poets, as the pattern of poetic composition, but to study the beauties of all. All good poems have their peculiar merits and faults, all great poets their points of strength and weakness, all schools of poetry their agreements with good taste and their offences against it. To confine the attention and limit the admiration to one particular sort of excellence, not only tends to narrow the range of the intellectual powers, but most surely brings along with it the peculiar defects to which that sort of excellence is allied, and into which it is most apt to deviate. Thus, a poet of the Lake school, by endeavoring too earnestly after simplicity, may run into childishness; a follower of Byron, in his pursuit of energy of thought, and the intense expression of passion, may degenerate into abruptness, extravagance, or obscurity; a disciple of Scott, in his zeal for easy writing, may find himself inditing something little better than doggerel, or, at least, very dull and feeble verse; an imitator of Leigh Hunt, too intent on keeping up the vivacity and joyousness of the poetic temperament, may forget his common sense; and a poet of the school of Pope may write very polished, well-balanced verses with a great deal of antithesis and very little true feeling.

Still, these several schools have all their excellences; they have all some qualities to be admired and loved and dwelt upon. Let the student of poetry dwell upon them as long as he pleases, let him study them until they are incorporated into his mind, but let him give his admiration to no one of them exclusively. It is remarkable to what a degree the great founders of the several styles of English poetry, even of the least lofty, varied, and original, have pursued this universal search after excellence. When Pope—brilliant, witty, harmonious, and, within a certain compass, a great master of language—had fixed the poetical taste of his age, we all know what a crowd of imitators arose in his train, and how rapidly poetry declined. But the imitators of Pope failed to do what Pope did. Great as was his partiality for the French school, and closely as he had formed himself on the model of Boileau, he yet disdained not to learn much from other instructors. He went back for gems of thought and graces of style to the earlier writers of English verse—to the poets of the Elizabethan age, and, farther still, to the venerable Chaucer. He was a passionate admirer and a restorer of Shakespeare, and, by recommending him to the English people, prepared the way for the downfall of his own school, but not, I hope, for the oblivion of his own writings.

This relish of poetic excellence in all its forms, and in whatever school or style of poetry it is found, does not, I apprehend, lead to a less lively apprehension of the several merits of these styles, while at the same time it opens the eyes of the student to their several defects and errors. In this way the mind forms to itself a higher standard of excellence than exists in any of them—a standard compounded of the characteristic merits of all, and free from any of their imperfections. To this standard it will refer all their compositions; to this it will naturally aspire; and, by the contemplation of this, it will divest itself of that blind and idolatrous reverence for certain models of composition and certain dogmas of ancient criticism which are the death of the hopes and inspirations of the poet.

It is long since the authority of great names was disregarded in matters of science. Ages ago the schools shook themselves loose from the fetters of Aristotle. He no more now delivers the oracles of philosophy than the priests of Apollo deliver the oracles of religion. Why should the chains of authority be worn any longer by the heart and the imagination than by the reason? This is a question which the age has already answered. The genius of modern times has gone out in every direction in search of originality. Its ardor has not always been compensated by the discovery of its object, but under its auspices a fresh, vigorous, and highly original poetry has grown up. The fertile soil of modern literature has thrown up, it is true, weeds among the flowers, but the flowers are of immortal bloom and fragrance, and the weeds are soon outworn. It is no longer necessary that a narrative poem should be written on the model of the ancient epic; a lyric composition is not relished the more, perhaps not so much, for being Pindaric or Horatian; and it is not required that a satire should remind the reader of Juvenal. It is enough for the age if beautiful diction, glowing imagery, strong emotion, and fine thought are so combined as to give them their fullest effect upon the mind. The end of poetry is then attained, no matter by what system of rules.

If it were to be asked which is the more likely to produce specimens of poetry worthy of going down to posterity, which

is the more favorable to the enlargement of the human mind
and the vigorous action of all its faculties on the variety of
objects and their relations by which it is surrounded—an age
distinguished for too great carefulness of imitation, or an
age remarkable for an excessive ambition of originality—I
think that a wise decision must be in favor of the latter. Whatever errors in taste may spring from the zeal for new developments of genius and the disdain of imitation, their influence
is of short duration. The fantastic brood of extravagances and
absurdities to which they give birth soon die and are forgotten, for nothing is immortal in literature but what is truly
excellent. On the other hand, such an age may and does produce poems worthy to live. The works of the early Italian
poets were composed in such an age; the proudest monuments
of English verse are the growth of such a spirit; the old poetry
of Spain, the modern poetry of Germany, grew into beauty
and strength under such auspices. Men walked, as they should
ever do, with a confident step by the side of these ancient
masters, of whom they learned this art; they studied their
works, not that they might resemble, but that they might surpass them.

But one of the best fruits of such an age is the remarkable
activity into which it calls the human intellect. Those things
which are ours rather by memory than by the natural growth
of the mind lie on its surface, already wrought into distinct
shape, and are brought into use with little effort. But for the
native conceptions of the mind, the offspring of strong mental
excitement, it is necessary to go deeper and to toil more intensely. It is not without a vigorous exercise that the intellect
searches for these among its stores, extricates them from the
obscurity in which they are first beheld, ascertains their parts
and detains them until they are moulded into distinctness and
symmetry, and embodied in language.

But when once a tame and frigid taste has possessed the
tribe of poets, when all their powers are employed in servilely
copying the works of their predecessors, it is not only impossible that any great work should be produced among them, but

the period of a literary reformation, of the awakening of genius, is postponed to a distant futurity. It is the quality of such a state of literature, by the imposing precision of its rules and the ridicule it throws on everything out of its own beaten track, to perpetuate itself indefinitely. The happy appearance of some extraordinary genius, educated under different influences than those operating on the age, and compelling admiration by the force of his talents, or perhaps some great moral or political revolution, by unsettling old opinions and familiarizing men to daring speculations—can alone have any effect to remove it. The mind grows indolent, or, at least, enfeebled, by the want of those higher exercises to which it was destined. At the same time, the spirit of poetry, as seen in its power of elevating the mind, of humanizing the affections, and expelling sordid appetites, is no longer felt, or only felt by a few, who conceal in their own bosoms the secret of its power over them.

EDGAR ALLAN POE

Edgar Allan Poe (1809-1849) was born in Boston, Massachusetts, orphaned at the age of two, and, after growing up in the household of his wealthy foster parents, Mr. and Mrs. John Foster Allan, in Richmond, Virginia, spent the rest of his short life in poor health, incurable poverty, and a depressed state of mind. Having attended English schools for five years, Poe later spent a year at the University of Virginia and, after his enlistment in the United States army, a year at the military academy at West Point. Abandoning his schooling, Poe became a free-lance writer and reviewer, variously in New York, Philadelphia, and Baltimore. He worked in an editorial capacity for the *Southern Literary Messenger* (1835-37), *Burton's Gentleman's Magazine* (1839-40), *Graham's Magazine* (1841-42), the *New-York Mirror* (1844-45), and the *Broadway Journal* (1845). He was the proprietor of the last of these, although his contributions to *Graham's* were what primarily established him as an influence in contemporary letters. Although Poe was never able to establish his own magazine, his prospectus for such a journal reveals his understanding of the marketing of literary wares. His polemical reviews bear this out, but his polemics were his professional undoing. Consequent unemployment and long spells of drinking further demoralized him. After the death of his child-wife and his unsuccessful courtship of several women, with attendant melancholy and alcohol, he died and was buried in Baltimore, Maryland, presumably the victim of a political gang.

Poe was primarily a journalist, and most of his writing appeared only in magazines. From 1827, when he subsidized and anonymously issued *Tamerlane,* his first volume of verse, until 1848, when he brought out *Eureka: A Prose Poem,* Poe published ten titles—only a fraction of his prose fiction and verse, and none of his literary criticism. The most complete collection of Poe's works is the Virginia Edition: James A. Harrison, *The Complete Works of Edgar Allan Poe* (17 vols., 1902).

The text for "Review of New Books" is taken from *Gra-*

ham's Magazine, January 1842. Although it originally appeared under this title, Poe's editors have since entitled the essay "Exordium." The quotation Poe cites appeared as a preface to *Arcturus* (1841), and was written by the editors of that magazine, Cornelius Mathews and Evart A. Duyckinck.

The text of "Tale Writing—Mr. Hawthorne" is taken from *Godey's Magazine and Lady's Book,* November 1847, and is a review of Hawthorne's *Twice-Told Tales* (1842) and *Mosses from an Old Manse* (1846). Poe's habit of rearranging and refining his ideas accounted for the several subjects of this essay and for its appearance, as partly a catalogue and partly a development of his other essays, among them, his first review (1842) of Hawthorne's tales, the preface to his *Poems* (1831), and his lecture, "The Poetic Principle" (1848).

REVIEW OF NEW BOOKS

In commencing, with the New Year, a New Volume, we shall be permitted to say a very few words by way of *exordium* to our usual chapter of Reviews, or, as we should prefer calling them, of Critical Notices. Yet we speak *not* for the sake of the *exordium,* but because we have really something to say, and know not when or where better to say it.

That the public attention in America has, of late days, been more than usually directed to the matter of literary criticism is plainly apparent. Our periodicals are beginning to acknowledge the importance of the science (shall we so term it?) and to disdain the flippant *opinion* which so long has been made its substitute.

Time was when we imported our critical decisions from the mother country. For many years we enacted a perfect farce of subserviency to the *dicta* of Great Britain. At last a revulsion of feeling, with self-disgust, necessarily ensued. Urged by these, we plunged into the opposite extreme. In throwing *totally* off that "authority," whose voice had so long been so sacred, we even surpassed, and by much, our original folly. But the

watchword now was, "a national literature!"—as if any true
literature *could be* "national"—as if the world at large were
not the only proper stage for the literary *histrie*. We became,
suddenly, the merest and maddest *partizans* in letters. Our
papers spoke of "tariffs" and "protection." Our Magazines had
habitual passages about that "truly native novelist, Mr.
Cooper," or that "staunch American genius, Mr. Paulding."
Unmindful of the spirit of the axioms that "a prophet has no
honor in his own land" and that "a hero is never a hero to his
valet-de-chambre"—axioms founded in reason and in truth—
our reviews urged the propriety, our booksellers the necessity,
of strictly "American" themes. A foreign subject, at this epoch,
was a weight more than enough to drag down into the very
depths of critical damnation the finest writer owning nativity
in the States; while, on the reverse, we found ourselves daily
in the paradoxical dilemma of liking, or pretending to like, a
stupid book the better because (sure enough) its stupidity was
of our own growth, and discussed our own affairs.

It is, in fact, but very lately that this anomalous state of
feeling has shown any signs of subsidence. Still it *is* subsiding.
Our views of literature in general having expanded, we begin
to demand the use—to inquire into the offices and provinces of
criticism—to regard it more as an art based immovably in
nature, less as a mere system of fluctuating and conventional
dogmas. And, with the prevalence of these ideas, has arrived a
distaste even to the home-dictation of the bookseller-*coteries*.
If our editors are not as yet *all* independent of the will of a
publisher, a majority of them scruple, at least, to *confess* a sub-
servience, and enter into no positive combinations against the
minority who despise and discard it. And this is a *very* great
improvement of exceedingly late date.

Escaping these quicksands, our criticism is nevertheless in
some danger—some very little danger—of falling into the pit
of a most detestable species of cant—the cant of *generality*.
This tendency has been given it, in the first instance, by the
onward and tumultuous spirit of the age. With the increase of

the thinking-material comes the desire, if not the necessity, of abandoning particulars for masses. Yet in our individual case, as a nation, we seem merely to have adopted this bias from the British Quarterly Reviews, upon which our own Quarterlies have been slavishly and pertinaciously modelled. In the foreign journal, the review or criticism properly so termed has gradually yet steadily degenerated into what we see it at present—that is to say, into anything but criticism. Originally a "review" was not so called as *lucus a non lucendo*. Its name conveyed a just idea of its design. It reviewed, or surveyed the book whose title formed its text, and, giving an analysis of its contents, passed judgment upon its merits or defects. But, through the system of anonymous contribution, this natural process lost ground from day to day. The name of a writer being known only to a few, it became to him an object not so much to write well as to write fluently, at so many guineas per sheet. The analysis of a book is a matter of time and of mental exertion. For many classes of composition there is required a deliberate perusal, with notes, and subsequent generalization. An easy substitute for this labor was found in a digest or compendium of the work noticed, with copious extracts—or a still easier, in random comments upon such passages as accidentally met the eye of the critic, with the passages themselves copied at full length. The mode of reviewing most in favor, however, because carrying with it the greatest *semblance* of care, was that of diffuse essay upon the subject matter of the publication, the reviewer (?) using the facts alone which the publication supplied, and using them as material for some theory, the sole concern, bearing, and intention of which, was mere difference of opinion with the author. These came at length to be understood and habitually practised as the customary or conventional *fashions* of review; and although the nobler order of intellects did not fall into the full heresy of these fashions—we may still assert that even Macaulay's nearest approach to criticism in its legitimate sense is to be found in his article upon Ranke's "History of the Popes"—an article in which the whole strength of the reviewer is put forth *to account* for a single fact—the progress of Romanism—which the book under discussion has established.

Now, while we do not mean to deny that a good essay is a good thing, we yet assert that these papers on general topics have nothing whatever to do with that *criticism* which their evil example has nevertheless infected *in se*. Because these dogmatising pamphlets, which *were once* "Reviews," have lapsed from their original faith, it does not follow that the faith itself is extinct—that "there shall be no more cakes and ale"—that criticism, in its old acceptation, does not exist. But we complain of a growing inclination on the part of our lighter journals to believe, on such grounds, that such is the fact— that because the British quarterlies, through supineness, and our own, through a degrading imitation, have come to merge all varieties of vague generalization in the one title of "Review," it therefore results that criticism, being everything in the universe, is, consequently, nothing whatever in fact. For to this end, and to none other conceivable, is the tendency of such propositions, for example, as we find in a late number of that very clever monthly magazine, Arcturus.

"But *now*" (the emphasis on the *now* is our own)—"But *now*," says Mr. Mathews, in the preface to the first volume of his journal, "criticism has a wider scope and a universal interest. It dismisses errors of grammar, and hands over an imperfect rhyme or a false quantity to the proof-reader; it looks *now* to the heart of the subject and the author's design. It is a test of opinion. Its acuteness is not pedantic, but philosophical; it unravels the web of the author's mystery to interpret his meaning to others; it detects his sophistry, because sophistry is injurious to the heart and life; it promulgates his beauties with liberal, generous praise, because this is its true duty as the servant of truth. Good criticism may be well asked for, since it is the type of the literature of the day. It gives method to the universal inquisitiveness on every topic relating to life or action. A criticism, *now*, includes every form of literature, except perhaps the imaginative and the strictly dramatic. It is an essay, a sermon, an oration, a chapter in history, a philosophical speculation, a prose-poem, an art-novel, a dialogue; it admits of humor, pathos, the personal feelings of auto-biography, the broadest views of statesmanship. As the ballad and the epic were the productions of the days of Homer, the review is the native characteristic growth of the nineteenth century." [Poe's italics.]

We respect the talents of Mr. Mathews, but must dissent from nearly all that he here says. The species of "review" which he designates as the "characteristic growth of the nineteenth century" is only the growth of the last twenty or thirty years *in Great Britain*. The French Reviews, for example, which are *not* anonymous, are very different things, and preserve the *unique* spirit of true criticism. And what need we say of the Germans?—what of Winkelmann, of Novalis, of Schelling, of Goethe, of Augustus William, and of Frederick Schlegel?—that their magnificent *critiques raisonnées* differ from those of Kaimes, of Johnson, and of Blair, in principle not at all, (for the principles of these artists will not fail until Nature herself expires,) but solely in their more careful elaboration, their greater thoroughness, their more profound analysis and application of the principles themselves. That a criticism *"now"* should be different in spirit, as Mr. Mathews supposes, from a criticism at any previous period, is to insinuate a charge of variability in laws that cannot vary—the laws of man's heart and intellect—for these are the sole basis upon which the true critical art is established. And this art *"now"* no more than in the days of the "Dunciad," can, without neglect of its duty, "dismiss errors of grammar," or "hand over an imperfect rhyme or a false quantity to the proof-reader." What is meant by a "test of opinion" in the connection here given the words by Mr. M., we do not comprehend as clearly as we could desire. By this phrase we are as completely enveloped in doubt as was Mirabeau in the castle of *If*. To our imperfect appreciation it seems to form a portion of that general vagueness which is the *tone* of the whole philosophy at this point:—but all that which our journalist describes a criticism to be is all that which we sturdily maintain it *is not*. Criticism is *not*, we think, an essay, nor a sermon, nor an oration, nor a chapter in history, nor a philosophical speculation, nor a prose-poem, nor an art novel, nor a dialogue. In fact, it *can be* nothing in the world but—a criticism. But if it were all that Arcturus imagines, it is not very clear why it might not be equally "imaginative" or "dramatic"—a romance or a melodrama, or both. That it would be a farce cannot be doubted.

It is against this frantic spirit of *generalization* that we protest. We have a word, "criticism," whose import is sufficiently distinct, through long usage, at least; and we have an art of high importance and clearly ascertained limit, which this word is quite well enough understood to represent. Of that conglomerate science to which Mr. Mathews so eloquently alludes, and of which we are instructed that it is anything and everything at once—of this science we know nothing, and really wish to know less; but we object to our contemporary's appropriation in its behalf, of a term to which we, in common with a large majority of mankind, have been accustomed to attach a certain and very definitive idea. Is there no word but "criticism" which may be made to serve the purposes of Arcturus? Has it any objection to Orphicism, or Dialism, or Emersonism, or any other pregnant compound indicative of confusion worse confounded?

Still, we must not pretend a total misapprehension of the idea of Mr. Mathews, and we should be sorry that he misunderstood *us*. It may be granted that we differ only in terms—although the difference will yet be found not unimportant in effect. Following the highest authority, we would wish, in a word, to limit literary criticism to comment upon *Art*. A book is written—and it is only *as the book* that we subject it to review. With the opinions of the work, considered otherwise than in their relation to the work itself, the critic has really nothing to do. It is his part simply to decide upon *the mode* in which these opinions are brought to bear. Criticism is thus no "test of opinion." For this test, the work, divested of its pretensions as an *art-product*, is turned over for discussion to the world at large—and first, to that class which it especially addresses—if a history, to the historian—if a metaphysical treatise, to the moralist. In this, the only true and intelligible sense, it will be seen that criticism, the test or analysis of *Art*, (*not* of opinion,) is only properly employed upon productions which have their basis in art itself, and although the journalist (whose duties and objects are multiform) may turn aside, at pleasure, from the *mode* or vehicle of opinion to discussion of the opinion conveyed—it is still clear that he is "critical" only in so much as he deviates from his true province not at all.

And of the critic himself what shall we say?—for as yet we have spoken only the *proem* to the true *epopea*. What *can* we better say of him than, with Bulwer, that "he must have courage to blame boldly, magnanimity to eschew envy, genius to appreciate, learning to compare, an eye for beauty, an ear for music, and a heart for feeling." Let us add, a talent for analysis and a solemn indifference to abuse.

TALE WRITING—MR. HAWTHORNE

I N the preface to my sketches of New York Literati, while speaking of the broad distinction between the seeming public and real private opinion respecting our authors, I thus alluded to Nathaniel Hawthorne:—

"For example, Mr. Hawthorne, the author of 'Twice-Told Tales,' is scarcely recognized by the press or by the public, and when noticed at all, is noticed merely to be damned by faint praise. Now, my opinion of him is, that although his walk is limited and he is fairly to be charged with mannerism, treating all subjects in a similar tone of dreamy *innuendo,* yet in this walk he evinces extraordinary genius, having no rival either in America or elsewhere; and this opinion I have never heard gainsaid by any one literary person in the country. That this opinion, however, is a spoken and not a written one, is referable to the facts, first, that Mr. Hawthorne *is* a poor man, and, secondly, that he *is not* an ubiquitous quack."

The reputation of the author of "Twice-Told Tales" has been confined, indeed, until very lately, to literary society; and

I have not been wrong, perhaps, in citing him as *the* example,
par excellence, in this country, of the privately admired and
publicly unappreciated man of genius. Within the last year or
two, it is true, an occasional critic has been urged, by honest
indignation, into very warm approval. Mr. Webber, for instance, (than whom no one has a keener relish for that kind of
writing which Mr. Hawthorne has best illustrated,) gave us,
in a late number of The American Review, a cordial and certainly a full tribute to his talents; and since the issue of the
"Mosses from an Old Manse," criticisms of similar tone have
been by no means infrequent in our more authoritative journals. I can call to mind few reviews of Hawthorne published
before the "Mosses." One I remember in Arcturus (edited by
Mathews and Duyckinck) for May, 1841; another in the American Monthly (edited by Hoffman and Herbert) for March,
1838; a third in the ninety-sixth number of the North American Review. These criticisms, however, seemed to have little
effect on the popular taste—at least, if we are to form any idea
of the popular taste by reference to its expression in the newspapers, or by the sale of the author's book. It was never the
fashion (until lately) to speak of him in any summary of our
best authors. The daily critics would say, on such occasions,
"Is there not Irving and Cooper, and Bryant and Paulding,
and—Smith?" or "Have we not Halleck and Dana, and Longfellow and—Thompson?" or "Can we not point triumphantly
to our own Sprague, Willis, Channing, Bancroft, Prescott and—
Jenkins?" but these unanswerable queries were never wound
up by the name of Hawthorne.

Beyond doubt, this inappreciation of him on the part of the
public arose chiefly from the two causes to which I have referred—from the facts that he is neither a man of wealth nor
a quack;—but these are insufficient to account for the whole
effect. No small portion of it is attributable to the very marked
idiosyncrasy of Mr. Hawthorne himself. In one sense, and in
great measure, to be peculiar is to be original, and than the
true originality there is no higher literary virtue. This true or
commendable originality, however, implies not the uniform,

but the continuous peculiarity—a peculiarity springing from
ever-active vigor of fancy—better still if from ever-present force
of imagination, giving its own hue, its own character to everything it touches, and, especially, *self impelled to touch everything.*

It is often said, inconsiderately, that very original writers
always fail in popularity—that such and such persons are too
original to be comprehended by the mass. "Too peculiar,"
should be the phrase, "too idiosyncratic." It is, in fact, the
excitable, undisciplined and child-like popular mind which
most keenly feels the original. The criticism of the conserva-
tives, of the hackneys, of the cultivated old clergymen of the
North American Review, is precisely the criticism which condemns and alone condemns it. "It becometh not a divine,"
saith Lord Coke, "to be of a fiery and salamandrine spirit."
Their conscience allowing them to move nothing themselves,
these dignitaries have a holy horror of being moved. "Give us
quietude," they say. Opening their mouths with proper caution, they sigh forth the word *"Repose."* And this is, indeed,
the one thing they should be permitted to enjoy, if only upon
the Christian principle of give and take.

The fact is that, if Mr. Hawthorne were really original, he
could not fail of making himself felt by the public. But the
fact is, he is *not* original in any sense. Those who speak of him
as original mean nothing more than that he differs in his manner or tone, and in his choice of subjects, from any author of
their acquaintance—their acquaintance not extending to the
German Tieck, whose manner, in *some* of his works, is absolutely identical with that *habitual* to Hawthorne. But it is
clear that the element of the literary originality is novelty. The
element of its appreciation by the reader is the reader's sense
of the new. Whatever gives him a new and insomuch a pleasurable emotion, he considers original, and whoever frequently
gives him such emotion, he considers an original writer. In a
word, it is by the sum total of these emotions that he decides
upon the writer's claim to originality. I may observe here,
however, that there is clearly a point at which even novelty

itself would cease to produce the legitimate originality, if we judge this originality, as we should, by the effect designed: this point is that at which *novelty becomes nothing novel;* and here the artist, *to preserve his originality,* will subside into the common-place. No one, I think, has noticed that, merely through inattention to this matter, Moore has comparatively failed in his "Lalla Rookh." Few readers, and indeed few critics, have commended this poem for originality—and, in fact, the effect, originality, is not produced by it—yet no work of equal size so abounds in the happiest originalities, individually considered. They are so excessive, as, in the end, to deaden in the reader all capacity for their appreciation.

These points properly understood, it will be seen that the critic (unacquainted with Tieck) who reads a single tale or essay by Hawthorne, may be justified in thinking him original; but the tone, or manner, or choice of subject, which induces in this critic the sense of the new, will—if not in a second tale, at least in a third and all subsequent ones—not only fail of inducing it, but bring about an exactly antagonistic impression. In concluding a volume, and more especially in concluding all the volumes of the author, the critic will abandon his first design of calling him "original," and content himself with styling him "peculiar."

With the vague opinion that to be original is to be popular, I could, indeed, agree, were I to adopt an understanding of originality which, to my surprise, I have known adopted by many who have a right to be called critical. They have limited, in a love for mere words, the literary to the metaphysical originality. They regard as original in letters only such combinations of thought, of incident, and so forth, as are, in fact, absolutely novel. It is clear, however, not only that it is the novelty of *effect* alone which is worth consideration, but that this effect is *best* wrought, for the end of all fictitious composition, pleasure, by shunning rather than by seeking the absolute novelty of combination. Originality, thus understood, tasks and startles the intellect, and so brings into undue action the faculties to which, in the lighter literature, we least appeal.

And thus understood, it cannot fail to prove unpopular with the masses, who, seeking in this literature amusement, are positively offended by instruction. But the true originality—true in respect of its purposes—is that which, in bringing out the half-formed, the reluctant, or the unexpressed fancies of mankind, or in exciting the more delicate pulses of the heart's passion, or in giving birth to some universal sentiment or instinct in embryo, thus combines with the pleasurable effect of *apparent* novelty, a real egoistic delight. The reader, in the case first supposed, (that of the absolute novelty,) is excited, but embarrassed, disturbed, in some degree even pained at his own want of perception, at his own folly in not having himself hit upon the idea. In the second case, his pleasure is doubled. He is filled with intrinsic and extrinsic delight. He feels and intensely enjoys the seeming novelty of the thought, enjoys it as really novel, as absolutely original with the writer—*and himself.* They two, he fancies, have alone of all men, thought thus. They two have, together, created this thing. Henceforward there is a bond of sympathy between them, a sympathy which irradiates every subsequent page of the book.

There is a species of writing which, with some difficulty, may be admitted as a lower degree of what I have called the true original. In its perusal, we say to ourselves not "how original this is!" nor "here is an idea which I and the author have alone entertained," but "here is a charmingly obvious fancy," or sometimes even "here is a thought which I am not sure has ever occurred to myself, but which, of course, has occurred to all the rest of the world." This kind of composition (which still appertains to a high order) is usually designated as "the natural." It has little external resemblance, but strong internal affinity to the true original, if , indeed, as I have suggested, it is not of this latter an inferior degree. It is best exemplified, among English writers, in Addison, Irving, and *Hawthorne.* The "ease" which is so often spoken of as its distinguishing feature, it has been the fashion to regard as ease in appearance alone, as a point of really difficult attainment. This idea, however, must be received with some reservation. The natural style is difficult only to those who should never intermeddle with it—to the unnatural. It is but the result of writing with the understanding, or with the instinct, that the *tone,* in composition, should be that which, at any given point or upon any given topic, would be the tone of the great mass of humanity. The author who, after the manner of the North Americans, is merely at *all* times *quiet* is, of course, upon *most* occasions merely silly or stupid, and has no more right to be thought "easy" or "natural" than has a cockney exquisite or the sleeping beauty in the waxworks.

The "peculiarity" or sameness or monotone of Hawthorne would, in its mere character of "peculiarity," and without reference to what *is* the peculiarity, suffice to deprive him of all chance of popular appreciation. But at his failure to be appreciated we can, *of course,* no longer wonder, when we find him monotonous at decidedly the worst of all possible points— at that point which, having the least concern with Nature, is the farthest removed from the popular intellect, from the popular sentiment, and from the popular taste. I allude to the strain of allegory which completely overwhelms the greatest number of his subjects, and which in some measure interferes with the direct conduct of absolutely all.

In defence of allegory (however, or for whatever object employed,) there is scarcely one respectable word to be said. Its best appeals are made to the fancy—that is to say, to our sense of adaptation, not of matters proper, but of matters improper for the purpose, of the real with the unreal; having never more of intelligible connection than has something with nothing, never half so much of effective affinity as has the substance for the shadow. The deepest emotion aroused within us by the happiest allegory, *as* allegory, is a very, very imperfectly satisfied sense of the writer's ingenuity in overcoming a difficulty we should have preferred his not having attempted to overcome. The fallacy of the idea that allegory, in any of its moods, can be made to enforce a truth—that metaphor, for example, may illustrate as well as embellish an argument— could be promptly demonstrated: the converse of the supposed fact might be shown, indeed, with very little trouble—but these are topics foreign to my present purpose. One thing is clear, that if allegory ever establishes a fact, it is by dint of overcoming a fiction. Where the suggested meaning runs through the obvious one in a *very* profound under-current, so as never to interfere with the upper one without our own volition, so as never to show itself unless *called* to the surface, there only, for the proper uses of fictitious narrative, is it available at all. Under the best circumstances, it must always interfere with that unity of effect which, to the artist, is worth all the allegory in the world. Its vital injury, however, is rendered to the most vitally important point in fiction—that of earnestness or verisimilitude. That "The Pilgrim's Progress" is a ludicrously over-rated book, owing its seeming popularity to one or two of those accidents in critical literature which by the critical are sufficiently well understood, is a matter upon which no two thinking people disagree; but the pleasure derivable from it, in any sense, will be found in the direct ratio of the reader's capacity to smother its true purpose, in the direct ratio of his ability to keep the allegory out of sight, or of his *in*ability to comprehend it. Of allegory properly handled, judiciously subdued, seen only as a shadow or by suggestive glimpses, and making its nearest approach to truth in a not obtrusive and therefore not unpleasant *appositeness,* the "Undine" of De La Motte Fouque is the best, and undoubtedly a very remarkable specimen.

The obvious causes, however, which have prevented Mr. Hawthorne's *popularity,* do not suffice to condemn him in the eyes of the few who belong properly to books, and to whom books, perhaps, do not quite so properly belong. These few estimate an author, not as do the public, altogether by what he does, but in a great measure—indeed, even in the greatest measure—by what he evinces a capability of doing. In this view, Hawthorne stands among literary people in America much in the same light as did Coleridge in England. The few, also, through a certain warping of the taste, which long pon-

dering upon books as books merely never fails to induce, are
not in condition to view the errors of a scholar as errors altogether. At any time these gentlemen are prone to think the
public not right rather than an educated author wrong. But
the simple truth is that the writer who aims at impressing the
people is *always* wrong when he fails in forcing that people to
receive the impression. How far Mr. Hawthorne has addressed
the people at all is, of course, not a question for me to decide.
His books afford strong internal evidence of having been
written to himself and his particular friends alone.

There has long existed in literature a fatal and unfounded
prejudice which it will be the office of this age to overthrow—
the idea that the mere bulk of a work must enter largely into
our estimate of its merit. I do not suppose even the weakest
of the Quarterly reviewers weak enough to maintain that in a
book's size or mass, abstractly considered, there is anything
which especially calls for our admiration. A mountain, simply
through the sensation of physical magnitude which it conveys,
does, indeed, affect us with a sense of the sublime, but we cannot admit any such influence in the contemplation even of
"The Columbiad." The Quarterlies themselves will not admit
it. And yet, what else are we to understand by their continual
prating about "sustained effort"? Granted that this sustained
effort has accomplished an epic—let us then admire the effort,
(if this be a thing admirable,) but certainly not the epic on the
effort's account. Common sense, in the time to come, may
possibly insist upon measuring a work of art rather by the
object it fulfils, by the impression it makes, than by the time
it took to fulfil the object, or by the extent of "sustained
effort" which became necessary to produce the impression. The
fact is, that perseverance is one thing and genius quite another;
nor can all the transcendentalists in Heathendom confound
them.

Full of its bulky ideas, the last number of the North American Review, in what it imagines a criticism on Simms, "honestly
avows that it has little opinion of the mere tale"; and the

honesty of the avowal is in no slight degree guaranteed by the fact that this Review has never yet been known to put forth an opinion which was *not* a very little one indeed.

The tale proper affords the fairest field which can be afforded by the wide domains of mere prose for the exercise of the highest genius. Were I bidden to say how this genius could be most advantageously employed for the best display of its powers, I should answer, without hesitation, "in the composition of a rhymed poem not to exceed in length what might be perused in an hour." Within this limit alone can the noblest order of poetry exist. I have discussed this topic elsewhere, and need here repeat only that the phrase "a long poem" embodies a paradox. A poem must intensely excite. Excitement is its providence, its essentiality. Its value is in the ratio of its (elevating) excitement. But all excitement is, from a psychal necessity, transient. It cannot be sustained through a poem of great length. In the course of an hour's reading, at most, it flags, fails; and then the poem is, in effect, no longer such. Men admire, but are wearied with the "Paradise Lost"; for platitude follows platitude, *inevitably,* at regular interspaces, (the depressions between the waves of excitement), until the poem, (which, properly considered, is but a succession of brief poems,) having been brought to an end, we discover that the sums of our pleasure and of displeasure have been very nearly equal. The absolute, ultimate, or aggregate effect of any epic under the sun is, for these reasons, a nullity. "The Iliad," in its form of epic, has but an imaginary existence; granting it real, however, I can only say of it that it is based on a primitive sense of Art. Of the modern epic nothing can be so well said as that it is a blindfold imitation of a "come-by-chance." By and by these propositions will be understood as self-evident, and in the meantime will not be essentially damaged as truths by being generally condemned as falsities.

A poem *too* brief, on the other hand, may produce a sharp or vivid, but never a profound or enduring impression. Without a certain continuity, without a certain duration or repetition of the cause, the soul is seldom moved to the effect. There must be the dropping of the water on the rock. There must be the pressing steadily down of the stamp upon the wax. De Béranger has wrought brilliant things, pungent and spirit-stirring, but most of them are too immassive to have *momentum,* and, as so many feathers of fancy, have been blown aloft only to be whistled down the wind. Brevity, indeed, may degenerate into epigrammatism, but this danger does not prevent extreme length from being the one unpardonable sin.

Were I called upon, however, to designate that class of composition which, next to such a poem as I have suggested, should best fulfil the demands and serve the purposes of ambitious genius, should offer it the most advantageous field of exertion, and afford it the fairest opportunity of display, I should speak at once of the brief prose tale. History, philosophy, and other matters of that kind we leave out of the question, of course. *Of course,* I say, and in spite of the graybeards. These graver topics, to the end of time, will be best illustrated by what a discriminating world, turning up its nose at the drab pamphlets, has agreed to understand as *talent.* The ordinary novel is objectionable, from its length, for reasons analogous to those which render length objectionable in the poem. As the novel cannot be read at one sitting, it cannot avail itself of the immense benefit of *totality.* Worldly interests, intervening during the pauses of perusal, modify, counteract and annul the impressions intended. But simple cessation in reading would, of itself, be sufficient to destroy the true unity. In the brief tale, however, the author is enabled to carry out his full design without interruption. During the hour of perusal, the soul of the reader is at the writer's control.

A skillful artist has constructed a tale. He has not fashioned his thoughts to accommodate his incidents, but having deliberately conceived a certain *single effect* to be wrought, he then invents such incidents, he then combines such events, and discusses them in such tone as may best serve him in establishing this preconceived effect. If his very first sentence tend not to the outbringing of this effect, then in his very first step has he committed a blunder. In the whole composition there should be no word written of which the tendency, direct or indirect, is not to the one pre-established design. And by such means, with such care and skill, a picture is at length painted which leaves in the mind of him who contemplates it with a kindred art a sense of the fullest satisfaction. The idea of the tale, its thesis, has been presented unblemished, because undisturbed —an end absolutely demanded, yet, in the novel, altogether unattainable.

Of skillfully constructed tales—I speak now without reference to other points, some of them more important than construction—there are very few American specimens. I am acquainted with no better one, upon the whole, than the "Murder Will Out" of Mr. Simms, and this has some glaring defects. The "Tales of a Traveler," by Irving, are graceful and impressive narratives—"The Young Italian" is especially good —but there is not one of the series which can be commended as a whole. In many of them the interest is subdivided and frittered away, and their conclusions are insufficiently *climactic*. In the higher requisites of composition, John Neal's magazine stories excel—I mean in vigor of thought, picturesque combination of incident, and so forth—but they ramble too much, and invariably break down just before coming to an end, as if the writer had received a sudden and irresistible summons to dinner, and thought it incumbent upon him to make a finish of his story before going. One of the happiest and best-sustained tales I have seen is "Jack Long; or, The Shot in the Eye," by Charles W. Webber, the assistant editor of Mr. Colton's American Review. But in general skill of construction, the tales of Willis, I think, surpass those of any American writer—with the exception of Mr. Hawthorne.

I must defer to the better opportunity of a volume now in hand a full discussion of his individual pieces, and hasten to conclude this paper with a summary of his merits and demerits.

He is peculiar and *not* original—unless in those detailed fancies and detached thoughts which his want of general originality will deprive of the appreciation due to them, in preventing them forever reaching the *public eye*. He is infinitely too fond of allegory, and can never hope for popularity so long as he persists in it. This he will not do, for allegory is at war with the whole tone of his nature, which disports itself never so well as when escaping from the mysticism of his Goodman Browns and White Old Maids into the hearty, genial, but still Indian-summer sunshine of his Wakefields and Little Annie's Rambles. Indeed, *his* spirit of "metaphor run mad" is clearly imbibed from the phalanx and phalanstery atmosphere in which he has been so long struggling for breath. He has not half the material for the exclusiveness of authorship that he possesses for its universality. He has the purest style, the finest taste, the most available scholarship, the most delicate humor, the most touching pathos, the most radiant imagination, the most consummate ingenuity; and with these varied good qualities he has done *well* as a mystic. But is there any one of these qualities which should prevent his doing doubly as well in a career of honest, upright, sensible, prehensible and comprehensible things? Let him mend his pen, get a bottle of visible ink, come out from the Old Manse, cut Mr. Alcott, hang (if possible) the editor of The Dial, and throw out of the window to the pigs all his old numbers of The North American Review.

RALPH WALDO EMERSON

Ralph Waldo Emerson (1803-1882) was born in Boston and raised in a Unitarian household. He was graduated from Harvard and, after several years of teaching school, from the Harvard Divinity School. In 1832 he resigned his pulpit at the Second [Unitarian] Church of Boston, because he could no longer serve the sacrament of Communion. He traveled in Europe for two years, and began to absorb philosophical ideas of Coleridge, Carlyle, and the German idealists. Because of these associations, his study compassed Platonism, Neo-Platonism, Eastern religion, and the teaching of Swedenborg. Upon his return to Boston, armed with his new convictions and with the entries in his journal, which he had continued since his undergraduate days, Emerson began a lecturing career.

His long essay, *Nature* (1836), and his orations, *The American Scholar* (1837) and *An Address Delivered Before the Senior Class in Divinity College, Cambridge* (1838), established his premises for the doctrine of Transcendentalism and the principles of his whole canon of writing. Two series of essays (1841, 1844), and *Representative Men: Seven Lectures* (1850) variously dramatized these principles and acknowledged their implications. Three volumes of poems (1847, 1867, 1876) and a dozen other titles of lectures and essays comprise most of Emerson's published writing.

After about 1870, Emerson's declining health and mental abilities limited his activities. Five more titles, comprising essays, ten volumes of Emerson's journals, and six volumes of his letters were posthumously published. The standard edition of his works is the Centenary Edition prepared by his son: Edward Waldo Emerson, *The Complete Works of Ralph Waldo Emerson* (12 vols., 1903-04).

This text of "The Poet" is from *Essays, Second Series* (1883), first published in 1844. This is the most complete statement of Emerson's earlier theory that symbolic language, which expresses the unity of all phenomena, is the poet's instrument for liberating men. The essay itself is an example of the kind of myth-making Emerson celebrated in the poet.

THE POET

THOSE who are esteemed umpires of taste are often persons who have acquired some knowledge of admired pictures or sculptures, and have an inclination for whatever is elegant; but if you inquire whether they are beautiful souls, and whether their own acts are like fair pictures, you learn that they are selfish and sensual. Their cultivation is local, as if you should rub a log of dry wood in one spot to produce fire, all the rest remaining cold. Their knowledge of the fine arts is some study of rules and particulars, or some limited judgment of color or form, which is exercised for amusement or for show. It is a proof of the shallowness of the doctrine of beauty as it lies in the minds of our amateurs, that men seem to have lost the perception of the instant dependence of form upon soul. There is no doctrine of forms in our philosophy. We were put into our bodies, as fire is put into a pan to be carried about; but there is no accurate adjustment between the spirit and the organ, much less is the latter the germination of the former. So in regard to other forms, the intellectual men do not believe in any essential dependence of the material world on thought and volition. Theologians think it a pretty air-castle to talk of the spiritual meaning of a ship or a cloud, of a city or a contract, but they prefer to come again to the solid ground of historical evidence; and even the poets are contented with a civil and conformed manner of living, and to write poems from the fancy, at a safe distance from their own experience. But the highest minds of the world have never ceased to explore the double meaning, or shall I say the quadruple or the centuple or much more manifold meaning, of every sensuous fact; Orpheus, Empedocles, Heraclitus, Plato, Plutarch, Dante, Swedenborg, and the masters of sculpture, picture, and poetry. For we are not pans and barrows, nor even porters of the fire and torch-bearers, but children of the fire, made of it, and only the same divinity transmuted and at two or three removes, when we know least about it. And this hidden truth, that the fountains whence all this river of Time and its creatures floweth are intrinsically ideal and beautiful, draws us to the consideration of the nature and functions of the Poet, or the man of Beauty; to the means and materials he uses, and to the general aspect of the art in the present time.

The breadth of the problem is great, for the poet is representative. He stands among partial men for the complete man, and apprises us not of his wealth, but of the common wealth. The young man reveres men of genius, because, to speak truly, they are more himself than he is. They receive of the soul as he also receives, but they more. Nature enhances her beauty, to the eye of loving men, from their belief that the poet is beholding her shows at the same time. He is isolated among his contemporaries by truth and by his art, but with this consolation in his pursuits, that they will draw all men sooner or later. For all men live by truth and stand in need of expression. In love, in art, in avarice, in politics, in labor, in games, we study to utter our painful secret. The man is only half himself, the other half is his expression.

Notwithstanding this necessity to be published, adequate expression is rare. I know not how it is that we need an interpreter, but the great majority of men seem to be minors, who have not yet come into possession of their own, or mutes, who cannot report the conversation they have had with nature. There is no man who does not anticipate a supersensual utility in the sun and stars, earth and water. These stand and wait to render him a peculiar service. But there is some obstruction or some excess of phlegm in our constitution, which does not suffer them to yield the due effect. Too feeble fall the impressions of nature on us to make us artists. Every touch should thrill. Every man should be so much an artist that he could report in conversation what had befallen him. Yet, in our experience, the rays or appulses have sufficient force to arrive at the senses, but not enough to reach the quick and compel the reproduction of themselves in speech. The poet is the person in whom these powers are in balance, the man without impediment, who sees and handles that which others dream of, traverses the whole scale of experience, and is representative of man, in virtue of being the largest power to receive and to impart.

For the Universe has three children, born at one time, which reappear under different names in every system of thought, whether they be called cause, operation, and effect; or, more poetically, Jove, Pluto, Neptune; or, theologically, the Father, the Spirit, and the Son; but which we will call here the Knower, the Doer, and the Sayer. These stand respectively for the love of truth, for the love of good, and for the love of beauty. These three are equal. Each is that which he is, essentially, so that he cannot be surmounted or analyzed, and each of these three has the power of the others latent in him, and his own, patent.

The poet is the sayer, the namer, and represents beauty. He is a sovereign, and stands on the centre. For the world is not painted or adorned, but is from the beginning beautiful; and God has not made some beautiful things, but Beauty is the creator of the universe. Therefore the poet is not any permissive potentate, but is emperor in his own right. Criticism is infested with a cant of materialism, which assumes that manual skill and activity is the first merit of all men, and disparages such as say and do not, overlooking the fact that some men, namely poets, are natural sayers, sent into the world to the end of expression, and confounds them with those whose province is action but who quit it to imitate the sayers. But Homer's words are as costly and admirable to Homer as Agamemnon's victories are to Agamemnon. The poet does not wait for the hero or the sage, but, as they act and think primarily, so he writes primarily what will and must be spoken, reckoning the others, though primaries also, yet, in respect to him, secondaries and servants; as sitters or models in the studio of a painter, or as assistants who bring building-materials to an architect.

For poetry was all written before time was, and whenever

we are so finely organized that we can penetrate into that region where the air is music, we hear those primal warblings and attempt to write them down, but we lose ever and anon a word or a verse and substitute something of our own, and thus miswrite the poem. The men of more delicate ear write down these cadences more faithfully, and these transcripts, though imperfect, become the songs of the nations. For nature is as truly beautiful as it is good, or as it is reasonable, and must as much appear as it must be done, or be known. Words and deeds are quite indifferent modes of the divine energy. Words are also actions, and actions are a kind of words.

The sign and credentials of the poet are that he announces that which no man foretold. He is the true and only doctor; he knows and tells; he is the only teller of news, for he was present and privy to the appearance which he describes. He is a beholder of ideas and an utterer of the necessary and causal. For we do not speak now of men of poetical talents, or of industry and skill in metre, but of the true poet. I took part in a conversation the other day concerning a recent writer of lyrics, a man of subtle mind, whose head appeared to be a music-box of delicate tunes and rhythm, and whose skill and command of language we could not sufficiently praise. But when the question arose whether he was not only a lyrist but a poet, we were obliged to confess that he is plainly a contemporary, not an eternal man. He does not stand out of our low limitations, like a Chimborazo under the line, running up from a torrid base through all the climates of the globe, with belts of the herbage of every latitude on its high and mottled sides; but this genius is the landscape-garden of a modern house, adorned with fountains and statues, with well-bred men and women standing and sitting in the walks and terraces. We hear, through all the varied music, the ground-tone of conventional life. Our poets are men of talents who sing, and not the children of music. The argument is secondary, the finish of the verses is primary.

For it is not metres, but a metre-making argument that

makes a poem,—a thought so passionate and alive that like the spirit of a plant or an animal it has an architecture of its own, and adorns nature with a new thing. The thought and the form are equal in the order of time, but in the order of genesis the thought is prior to the form. The poet has a new thought; he has a whole new experience to unfold; he will tell us how it was with him, and all men will be the richer in his fortune. For the experience of each new age requires a new confession, and the world seems always waiting for its poet. I remember when I was young how much I was moved one morning by tidings that genius had appeared in a youth who sat near me at table. He had left his work and gone rambling none knew whither, and had written hundreds of lines, but could not tell whether that which was in him was therein told; he could tell nothing but that all was changed,—man, beast, heaven, earth, and sea. How gladly we listened! how credulous! Society seemed to be compromised. We sat in the aurora of a sunrise which was to put out all the stars. Boston seemed to be at twice the distance it had the night before, or was much farther than that. Rome,—what was Rome? Plutarch and Shakspeare were in the yellow leaf, and Homer no more should be heard of. It is much to know that poetry has been written this very day, under this very roof, by your side. What! that wonderful spirit has not expired! These stony moments are still sparkling and animated! I had fancied that the oracles were all silent, and nature had spent her fires; and behold! all night, from every pore, these fine auroras have been streaming. Everyone has some interest in the advent of the poet, and no one knows how much it may concern him. We know that the secret of the world is profound, but who or what shall be our interpreter, we know not. A mountain ramble, a new style of face, a new person, may put the key into our hands. Of course the value of genius to us is in the veracity of its report. Talent may frolic and juggle; genius realizes and adds. Mankind in good earnest have availed so far in understanding themselves and their work, that the foremost watchman on the peak announces his news. It is the truest word ever spoken, and the phrase will be the fittest, most musical, and the unerring voice of the world for that time.

All that we call sacred history attests that the birth of a poet is the principal event in chronology. Man, never so often deceived, still watches for the arrival of a brother who can hold him steady to a truth until he has made it his own. With what joy I begin to read a poem which I confide in as an inspiration! And now my chains are to be broken; I shall mount above these clouds and opaque airs in which I live,—opaque, though they seem transparent,—and from the heaven of truth I shall see and comprehend my relations. That will reconcile me to life and renovate nature, to see trifles animated by a tendency, and to know what I am doing. Life will no more be a noise; now I shall see men and women, and know the signs by which they may be discerned from fools and satans. This day shall be better than my birthday: then I became an animal; now I am invited into the science of the real. Such is the hope, but the fruition is postponed. Oftener it falls that this winged man, who will carry me into the heaven, whirls me into mists, then leaps and frisks about with me as it were from cloud to cloud, still affirming that he is bound heavenward; and I, being myself a novice, am slow in perceiving that he does not know the way into the heavens, and is merely bent that I should admire his skill to rise like a fowl or a flying fish a little way from the ground or the water; but the all-piercing, all-feeding, and ocular air of heaven that man shall never inhabit. I tumble down again soon into my old nooks, and lead the life of exaggerations as before, and have lost my faith in the possibility of any guide who can lead me thither where I would be.

But, leaving these victims of vanity, let us, with new hope, observe how nature, by worthier impulses, has insured the poet's fidelity to his office of announcement and affirming, namely by the beauty of things, which becomes a new and higher beauty when expressed. Nature offers all her creatures to him as a picture-language. Being used as a type, a second wonderful value appears in the object, far better than its old value; as the carpenter's stretched cord, if you hold your ear close enough, is musical in the breeze. "Things more excellent than every image," says Jamblichus, "are expressed through images." Things admit of being used as symbols because nature is a symbol, in the whole, and in every part. Every line we can draw in the sand has expression; and there is no body without its spirit or genius. All form is an effect of character; all condition, of the quality of the life; all harmony, of health; and for this reason a perception of beauty should be sympathetic, or proper only to the good. The beautiful rests on the foundations of the necessary. The soul makes the body, as the wise Spenser teaches:—

> So every spirit, as it is more pure,
> And hath in it the more of heavenly light,
> So it the fairer body doth procure
> To habit in, and it more fairly dight,
> With cheerful grace and amiable sight.
> For, of the soul, the body form doth take,
> For soul is form, and doth the body make.

Here we find ourselves suddenly not in a critical speculation but in a holy place, and should go very warily and reverently. We stand before the secret of the world, there where Being passes into Appearance and Unity into Variety.

The Universe is the externization of the soul. Wherever the life is, that bursts into appearance around it. Our science is sensual, and therefore superficial. The earth and the heavenly bodies, physics, and chemistry, we sensually treat, as if they were self-existent; but these are the retinue of that Being we have. "The mighty heaven," said Proclus, "exhibits, in its transfigurations, clear images of the splendor of intellectual perceptions; being moved in conjunction with the unapparent periods of intellectual natures." Therefore science always goes abreast with the just elevation of the man, keeping step with religion and metaphysics; or the state of science is an index of our self-knowledge. Since every thing in nature answers to a moral power, if any phenomenon remains brute and dark it is because the corresponding faculty in the observer is not yet active.

No wonder then, if these waters be so deep, that we hover over them with a religious regard. The beauty of the fable proves the importance of the sense; to the poet, and to all others; or, if you please, every man is so far a poet as to be susceptible of these enchantments of nature; for all men have the thoughts whereof the universe is the celebration. I find that the fascination resides in the symbol. Who loves nature? Who does not? Is it only poets, and men of leisure and culti-vation, who live with her? No; but also hunters, farmers, grooms, and butchers, though they express their affection in their choice of life and not in their choice of words. The writer wonders what the coachman or the hunter values in riding, in horses and dogs. It is not superficial qualities. When you talk with him he holds these at as slight a rate as you. His worship is sympathetic; he has no definitions, but he is commended in nature by the living power which he feels to be there present. No imitation or playing of these things would content him; he loves the earnest of the north wind, of rain, of stone, and wood, and iron. A beauty not explicable is dearer than a beauty which we can see to the end of. It is na-ture the symbol, nature certifying the supernatural, body overflowed by life which he worships with coarse but sincere rites.

The inwardness and mystery of this attachment drive men of every class to the use of emblems. The schools of poets and philosophers are not more intoxicated with their symbols than the populace with theirs. In our political parties, com-pute the power of badges and emblems. See the great ball which they roll from Baltimore to Bunker Hill! In the politi-cal processions, Lowell goes in a loom, and Lynn in a shoe, and Salem in a ship. Witness the cider-barrel, the log-cabin, the hickory-stick, the palmetto, and all the cognizances of party. See the power of national emblems. Some stars, lilies, leopards, a crescent, a lion, an eagle, or other figure which came into credit God knows how, on an old rag of bunting, blowing in the wind on a fort at the ends of the earth, shall make the blood tingle under the rudest or the most conventional exterior. The people fancy they hate poetry, and they are all poets and mystics!

Beyond this universality of the symbolic language, we are apprised of the divineness of this superior use of things, whereby the world is a temple whose walls are covered with emblems, pictures, and commandments of the Deity,—in this, that there is no fact in nature which does not carry the whole sense of nature; and the distinctions which we make in events and in affairs; of low and high, honest and base, disappear when nature is used as a symbol. Thought makes everything fit for use. The vocabulary of an omniscient man would embrace words and images excluded from polite conversation. What would be base, or even obscene, to the obscene, becomes illustrious, spoken in a new connection of thought. The piety of the Hebrew prophets purges their grossness. The circumcision is an example of the power of poetry to raise the low and offensive. Small and mean things serve as well as great symbols. The meaner the type by which a law is expressed, the more pungent it is, and the more lasting in the memories of men; just as we choose the smallest box or case in which any needful utensil can be carried. Bare lists of words are found suggestive to an imaginative and excited mind; as it is related of Lord Chatham that he was accustomed to read in Bailey's Dictionary when he was preparing to speak in Parliament. The poorest experience is rich enough for all the purposes of expressing thought. Why covet a knowledge of new facts? Day and night, house and garden, a few books, a few actions, serve us as well as would all trades and all spectacles. We are far from having exhausted the significance of the few symbols we use. We can come to use them yet with a terrible simplicity. It does not need that a poem should be long. Every word was once a poem. Every new relation is a new word. Also we use defects and deformities to a sacred purpose, so expressing our sense that the evils of the world are such only to the evil eye. In the old mythology, mythologists observe, defects are as-

cribed to divine natures, as lameness to Vulcan, blindness to
Cupid, and the like,—to signify exuberances.

For as it is dislocation and detachment from the life of God
that makes things ugly, the poet, who re-attaches things to nature and the Whole,—re-attaching even artificial things and
violations of nature, to nature, by a deeper insight,—disposes
very easily of the most disagreeable facts. Readers of poetry
see the factory-village and the railway, and fancy that the
poetry of the landscape is broken up by these; for these works
of art are not yet consecrated in their reading; but the poet
sees them fall within the great Order not less than the bee-
hive or the spider's geometrical web. Nature adopts them very
fast into her vital circles, and the gliding train of cars she
loves like her own. Besides, in a centred mind, it signifies nothing how many mechanical inventions you exhibit. Though
you add millions, and never so surprising, the fact of mechanics has not gained a grain's weight. The spiritual fact remains unalterable, by many or by few particulars; as no
mountain is of any appreciable height to break the curve of
the sphere. A shrewd country-boy goes to the city for the first
time, and the complacent citizen is not satisfied with his little
wonder. It is not that he does not see all the fine houses and
know that he never saw such before, but he disposes of them
as easily as the poet finds place for the railway. The chief
value of the new fact is to enhance the great and constant fact
of Life, which can dwarf any and every circumstance, and to
which the belt of wampum and the commerce of America are
alike.

The world being thus put under the mind for verb and
noun, the poet is he who can articulate it. For though life is
great, and fascinates and absorbs; and though all men are intelligent of the symbols through which it is named; yet they
cannot originally use them. We are symbols and inhabit symbols; workmen, work, and tools, words and things, birth and
death, all are emblems; but we sympathize with the symbols,
and being infatuated with the economical uses of things, we
do not know that they are thoughts. The poet, by an ulterior

intellectual perception, gives them a power which makes their old use forgotten, and puts eyes and a tongue into every dumb and inanimate object. He perceives the independence of the thought on the symbol, the stability of the thought, the accidency and fugacity of the symbol. As the eyes of Lyncaeus were said to see through the earth, so the poet turns the world to glass, and shows us all things in their right series and procession. For through that better perception he stands one step nearer to things, and sees the flowing or metamorphosis; perceives that thought is multiform; that within the form of every creature is a force impelling it to ascend into a higher form; and following with his eyes the life, uses the forms which express that life, and so his speech flows with the flowing of nature. All the facts of the animal economy, sex, nutriment, gestation, birth, growth, are symbols of the passage of the world into the soul of man, to suffer there a change and reappear a new and higher fact. He uses forms according to the life, and not according to the form. This is true science. The poet alone knows astronomy, chemistry, vegetation and animation, for he does not stop at these facts, but employs them as signs. He knows why the plain or meadow of space was strewn with these flowers we call suns and moons and stars; why the great deep is adorned with animals, with men, and gods; for in every word he speaks he rides on them as the horses of thought.

By virtue of this science the poet is the Namer or Language-maker, naming things sometimes after their appearance, sometimes after their essence, and giving to every one its own name and not another's, thereby rejoicing the intellect, which delights in detachment or boundary. The poets made all the words, and therefore language is the archives of history, and, if we must say it, a sort of tomb of the muses. For though the origin of most of our words is forgotten, each word was at first a stroke of genius, and obtained currency because for the moment it symbolized the world to the first speaker and to the hearer. The etymologist finds the deadest word to have been once a brilliant picture. Language is fossil poetry. As the lime-

stone of the continent consists of infinite masses of the shells
of animalcules, so language is made up of images or tropes,
which now, in their secondary use, have long ceased to remind
us of their poetic origin. But the poet names the thing because
he sees it, or comes one step nearer to it than any other. This
expression or naming is not art, but a second nature, grown
out of the first, as a leaf out of a tree. What we call nature is
a certain self-regulated motion or change; and nature does all
things by her own hands, and does not leave another to bap-
tize her but baptizes herself; and this through the metamorphosis again. I remember that a certain poet described it to
me thus:—

Genius is the activity which repairs the decays of things,
whether wholly or partly of a material and finite kind. Nature,
through all her kingdoms, insures herself. Nobody cares for
planting the poor fungus; so she shakes down from the gills of
one agaric countless spores, any one of which, being preserved,
transmits new billions of spores tomorrow or next day. The
new agaric of this hour has a chance which the old one had
not. This atom of seed is thrown into a new place, not subject
to the accidents which destroyed its parent two rods off. She
makes a man; and having brought him to ripe age, she will no
longer run the risk of losing this wonder at a blow, but she
detaches from him a new self, that the kind may be safe from
accidents to which the individual is exposed. So when the soul
of the poet has come to ripeness of thought, she detaches and
sends away from it its poems or songs,—a fearless, sleepless,
deathless progeny, which is not exposed to the accidents of
the weary kingdom of time; a fearless, vivacious offspring, clad
with wings (such was the virtue of the soul out of which they
came) which carry them fast and far, and infix them irrecover-
ably into the hearts of men. These wings are the beauty of the
poet's soul. The songs, thus flying immortal from their mortal
parent, are pursued by clamorous flights of censures, which
swarm in far greater numbers and threaten to devour them;
but these last are not winged. At the end of a very short leap
they fall plump down and rot, having received from the souls

out of which they came no beautiful wings. But the melodies
of the poet ascend and leap and pierce into the deeps of infinite time.

So far the bard taught me, using his freer speech. But nature
has a higher end, in the production of new individuals, than
security, namely *ascension,* or the passage of the soul into
higher forms. I knew in my younger days the sculptor who
made the statue of the youth which stands in the public garden. He was, as I remember, unable to tell directly what made
him happy or unhappy, but by wonderful indirections he
could tell. He rose one day, according to his habit, before the
dawn, and saw the morning break, grand as the eternity out
of which it came, and for many days after, he strove to express
this tranquillity, and lo! his chisel had fashioned out of marble the form of a beautiful youth, Phosphorus, whose aspect
is such that it is said all persons who look on it become silent.
The poet also resigns himself to his mood, and that thought
which agitated him is expressed, but *alter idem,* in a manner
totally new. The expression is organic, or the new type which
things themselves take when liberated. As, in the sun, objects
paint their images on the retina of the eye, so they, sharing
the aspiration of the whole universe, tend to paint a far more
delicate copy of their essence in his mind. Like the metamorphosis of things into higher organic forms is their change into
melodies. Over everything stands its daemon or soul, and, as
the form of the thing is reflected by the eye, so the soul of the
thing is reflected by a melody. The sea, the mountain-ridge,
Niagara, and every flower-bed, pre-exist or super-exist, in pre-
cantations, which sail like odors in the air, and when any man
goes by with an ear sufficiently fine, he overhears them and
endeavors to write down the notes without diluting or de-
praving them. And herein is the legitimation of criticism, in
the mind's faith that the poems are a corrupt version of some
text in nature with which they ought to be made to tally. A
rhyme in one of our sonnets should not be less pleasing than
the iterated nodes of a seashell, or the resembling difference of

a group of flowers. The pairing of the birds is an idyl, not tedious as our idyls are; a tempest is a rough ode, without falsehood or rant; a summer, with its harvest sown, reaped, and stored, is an epic song, subordinating how many admirably executed parts. Why should not the symmetry and truth that modulate these, glide into our spirits, and we participate the invention of nature?

This insight, which expresses itself by what is called Imagination, is a very high sort of seeing, which does not come by study, but by the intellect being where and what it sees; by sharing the path or circuit of things through forms, and so making them translucid to others. The path of things is silent. Will they suffer a speaker to go with them? A spy they will not suffer; a lover, a poet, is the transcendency of their own nature,—him they will suffer. The condition of true naming, on the poet's part, is his resigning himself to the divine *aura* which breathes through forms, and accompanying that.

It is a secret which every intellectual man quickly learns, that beyond the energy of his possessed and conscious intellect he is capable of a new energy (as of an intellect doubled on itself), by abandonment to the nature of things; that beside his privacy of power as an individual man, there is a great public power on which he can draw, by unlocking, at all risks, his human doors, and suffering the ethereal tides to roll and circulate through him; then he is caught up into the life of the Universe, his speech is thunder, his thought is law, and his words are universally intelligible as the plants and animals. The poet knows that he speaks adequately then only when he speaks somewhat wildly, or "with the flower of the mind"; not with the intellect used as an organ, but with the intellect released from all service and suffered to take its direction from its celestial life; or as the ancients were wont to express themselves, not with intellect alone but with the intellect inebriated by nectar. As the traveller who has lost his way throws his reins on his horse's neck and trusts to the instinct of the animal to find his road, so must we do with the divine animal who carries us through this world. For if in any manner we can stimulate this instinct, new passages are opened for us into nature; the mind flows into and through things hardest and highest, and the metamorphosis is possible.

This is the reason why bards love wine, mead, narcotics, coffee, tea, opium, the fumes of sandalwood and tobacco, or whatever other procurers of animal exhilaration. All men avail themselves of such means as they can, to add this extraordinary power to their normal powers; and to this end they prize conversation, music, pictures, sculpture, dancing, theatres, travelling, war, mobs, fires, gaming, politics, or love, or science, or animal intoxication,—which are several coarser or finer quasi-mechanical substitutes for the true nectar, which is the ravishment of the intellect by coming nearer to the fact. These are auxiliaries to the centrifugal tendency of a man, to his passage out into free space, and they help him to escape the custody of that body in which he is pent up, and of that jail-yard of individual relations in which he is enclosed. Hence a great number of such as were professionally expressers of Beauty, as painters, poets, musicians, and actors, have been more than others wont to lead a life of pleasure and indulgence; all but the few who received the true nectar; and, as it was a spurious mode of attaining freedom, as it was an emancipation not into the heavens but into the freedom of baser places, they were punished for that advantage they won, by a dissipation and deterioration. But never can any advantage be taken of nature by a trick. The spirit of the world, the great calm presence of the Creator, comes not forth to the sorceries of opium or of wine. The sublime vision comes to the pure and simple soul in a clean and chaste body. That is not an inspiration, which we owe to narcotics, but some counterfeit excitement and fury. Milton says that the lyric poet may drink wine and live generously, but the epic poet, he who shall sing of the Gods and their descent unto men, must drink water out of a wooden bowl. For poetry is not "Devil's wine," but God's wine. It is with this as it is with toys. We fill the hands and nurseries of our children with all manner of dolls, drums, and horses; withdrawing their eyes from the plain face and sufficing objects of nature, the sun, the moon, the animals, the water, and stones, which should be their toys. So the poet's habit of living should be set on a key so low that the common influences should delight him. His cheerfulness should be the gift of the sunlight; the air should suffice for his inspiration, and he should be tipsy with water. That spirit which suffices quiet hearts, which seems to come forth to such from every dry knoll of sere grass, from every pine-stump and half-imbedded stone on which the dull March sun shines, comes forth to the poor and hungry, and such as are of simple taste. If thou fill thy brain with Boston and New York, with fashion and covetousness, and wilt stimulate thy jaded senses with wine and French coffee, thou shalt find no radiance of wisdom in the lonely waste of the pinewoods.

If the imagination intoxicates the poet, it is not inactive in other men. The metamorphosis excites in the beholder an emotion of joy. The use of symbols has a certain power of emancipation and exhiliration for all men. We seem to be touched by a wand which makes us dance and run about happily, like children. We are like persons who come out of a cave or cellar into the open air. This is the effect on us of tropes, fables, oracles, and all poetic forms. Poets are thus liberating gods. Men have really got a new sense, and found within their world another world, or nest of worlds; for, the metamorphosis once seen, we divine that it does not stop. I will not now consider how much this makes the charm of algebra and the mathematics, which also have their tropes, but it is felt in every definition; as when Aristotle defines *space* to be an immovable vessel in which things are contained;—or when Plato defines a *line* to be a flowing point; or *figure* to be a bound of solid; and many the like. What a joyful sense of freedom we have when Vitruvius announces the old opinion of artists that no architect can build any house well who does not know something of anatomy. When Socrates, in Charmides, tells us that the soul is cured of its maladies by certain incantations, and that these incantations are beautiful reasons, from which temperance is generated in souls; when Plato calls the world an animal, and Timaeus affirms that the plants also are animals; or affirms a man to be a heavenly tree, growing with his root, which is his head, upward; and, as George Chapman, following him, writes,—

> So in our tree of man, whose nervie root
> Springs in his top;—

when Orpheus speaks of hoariness as "that white flower which marks extreme old age"; when Proclus calls the universe the statue of the intellect; when Chaucer, in his praise of "Gentilesse," compares good blood in mean condition to fire, which, though carried to the darkest house betwixt this and the mount of Caucasus, will yet hold its natural office and burn as bright as if twenty thousand men did it behold; when John saw, in the Apocalypse, the ruin of the world through evil, and the stars fall from heaven as the figtree casteth her untimely fruit; when Aesop reports the whole catalogue of common daily relations through the masquerade of birds and beasts;—we take the cheerful hint of the immortality of our essence and its versatile habit and escapes, as when the gypsies say of themselves, "It is in vain to hang them, they cannot die."

The poets are thus liberating gods. The ancient British bards had for the title of their order, "Those who are free throughout the world." They are free, and they make free. An imaginative book renders us much more service at first, by stimulating us through its tropes, than afterward when we arrive at the precise sense of the author. I think nothing is of any value in books excepting the transcendental and extraordinary. If a man is inflamed and carried away by his thought, to that degree that he forgets the authors and the public and heeds only this one dream which holds him like an insanity, let me read his paper, and you may have all the arguments and histories and criticism. All the value which attaches to Pythagoras, Paracelsus, Cornelius Agrippa, Cardan, Kepler, Swedenborg, Schelling, Oken, or any other who introduces questionable facts into his cosmogony, as angels, devils, magic, astrology, palmistry, mesmerism, and so on, is the certificate we have of departure from routine, and that here is a new witness. That also is the best success in conversation, the magic of liberty, which puts the world like a ball in our hands. How cheap even the liberty then seems; how mean to study, when an emotion communicates to the intellect the power to sap and upheave nature; how great the perspective! nations, times, systems, enter and disappear like threads in tapestry of large figure and many colors; dream delivers us to dream, and while the drunkenness lasts we will sell our bed, our philosophy, our religion, in our opulence.

There is good reason why we should prize this liberation. The fate of the poor shepherd, who, blinded and lost in the snow-storm, perishes in a drift within a few feet of his cottage door, is an emblem of the state of man. On the brink of the waters of life and truth, we are miserably dying. The inaccessibleness of every thought but that we are in, is wonderful. What if you come near to it; you are as remote when you are nearest as when you are farthest. Every thought is also a prison; every heaven is also a prison. Therefore we love the poet, the inventor, who in any form, whether in an ode or in an action or in looks and behavior, has yielded us a new thought. He unlocks our chains and admits us to a new scene.

This emancipation is dear to all men, and the power to impart it, as it must come from greater depth and scope of thought, is a measure of intellect. Therefore all books of the imagination endure, all which ascend to that truth that the writer sees nature beneath him, and uses it as his exponent. Every verse or sentence possessing this virtue will take care of its own immortality. The religions of the world are the ejaculations of a few imaginative men.

But the quality of the imagination is to flow, and not to freeze. The poet did not stop at the color or the form, but read their meaning; neither may he rest in this meaning, but he makes the same objects exponents of his new thought. Here is the difference betwixt the poet and the mystic, that the last nails a symbol to one sense, which was a true sense for a moment, but soon becomes old and false. For all symbols are fluxional; all language is vehicular and transitive, and is good, as ferries and horses are, for conveyance, not as farms and houses are, for homestead. Mysticism consists in the mistake of an accidental and individual symbol for an universal one. The morning-redness happens to be the favorite meteor to the eyes of Jacob Behmen, and comes to stand to him for truth and faith; and, he believes, should stand for the same realities to every reader. But the first reader prefers as naturally the symbol of a mother and child, or a gardener and his bulb, or a jeweller polishing a gem. Either of these, or of a myriad more, are equally good to the person to whom they are significant. Only they must be held lightly, and be very willingly translated into the equivalent terms which others use. And the mystic must be steadily told,—All that you say is just as true without the tedious use of that symbol as with it. Let us have a little algebra, instead of this trite rhetoric,—universal signs, instead of these village symbols,—and we shall both be gainers. The history of hierarchies seems to show that all religious error consisted in making the symbol too stark and solid, and was at last nothing but an excess of the organ of language.

Swedenborg, of all men in the recent ages, stands eminently for the translator of nature into thought. I do not know the man in history to whom things stood so uniformly for words. Before him the metamorphosis continually plays. Everything on which his eye rests obeys the impulses of moral nature. The figs become grapes whilst he eats them. When some of his angels affirmed a truth, the laurel twig which they held blossomed in their hands. The noise which at a distance appeared like gnashing and thumping, on coming nearer was found to be the voice of disputants. The men in one of his visions, seen in heavenly light, appeared like dragons, and seemed in darkness; but to each other they appeared as men, and when the light from heaven shone into their cabin, they complained of the darkness, and were compelled to shut the window that they might see.

There was this perception in him which makes the poet or seer an object of awe and terror, namely that the same man or society of men may wear one aspect to themselves and their companions, and a different aspect to higher intelligences. Certain priests, whom he describes as conversing very learnedly together, appeared to the children who were at some distance like dead horses; and many the like misappearances. And instantly the mind inquires whether these fishes under the bridge, yonder oxen in the pasture, those dogs in the yard, are immutably fishes, oxen, and dogs, or only so appear to me, and perchance to themselves appear upright men; and whether I appear as a man to all eyes. The Bramins and Pythagoras propounded the same question, and if any poet has witnessed the transformation he doubtless found it in harmony with various experiences. We have all seen changes as considerable in wheat and caterpillars. He is the poet and shall draw us with love and terror, who sees through the flowing vest the firm nature, and can declare it.

I look in vain for the poet whom I describe. We do not with sufficient plainness or sufficient profoundness address ourselves to life, nor dare we chaunt our own times and social circumstance. If we filled the day with bravery, we should not shrink from celebrating it. Time and nature yield us many gifts, but not yet the timely man, the new religion, the reconciler, whom all things await. Dante's praise is that he dared to write his autobiography in colossal cipher, or into universality. We have yet had no genius in America, with tyrannous eye, which knew the value of our incomparable materials, and saw, in the barbarism and materialism of the times, another carnival of the same gods whose picture he so much admires in Homer; then in the Middle Age; then in Calvinism. Banks and tariffs, the newspaper and caucus, Methodism and Unitarianism, are flat and dull to dull people, but rest on the same foundations of wonder as the town of Troy and the temple of Delphi, and are as swiftly passing away. Our log-rolling, our stumps and their politics, our fisheries, our Negroes and Indians, our boasts and our repudiations, the wrath of rogues and the pusillanimity of honest men, the northern trade, the southern planting, the western clearing, Oregon and Texas, are yet unsung. Yet

America is a poem in our eyes; its ample geography dazzles the imagination, and it will not wait long for metres. If I have not found that excellent combination of gifts in my countrymen which I seek, neither could I aid myself to fix the idea of the poet by reading now and then in Chalmers's collection of five centuries of English poets. These are wits more than poets, though there have been poets among them. But when we adhere to the ideal of the poet, we have our difficulties even with Milton and Homer. Milton is too literary, and Homer too literal and historical.

But I am not wise enough for a national criticism, and must use the old largeness a little longer, to discharge my errand from the muse to the poet concerning his art.

Art is the path of the creator to his work. The paths or methods are ideal and eternal, though few men ever see them; not the artist himself for years, or for a lifetime, unless he come into the conditions. The painter, the sculptor, the composer, the epic rhapsodist, the orator, all partake one desire, namely to express themselves symmetrically and abundantly, not dwarfishly and fragmentarily. They found or put themselves in certain conditions, as the painter and sculptor before some impressive human figures; the orator, into the assembly of the people; and the others in such scenes as each has found exciting to his intellect; and each presently feels the new desire. He hears a voice, he sees a beckoning. Then he is apprised, with wonder, what herds of daemons hem him in. He can no more rest; he says, with the old painter, "By God it is in me and must go forth of me." He pursues a beauty, half seen, which flies before him. The poet pours out verses in every solitude. Most of the things he says are conventional, no doubt; but by and by he says something which is original and beautiful. That charms him. He would say nothing else but such things. In our way of talking we say, "That is yours, this is mine"; but the poet knows well that it is not his; that it is as strange and beautiful to him as to you; he would fain hear the like eloquence at length. Once having tasted this immortal ichor, he cannot have enough of it, and as an admirable crea-

tive power exists in these intellections, it is of the last importance that these things get spoken. What a little of all we
know is said! What drops of all the sea of our science are baled
up! and by what accident it is that these are exposed, when so
many secrets sleep in nature. Hence the necessity of speech and
song; hence these throbs and heart-beatings in the orator, at
the door of the assembly, to the end namely that thought may
be ejaculated as Logos, or Word.

Doubt not, O poet, but persist. Say "It is in me, and shall
out." Stand there, balked and dumb, stuttering and stammer-
ing, hissed and hooted, stand and strive, until at last rage draw
out of thee that *dream*-power which every night shows thee is
thine own; a power transcending all limit and privacy, and by
virtue of which a man is the conductor of the whole river of
electricity. Nothing walks, or creeps, or grows, or exists, which
must not in turn arise and walk before him as exponent of his
meaning. Comes he to that power, his genius is no longer
exhaustible. All the creatures by pairs and by tribes pour into
his mind as into a Noah's ark, to come forth again to people
a new world. This is like the stock of air for our respiration
or for the combustion of our fireplace; not a measure of gal-
lons, but the entire atmosphere if wanted. And therefore the
rich poets, as Homer, Chaucer, Shakespeare, and Raphael,
have obviously no limits to their works except the limits of
their lifetime, and resemble a mirror carried through the
street, ready to render an image of every created thing.

O poet! a new nobility is conferred in groves and pastures,
and not in castles or by the sword-blade any longer. The conditions are hard, but equal. Thou shalt leave the world, and
know the muse only. Thou shalt not know any longer the
times, customs, graces, politics, or opinions of men, but shalt
take all from the muse. For the time of towns is tolled from
the world by funereal chimes, but in nature the universal
hours are counted by succeeding tribes of animals and plants,
and by growth of joy on joy. God wills also that thou abdicate
a manifold and duplex life, and that thou be content that
others speak for thee. Others shall be thy gentlemen and shall

represent all courtesy and worldly life for thee; others shall do the great and resounding actions also. Thou shalt lie close hid with nature, and canst not be afforded to the Capitol or the Exchange. The world is full of renunciations and apprenticeships, and this is thine; thou must pass for a fool and a churl for a long season. This is the screen and sheath in which Pan has protected his well-beloved flower, and thou shalt be known only to thine own, and they shall console thee with tenderest love. And thou shalt not be able to rehearse the names of thy friends in thy verse, for an old shame before the holy ideal. And this is the reward; that the ideal shall be real to thee, and the impressions of the actual world shall fall like summer rain, copious, but not troublesome to thy invulnerable essence. Thou shalt have the whole land for thy park and manor, the sea for thy bath and navigation, without tax and without envy; the woods and the rivers thou shalt own, and thou shalt possess that wherein others are only tenants and boarders. Thou true land-lord! sea-lord! air-lord! Wherever snow falls or water flows or birds fly, wherever day and night meet in twilight, wherever the blue heaven is hung by clouds or sown with stars, wherever are forms with transparent boundaries, wherever are outlets into celestial space, wherever is danger, and awe, and love,—there is Beauty, plenteous as rain, shed for thee, and though thou shouldst walk the world over, thou shalt not be able to find a condition inopportune or ignoble.

E. P. WHIPPLE

Edwin Percy Whipple (1819-1886) was born in Gloucester, Massachusetts. After leaving high school in Salem, where he also worked in a local bank and wrote for newspapers, he went to Boston, the employee of a brokerage house and, later, superintendent of the Merchants' Exchange. He began to write critical reviews as soon as he arrived in Boston, and in 1843 he published, in *Boston Miscellany,* an essay on Thomas Babington Macaulay which won even Macaulay's commendation. This essay was included in Whipple's two-volume collection, *Essays and Reviews* (1848-49). The following year Whipple published another volume of lectures on literary subjects. Although these writings established Whipple's considerable reputation as a literary critic—Whittier called him "one of the ablest critical essayists" of the times— Whipple maintained his business career until 1860, when he became a professional lecturer. He published three more volumes of essays, one of which contained the Lowell Lectures of 1869. He was the literary editor (1872) of the Boston *Daily Globe,* and he edited an anthology of poetry and the writings of several colleagues. Three volumes of lectures and papers on society, literature, and literary personalities were posthumously published. There is no collected edition of his writing.

First printed as "Criticisms: Coleridge," in the *American Review,* June 1846, Whipple's essay was reprinted in *Essays and Reviews* (1849), from which this text is taken. Whipple's cogent summary of Coleridge's critical thought anticipated his own practice, in reviewing, of seeking out what he called the life-principle of a work as a basis for criticism.

COLERIDGE AS A PHILOSOPHICAL CRITIC

THE present century has been eminently characterized by its critical spirit. Institutions and opinions, men, manners, and literature, have all been subjected to the most exhausting analysis. The moment a thing becomes a fixed fact in the community, criticism breaks it to pieces, curious to scan its elements. It is not content to admire the man until satisfied with his appearance as a skeleton. The science of criticism is thus in danger of becoming a kind of intellectual anatomy. The living body of a poem or institution is dissected, and its principle of life sought in a process which annihilates life at its first step. An analysis thus employing no other implements but those furnished by the understanding, must imperfectly interpret what has proceeded from the imagination. The soul ever eludes the knife of the dissector, however keen and cunning.

The charlatanism, which spreads and sprawls in almost every department of literature and life, is doubtless one cause of this analytical spirit. A man placed in our century finds himself surrounded by quackeries. Collision with these begets in him a feeling of impatience and petulant opposition, and ends often in forcing him to apply individual tests to all outward things. By this course he, at least, preserves his own personality amid the whiz and burr around him. None of that spurious toleration which comes from feebleness of thought, or laxity of will, or indifference to truth, makes him lend his ear to every moan of the noodle, and every promise of the quack. But this self-consciousness, so jealous of encroachment and battling against all external influences, shuts his mind to new truth as well as old error. He preserves his common sense at the expense of his comprehension. He is sensible and barren. His tiresome self-repetition becomes, at last, as hollow a mockery as the clap-trap of the charlatan.

This tendency to individualism—this testing the value of all things by their agreement or discordance with individual modes of thinking—subjects the author to hard conditions. He is necessarily viewed from an antagonistic position, and considered an impostor until proved a reality. We think he is determined to fool us if he can, and are therefore most delighted and refreshed when we have analyzed the seeming genius down into the real quack. The life of the intellect thus becomes negative rather than positive—devoted to the exposure of error, not to the assimilation of truth. Men of strong minds in this generation have established a sort of intellectual feudal system—each baron walled in from approach, and sallying out only to prey upon his brothers. Everybody is on his guard against everybody else. An author has to fight his way into esteem. He must have sufficient force of being to be victorious over others: his readers are the spoils of his conquest. He attacks minds intrenched in their own thoughts and prejudices, and determined not to yield as long as their defences will hold out. The poetaster in Wycherley's play binds the widow to a chair, in order that she may be compelled to listen to his well-penned verses. A resisting criticism, somewhat after the manner of the widow, is practiced unconsciously by most educated readers. It is mortifying to become the vassal of a superior nature; to feel the understanding bowed and bent before a conquering intellect, and be at once petulant and impotent. Butler's reasoning and Milton's rhetoric, fastening themselves as they do on the mind or heart, become at times distasteful, from the fact of our incapacity to resist their power. It is from men of education and ability that great genius experiences most opposition. The multitude can scarcely resist a powerful nature, but are forced into the current of its thoughts and impulses. The educated, on the contrary, have implements of defence. Their minds have become formal and hardened. Coleridge felt this deeply, when he exclaimed, "Who will dare to force his way out of the crowd—not of the mere vulgar, but of the *vain and banded aristocracy of intellect*—and presume to join the almost supernatural beings that stand by themselves aloof?" This aristocracy furnishes generally the cham-

pions of accredited opinions and processes. It flouts the inno-
vations of genius and philanthropy, as well as the fooleries of
knavery and ignorance. It desires nothing new, good or bad.

The influence of this spirit on criticism in the present century has been incalculable. In those cases where personal and
partisan feelings have not converted literary judgments into
puffs or libels, the analytical and unsympathizing mode in
which critical inquiries have been prosecuted has been unjust
to original genius. Poets have been tried by tests which their
writings were never intended to meet. Where a work is a
mere collection of parts, loosely strung together, and animated
by no central principle of vitality, analysis has only to cut the
string to destroy its rickety appearance of life. As a large majority of productions, purporting to come from the human
mind, are heterogeneous, not homogeneous; mechanical, not
organic—the works of what Fichte calls the *hodmen* of letters
—the course pursued by the critic at least exposes deception.
But the process by which imposture may be exposed is not
necessarily that by which truth can be evolved. A life spent in
examining deceptions and quackeries produces little fruit. A
well-trained power to discern excellence would include all the
negative advantages of the other, and end also in the positive
benefit of mental enlargement and elevation. Reading and
judgment result in nothing but barrenness when they simply
confirm the critic's opinion of himself. The mind is enriched
only by assimilation, and true intellectual independence comes
not from the complacent dullness of the egotist. The mind
that would be monarchical should not be content with a petty
domain, but have whole provinces of thought for its depend-
encies. To comprehend another mind, we must first be tolerant to its peculiarities, and place ourselves in the attitude of
learners. After that our judgment will be of value. The thing
itself must be known before its excellence can be estimated;
and it must be reproduced before it can be known. By contemplation rather than analysis, by self-forgetfulness rather
than self-confidence, does the elusive and ethereal life of genius yield itself to the mind of the critic.

If we examine the writings of some of the most popular critics of the present century, we shall find continual proofs of the narrowness to which we have referred. In a vast majority of cases, the criticism is merely the grating of one individual mind against another. The critic understands little but himself, and his skill consists in a dexterous substitution of his own peculiarities for the laws of taste and beauty, or in sneeringly alluding to the difference between the work he is reviewing and works of established fame. Lord Jeffrey is an instance. The position in which he was placed, as editor of the most influential Review ever published, was one requiring the most comprehensive thought and the most various attainments. At the period the Edinburgh Review was started, the literary republic swarmed with a host of vain and feeble poetasters, whose worthlessness invited destruction; but in the midst of these there were others, the exponents of a new and original school of poetry, whose genius required interpretation. Now the test to be applied to a critic, under such circumstances, is plain. Was his taste catholic? Did he perceive and elucidate excellence, as well as detect and punish pretension? Did he see the dawn on the mountain tops, as well as the will-o'-the-wisps in the bogs beneath? Did he have any principles on which to ground his judgments, apart from the impertinences of his personality? We think not. Not in his writings are we to look for a philosophy of criticism. He could see that the consumptive hectic on the cheek of mediocrity was not the ruddy glow of genius. He could torture feebleness and folly on the rack of his ridicule. He could demonstrate that Mr. William Hayley and Mr. Robert Merry were poor successors of Pope and Dryden. But when he came to consider men like Wordsworth and Coleridge, we find the nimble-witted critic to be, after all, blind in one eye. Here were authors destined to work a great poetical revolution, to give a peculiar character to the literature of a generation, to have followers even among men of genius. In their earlier efforts, doubtless grave faults might have been discovered. Their thoughts were often vitiated by mental bombast; their expression, by simplicity that bordered on silliness, by obscurity that sometimes tumbled into the void inane. But amidst all their errors, indications were continually given of the vital powers of genius; of minds which, to the mere forms and colors of nature, could

> Add the gleam,
> The light that never was on sea or land,
> The consecration and the poet's dream.

Now these poets Jeffrey judged before he interpreted. His quick glance over the superficies of things, and his faculty of rapid empirical generalization, enabled him to present their defects before the eye in exaggerated proportions; but their genius merely hummed in his ears. He was never borne along with the glad and exulting song in which they hymned the wondrousness and beauty of nature; his soul never lifted itself up to those regions where their spirits roved and shaped in the ecstasies of contemplation. In all his various *critiques,* he never touched the heart of their mystery—never comprehended their individuality, their humanity, their spirituality, the organic life of their works. He either could not, or would not, reproduce in his own mind those moods of thought and feeling, upon whose validity the truth of their poetry was to be tried; consequently, he merely shoots squibs when he seems to be delivering decisions. Though he could handle a wide variety of topics, and was generally adroit and plausible in their management, his comprehension was simply of the surfaces of things.

Now the man for whose opinions Jeffrey had the least regard is the true exponent of the philosophical criticism of the century—Coleridge. He was the first who made criticism interpretative both of the spirit and form of works of genius, the first who founded his principles in the nature of things. Though his views strikingly coincide with those of Schlegel, they were formed and publicly expressed before that author's lectures on the Drama were delivered. Hazlitt, who delighted to vex Coleridge, was still very indignant when the latter was accused of pilfering from Schlegel, testifying to the fact of his originality from the most positive knowledge. Amid a host of professional critics, it was reserved for a poet to declare the true principles on which literary judgments should be grounded.

Coleridge's mind was eminently interpretative. He never was contented with knowing merely the surfaces of things, but his intellect pierced beneath to their laws. He possessed the power of learning from other minds. A creed, a poem, an institution, which had met the wants of any body of people, required, in his view, to be explained before it was censured. The reason of its influence must be given. He was not contented with judging it from his own point of view, but looked at it from its author's position. He saw that, to understand the events of history and the masterpieces of art, it was necessary to bring to them a mind willing to learn—that knowledge began in self-distrust—that individual experience is a poor measure of the resources of the race—and that ideas and principles varied their forms with variations in the circumstances of mankind. He knew that "to appreciate the defects of a great mind, it was necessary to understand previously its characteristic excellencies." He had a clear notion of the difference, lying at the base of all poetic criticism, between *mechanical regularity* and *organic form;* and in the disregard of this distinction by critics, he saw the cause of the numberless fallacies and falsities which vitiated their judgments. The form or body of a work of genius he considered as physiognomical of the soul within; that it was not a collection of parts, cunningly put together, but a growth from a central principle of life; and that every production of the mind, which was animated with life, was to be judged by its *organic* laws. This, of course, brings the critic to the very heart of the matter—the consideration of the vital powers of genius; those mysterious powers of growth and production, which are identical with the laws by which they work, and whose products, therefore, are not to be tried by laws external to themselves. "Could a rule be given from without, poetry would cease to be poetry, and sink into a mechanical art."

Without this doctrine of vital powers, criticism becomes

mere gibberish. Animated and informed by these vital powers, commonplace becomes poetry, and ritual religion. The first thing to be settled in reviewing a composition, is its vitality. Has it life? Did it grow to its present shape, or was it merely put together? It is useless to criticise a corpse. Now if a poem have life, the principle of growth and assimilation, then criticism should first develop from within the laws of its being. The question of its relative excellence comes afterwards. We must first discover what it is, and not decide that by saying what it is not. We must pass into the mysterious depths of the mind in which it was matured, see the fountain springs of its thoughts and emotions, and discern its own laws of growth and production. The peculiar individuality of the man, the circumstances of *his* being, not *our* peculiar individuality and the circumstances of *our* being, must be investigated, and, in imagination, lived. We must learn from what point, and under what influences, he looked on nature and human life, in order rightly to interpret his production. A tree, growing by virtue of inward properties, has, we all feel, an independent existence, and is itself its own apology and defence. So with a true poem, instinct with vitality. To judge it simply on its agreement or disagreement with the form of other poems is about as wise as to flout the willow because it is not the oak. Besides, what are called the "rules" of poetry were once the organic laws of individual works. The first poet furnished the rules of the first critic. The essential originality and life of a poem consists in containing within itself the laws by which it is to be judged. To make these laws the tests of other poems, produced by different minds, under different circumstances, in different ages and countries, is to convert the results of freedom into the instruments of slavery, and doom the intellect to barrenness and death. In almost every instance where a man of genius has given the law to others, the literature formed on his model has dwindled into mechanical imitation, and only been resuscitated by rebellion.

Nature furnishes exhaustless arguments against the critical narrowness, which would kill new beauty by accredited reputations. The faculty of perceiving beauty in a variety of different objects and forms is the source of true delight and improvement in literature as in scenery. An everlasting sameness and repetition in either would be intolerable. In one sentence Coleridge has given the true method of investigation: "Follow nature in variety of kinds." As nature is inexhaustible in its variety, so are the possible combinations of the human mind. If we could see all the poems that exist potentially, nature and man being given, we should drop our critical rules, though they were as wide as Homer and Shakspeare. The man of true taste enlarges his apprehension to receive the new poem as readily as to receive the new landscape. The Alps breed in him no contempt of the prairies. He has something in him which answers to Lake Leman as well as to the ocean. He has no quarrel with Chaucer because he loves Wordsworth. He feels the unity of beauty, and love, and grandeur, amid all the differences of forms; feels it, indeed, all the more intensely, with every glimpse of it in a new object. The swan and dove are both beautiful, but it would be absurd, says Coleridge, pertinently, "to institute a comparison between their separate claims to beauty from any abstract rule common to both, *without reference to the life and being of the animals themselves;* or, as if having first seen the dove, we abstracted its outlines, gave them a false generalization, called them the principles or ideal of bird beauty, and proceeded to criticise the swan and the eagle." It was from a method similar to this that critics, mesmerized by Pope and Goldsmith, dictated laws to Wordsworth and Shelley, and measured the genius of Shakspeare and Spenser. It was this method which made two generations rest contented with that precious morsel of criticism on Shakspeare, that he was a man of great beauties balanced by great faults—a man of the supremest genius and execrable taste! In view of the stupidities into which acute but narrow understandings have fallen, when they have mistaken the range of their own perceptions for the extent of the universe, we may exclaim with Coleridge—"Oh! few have there been among critics, who have followed with *the eye of imagination* the imperishable and ever-wandering spirit of poetry through its various metempsychoses and consequent metamorphoses— or who have rejoiced in the light of a clear perception at beholding with each new birth, with each rare *avatar*, the human race form to itself a new body, by assimilating materials of nourishment out of its new circumstances, and work for itself new organs of power appropriate to the new sphere of its motion and activity."

We are convinced that the true philosophical principles of criticism are those implied in the instinctive processes of every tolerant reader of taste. The mind, untrammeled by forms and rules which bigotry has put into it, has a sense for the beauty of all new objects, and sees them in relation to their own laws. Imperfect intellectual statements of the inward sense of beauty, and the hardening down of feelings into rules, cannot altogether blunt the natural processes even of the critic's own imagination. Besides, the mode we have indicated does not ignore rules and principles, except when rules and principles are without foundation in nature. It deduces its canons of criticism from premises lying deep in the nature of man. It pierces to that mysterious region of the soul in which poetry and religion, and all that transcends actual life, have their home. It disregards individual dictation and petulance, and empirical rules; but it does not disregard the nature of things. It applies tests, and severe ones, but its tests are the laws, in obedience to which the creative and modifying powers of the soul act. And these laws it philosophically investigates and systematizes. It requires unity in every work of art, because unity is the mark of organization. It tolerates the widest variety of kinds, but it demands that each shall have organic life. It detects deviations in a composition from its own law. It discriminates between what properly belongs to a work of art— what in it has been developed from its central principle of vitality—and the accretions which may have stuck to it. When it condemns poems, it condemns them from their "inappropriateness to their own end and being, their want of significance as symbols or physiognomy." By assuming the writer's own point of view, it has a sense of those imperfections of which he himself is painfully conscious; discerns the distance between the law and its embodiment; and preserves the dignity of the ideal by knowing the possibilities as well as the products of the imagination. Every form of beauty in nature or art, suggests something higher than itself.

In Coleridge's criticisms on Shakspeare, in his "Biographia Literaria," and in portions of his other prose works, we have a distinct enunciation, often in sentences of great splendor and energy, of the leading principles of this philosophical criticism. His prose, to be sure, is full of provoking faults, which few mere readers can tolerate. It is sometimes diffuse, obscure and languid, branching off into episodes and digressions, and not always held together by any perceptible thread of thought. Most students bring little from it but headaches. He is at once one of the best, and one of the worst of writers. He continually gives evidence of a power of composition, of which his prose works, on the whole, are but imperfect exponents. Sentences, full of muscular life and energy, embodying principles of the deepest import—words which come bright and rapid as lightning, splitting the "unwedgable and gnarled" problem—are often seen in his writings, in connection with unintelligible profundities and disordered metaphysics. The "Biographia Literaria" no one can read without being enriched, and without being bored. Tried by his own critical principles, it wants unity, clearness and proportion. He expends page upon page of what most readers would consider meaningless, metaphysical disquisition, preparatory to a definition of imagination, and then stops short with saying that, at present, he can merely give the result of his inquiries. That result is darker than the processes. "The primary Imagination," he says, "I hold to be the living Power and prime Agent of all human Perception, and as a repetition in the finite mind of the eternal act of creation, in the infinite I AM." We do not say that this and other passages are without any meaning, but the meaning is not clear. It is not unfolded, but wrapped up. The words buzz and whirl in the brain, but give no distinct ideas. The writer does not really communicate his thought, and, therefore, the first object of writing is over-looked. There is no subordination of the parts to the whole, but a splendid confusion.

Still, in this book, but more especially in the fragments on Shakspeare, Coleridge has given us the results of his investigations into poetry and art, though his metaphysical analysis of the faculties to which they relate is imperfect. His statements are better than his disquisitions—his appeal to consciousness better than his reasonings. The truths that he grasped in contemplation he could not always succeed in legitimatizing in metaphysical forms. But his theory of the vital powers of genius; his definitions of imagination and fancy; his felicitous distinctions, such as that which he makes between illusion and delusion; his view of the nature, scope and object of poetry; his acute perception of the difference between the classical and romantic drama, the essence of the first consisting in "the sternest separation of the diverse in kind and the disparate in degree, whilst the other delights in interlacing by a rainbow-like transfusion of hues the one with the other"; his elaborate criticism on the genius of Wordsworth; his view of the mind of Shakspeare; his criticism of single dramas, and his "endeavor to make out the title of the English drama, as created by and existing in Shakspeare, to the supremacy of dramatic excellence in general"; his definition of poetry as the art of representing, in measured words, "external nature and human thoughts, both relatively to human affections, so as to cause the production of as great immediate pleasure in each part as is compatible with the largest possible sum of pleasure in the whole"; his explanation of the *sensuous* element of poetry as the "union, harmonious melting down and *fusion* of the *sensual* in the spiritual"—all are replete with knowledge and suggestive thought. When Coleridge speaks of the poetical powers, we are constantly reminded by his very language that he transcribes his own consciousness, and speaks from authority, not as the reviewers; as when he refers to the "violences of excitement"—"the laws of association of feeling with thought"—"*the starts and strange farflights* of the assimilative power on the slightest and least obvious likeness presented by thoughts, words and objects"—"the original gift of spreading the tone, the *atmosphere,* and with it, the depth and height of the ideal world around forms, incidents and situations, of which, for the common view, custom had bedimmed all the lustre, had dried up the sparkle and the dew-drops." Also, in speaking of the language of the highest poetry, he calls it intermediate between arbitrary language, mere "modes of *recalling* an object, seen or felt, and the language of nature—a subordinate *Logos*—that was in the beginning, and was with the thing it represented, and was the thing it represented. It is the blending arbitrary language with that of nature, not merely recalling the cold notion of a thing, but expressing the reality of it—language which is itself a part of that which it manifests." In reading this, and also Wordsworth's definition of language, as the *"Incarnation* of thought," not its *dress,* we feel that it is not observation but consciousness that speaks.

To Coleridge belongs the honor of emancipating Shaksperian criticism in England from its old bonds. He showed that the error of the classical critics consisted in "mistaking for the essentials of the Greek stage, certain rules which the wise poets imposed on themselves, in order to render all the remaining parts of the drama consistent with those which had been forced upon them by circumstances independent of their will; out of which circumstances the drama itself rose. The circumstances in Shakspeare's time were different, which it was equally out of his power to alter, and such as, in my opinion, allowed a far wider sphere, and a deeper and more human interest. Critics are too apt to forget that rules are but means to an end; consequently, where the ends are different, the rules must be likewise so. We must have ascertained what the end *is,* before we can determine what the rules *ought* to be. Judging under this impression," he adds, "I did not hesitate to declare my full conviction, that the consummate judgment of Shakspeare, not only in the general construction, but in all the *detail* of his dramas, impressed me with greater wonder than even the might of his genius, or the depth of his philosophy." In his criticisms on Shakspeare, he insists, with much felicity, on the unity of a work of art as its characteristic excellence. It must be a concrete whole, all its parts in just subordination to its leading idea or principle of life. Thus the imagination, in its tranquil and purely pleasurable operation, "acts chiefly by creating out of many things as they would have appeared in the description of an ordinary mind detailed in unimpassioned succession, a *oneness,* even as nature, the greatest of poets, acts upon us when we open our eyes upon an extended prospect." And again: the imagination, by combining many circumstances into one moment of consciousness, "tends to produce the ultimate end of all human thought and feeling, unity, and thereby the reduction of the spirit to its principles and fountain, who is always truly one." At the end of his notes on Shakspeare, he has a passage, full of power and meaning, incidentally referring to the same thought: "There are three powers: Wit, which discovers partial likeness hidden in general diversity; Subtlety, which discovers the diversity concealed in general apparent sameness; and Profundity, which discovers an essential unity under all the semblances of difference. Give to a subtle man fancy, and he is a wit; to a deep man imagination, and he is a philosopher. Add, again, pleasurable sensibility in the threefold form of sympathy, with the interesting in morals, the impressive in form, and the harmonious in sound, and you have the poet. But combine all, wit, subtlety, and fancy, with profundity, imagination, and moral and physical susceptibility of the pleasurable, and let the object of action be man universal, and we shall have—O rash prophecy! say, rather, we have—a Shakspeare!"

We have no space to refer to the details of Coleridge's interpretations of Shakspeare, and Wordsworth, and to his application of his theory of vital powers to society, and the forms of religion and government. Everything *organized* received from him a respectful consideration, when he could recognize its organic life and principle of growth. This, of course, did not prevent him from criticising it, and estimating its value, and placing it in its due rank in the sliding scale of excellence and importance. But it did prevent him from hastily deciding questions on shallow grounds. It tended to give his mind catholicity and comprehension. It made him willing to learn. When he was dogmatic, his dogmatism was the dogmatism of knowledge, not of ignorance. He showed that there are deeper principles involved in what men loosely reason upon, and carelessly praise or condemn, than are generally acknowledged. He was most disposed to examine a book or an institution, to discern its meaning, while others were joining the hue and cry against it. And, especially, he changed criticism from censorship into interpretation—evolving laws, whilst others were railing at forms. His influence in this respect has been great. He has revolutionized the tone of Jeffrey's own review, and Carlyle, Macaulay, Talfourd, all the most popular critics of the day, more or less follow his mode of judgment and investigation.

NATHANIEL HAWTHORNE

Nathaniel Hawthorne (1804-1864), who was born in Salem, Massachusetts, spent nearly all of his sixty years in New England. His public life does not immediately reinforce one's impression of his fiction. Graduated from Bowdoin College in 1825, he was later the editor of a popular magazine, the author of juvenile stories, an employee in the Boston Customs House, and Surveyor of the Port of Salem. Involved in politics, he was the author of a campaign biography of Franklin Pierce, and, for three years, United States consul at Liverpool, England.

One common denominator of these activities, nevertheless—his sense of commitment to contemporary affairs—squares with Hawthorne's fiction, which dramatized the process of finding out oneself and, in this introspective process, the problem of isolation from and reunion with one's society. Hawthorne's fiction consistently represented an incident or a pattern of events in the context of this need to define oneself, whether he wrote specifically of the artist and society, characteristically of the inheritance of a decayed Puritan system of ideas in New England, or generally of the Fall of Man. This preoccupation with self-definition, and with the attendant isolation from and reunion with society marks the four romances of Hawthorne's mature years, *The Scarlet Letter* (1850), *The House of the Seven Gables* (1851), *The Blithedale Romance* (1852) and *The Marble Faun* (1860), and his several volumes of tales; and there are signs of it in his notebooks, which were edited and published after his death, and in the four fragments of a romance about England and America, which Hawthorne could never finish.

Always Hawthorne narrated the incident for the sake of its implications. Speculating about how to dramatize an actual occurence in "Wakefield," Hawthorne wrote, "Thought has always its efficacy and every striking incident its moral." This habit of thought partly explains the theory of fiction which Hawthorne set down in his Preface to *The House of the Seven Gables* (1851). His continuing satisfaction with the theory of the romance, in this Preface, showed up in his Preface to *The Marble Faun,* nine years later, in which he wrote, "The author proposed to himself merely to write a fanciful story, evolving a thoughtful moral. . . ."

This text of the Preface is from the 1864 edition of the novel. The standard edition of Hawthorne's works is the Riverside Edition: George P. Lathrop, *The Complete Works of Nathaniel Hawthorne, with Introductory Notes* (12 vols., 1883).

PREFACE TO
THE HOUSE OF THE SEVEN GABLES

WHEN a writer calls his work a Romance, it need hardly be observed that he wishes to claim a certain latitude, both as to its fashion and material, which he would not have felt himself entitled to assume had he professed to be writing a Novel. The latter form of composition is presumed to aim at a very minute fidelity, not merely to the possible, but to the probable and ordinary course of man's experience. The former—while, as a work of art, it must rigidly subject itself to laws, and while it sins unpardonably so far as it may swerve aside from the truth of the human heart—has fairly a right to present that truth under circumstances, to a great extent, of the writer's own choosing or creation. If he think fit, also, he may so manage his atmospherical medium as to bring out or mellow the lights and deepen and enrich the shadows of the picture. He will be wise, no doubt, to make a very moderate use of the privileges here stated, and, especially, to mingle the Marvellous rather as a slight, delicate, and evanescent flavor, than as any portion of the actual substance of the dish offered to the public. He can hardly be said, however, to commit a literary crime even if he disregard this caution.

In the present work, the author has proposed to himself— but with what success, fortunately, it is not for him to judge— to keep undeviatingly within his immunities. The point of view in which this tale comes under the Romantic definition lies in the attempt to connect a bygone time with the very present that is flitting away from us. It is a legend prolonging itself, from an epoch now gray in the distance, down into our own broad daylight, and bringing along with it some of its legendary mist, which the reader, according to his pleasure, may either disregard, or allow it to float almost imperceptibly about the characters and events for the sake of a picturesque effect. The narrative, it may be, is woven of so humble a texture as to require this advantage, and, at the same time, to render it the more difficult of attainment.

Many writers lay very great stress upon some definite moral purpose, at which they profess to aim their works. Not to be deficient in this particular, the author has provided himself with a moral: the truth, namely, that the wrong-doing of one generation lives into the successive ones, and divesting itself of every temporary advantage, becomes a pure and uncontrollable mischief; and he would feel it a singular gratification, if this romance might effectually convince mankind—or, indeed, any one man—of the folly of tumbling down an avalanche of ill-gotten gold, or real estate, on the heads of an unfortunate posterity, thereby to maim and crush them, until the accumulated mass shall be scattered abroad in its original atoms. In good faith, however, he is not sufficiently imaginative to flatter himself with the slightest hope of this kind. When romances do really teach anything, or produce any effective operation, it is usually through a far more subtle process than the ostensible one. The author has considered it hardly worth his while, therefore, relentlessly to impale the story with its moral as with an iron rod,—or, rather, as by sticking a pin through a butterfly,—thus at once depriving it of life, and causing it to stiffen in an ungainly and unnatural attitude. A high truth, indeed, fairly, finely, and skilfully wrought out, brightening at every step, and crowning the final development of a work of fiction, may add an artistic glory, but is never any truer, and seldom any more evident, at the last page than at the first.

The reader may perhaps choose to assign an actual locality

to the imaginary events of this narrative. If permitted by the historical connection,—which, though slight, was essential to his plan,—the author would very willingly have avoided anything of this nature. Not to speak of other objections, it exposes the romance to an inflexible and exceedingly dangerous species of criticism, by bringing his fancy-pictures almost into positive contact with the realities of the moment. It has been no part of his object, however, to describe local manners, nor in any way to meddle with the characteristics of a community for whom he cherishes a proper respect and a natural regard. He trusts not to be considered as unpardonably offending by laying out a street that infringes upon nobody's private rights, and appropriating a lot of land which had no visible owner, and building a house of materials long in use for constructing castles in the air. The personages of the tale—though they give themselves out to be of ancient stability and considerable prominence—are really of the author's own making, or, at all events, of his own mixing; their virtues can shed no lustre, nor their defects redound, in the remotest degree, to the discredit of the venerable town of which they profess to be inhabitants. He would be glad, therefore, if—especially in the quarter to which he alludes—the book may be read strictly as a Romance, having a great deal more to do with the clouds overhead than with any portion of the actual soil of the County of Essex.

JAMES RUSSELL LOWELL

Born in Cambridge, Massachusetts, graduated from Harvard and trained for the law, James Russell Lowell (1819-1891) represented for most of his life those philosophical, literary, and academic ideals which came to be known as the genteel tradition. His marriage in 1844 to Maria White, poet, abolitionist, and liberal, tempered Lowell's conservatism and, until her death in 1853, engendered his most vigorous and significant writing. In 1843 Lowell founded the *Pioneer,* a short-lived monthly literary magazine dedicated to the cause of a national literature. In 1848-49 he was editor of the *National Anti-Slavery Standard.* He was the first editor of the *Atlantic Monthly* (1857-61), and an editor (1864), with Charles Eliot Norton, of the *North American Review.* In 1855 Lowell succeeded Longfellow as Smith Professor of French and Spanish at Harvard, a chair which he held until 1886, although during the last ten years of this period he served as minister to Spain (1877-80), and minister to England (1880-85).

From 1838 to 1891, excepting the sixteen years following the death of his wife, Lowell published twenty-three titles of poetry, criticism and political commentary, nearly all of which he first wrote as lectures or as essays for periodicals. The most comprehensive collection of these writings is the Elmwood Edition: Charles Eliot Norton, *The Complete Writings of James Russell Lowell* (16 vols., 1904).

"The Function of the Poet" was the concluding lecture in the course which Lowell read before the Lowell Institute in 1855, the year in which he joined the Harvard faculty. The essay was posthumously published in *The Century Magazine,* January 1894, from which this text is taken. It appeared with a brief introduction by Norton, who speculated that Lowell had never published the essay because he had probably realized, as he grew older, that its assertions were too absolute, and its style too rhetorical for print. Norton endorsed the spirit of this lecture, nevertheless, its enthusiasm, and its lofty conception of the poet, and he compared it favorably with Sidney's and with Shelley's "Defence of Poesy."

THE FUNCTION OF THE POET

WHETHER, as some philosophers assume, we possess only the fragments of a great cycle of knowledge in whose center stood the primeval man in friendly relation with the powers of the universe, and build our hovels out of the ruins of our ancestral palace; or whether, according to the development theory of others, we are rising gradually, and have come up out of an atom instead of descending from an Adam, so that the proudest pedigree might run up to a barnacle or a zoophyte at last, are questions that will keep for a good many centuries yet. Confining myself to what little we can learn from history, we find tribes rising slowly out of barbarism to a higher or lower point of culture and civility, and everywhere the poet also is found, under one name or other, changing in certain outward respects, but essentially the same.

And however far we go back, we shall find this also—that the poet and the priest were united originally in the same person; which means that the poet was he who was conscious of the world of spirit as well as that of sense, and was the ambassador of the gods to men. This was his highest function, and hence his name of "seer." He was the discoverer and declarer of the perennial beneath the deciduous. His were the *epea pteroenta,* the true "winged words" that fly down the unexplored future and carry the names of ancestral heroes, of the brave and wise and good. It was thus that the poet could reward virtue, and, by and by, as society grew more complex, could burn in the brand of shame. This is Homer's character of Demodocus, in the eighth book of the Odyssey, "whom the Muse loved and gave the good and ill"—the gift of conferring good or evil immortality. The first histories were in verse; and sung as they were at feasts and gatherings of the people, they awoke in men the desire of fame, which is the first promoter of courage and self-trust, because it teaches men by degrees to appeal from the present to the future. We may fancy what the influence of the early epics was when they were recited to men who claimed the heroes celebrated in them for their ancestors, by what Bouchardon, the sculptor, said, only two centuries ago: "When I read Homer, I feel as if I were twenty feet high." Nor have poets lost their power over the future in modern times. Dante lifts up by the hair the face of some petty traitor, the Smith or Brown of some provincial Italian town, lets the fire of his Inferno glare upon it for a moment, and it is printed forever on the memory of mankind. The historians may iron out the shoulders of Richard the Third as smooth as they can, they will never get over the wrench that Shakspere gave them.

The peculiarity of almost all early literature is that it seems to have a double meaning, that, underneath its natural, we find ourselves continually seeing or suspecting a supernatural meaning. In the older epics the characters seem to be half typical and only half historical. Thus did the early poets endeavor to make realities out of appearances; for, except a few typical men in whom certain ideas get embodied, the generations of mankind are mere apparitions who come out of the dark for a purposeless moment, and re-enter the dark again after they have performed the nothing they came for.

Gradually, however, the poet as the "seer" became secondary to the "maker." His office became that of entertainer rather than teacher. But always something of the old tradition was kept alive. And if he has now come to be looked upon merely as the best expresser, the gift of seeing is implied as necessarily antecedent to that, and of seeing very deep, too. If any man would seem to have written without any conscious moral, that man is Shakspere. But that must be a dull sense, indeed, which does not see through his tragic—yes, and his comic—masks awful eyes that flame with something intenser and deeper than a mere scenic meaning—a meaning out of the great deep that is behind and beyond all human and merely personal character. Nor was Shakspere himself unconscious of his place as a teacher and profound moralist: witness that sonnet in which

he bewails his having neglected sometimes the errand that was
laid upon him:

> Alas, 't is true I have gone here and there,
> And made myself a motley to the view,
> Gored mine own thoughts, sold cheap what is most dear,
> Made old offences of affections new;
> Most true it is that I have look'd on truth
> Askance and strangely;

the application of which is made clear by the next sonnet, in
which he distinctly alludes to his profession.

There is this unmistakable stamp on all the great poets—
that, however in little things they may fall below themselves,
whenever there comes a great and noble thing to say, they say
it greatly and nobly, and bear themselves most easily in the
royalties of thought and language. There is not a mature play
of Shakspere's in which great ideas do not jut up in mountain-
ous permanence, marking forever the boundary of provinces of
thought, and known afar to many kindreds of men.

And it is for this kind of sight, which we call *in*sight, and
not for any faculty of observation and description, that we
value the poet. It is in proportion as he has this that he is an
adequate expresser, and not a juggler with words. It is by
means of this that for every generation of man he plays the
part of "namer." Before him, as before Adam, the creation
passes to be named anew: first the material world; then the
world of passions and emotions; then the world of ideas. But
whenever a great imagination comes, however it may delight
itself with imaging the outward beauty of things, however it
may seem to flow thoughtlessly away in music like a brook,
yet the shadow of heaven lies also in its depth beneath the
shadow of earth. Continually the visible universe suggests
the invisible. We are forever feeling this in Shakspere. His
imagination went down to the very bases of things, and while
his characters are the most natural that poet ever created, they
are also perfectly ideal, and are more truly the personifications
of abstract thoughts and passions than those of any allegorical
writer whatever.

Even in what seems so purely a picturesque poem as the Iliad, we feel something of this. Beholding as Homer did, from the tower of contemplation, the eternal mutability and nothing permanent but change, he must look underneath the show for the reality. Great captains and conquerors came forth out of the eternal silence, entered it again with their trampling hosts, and shoutings, and trumpet-blasts, and were as utterly gone as those echoes of their deeds which he sang, and which faded with the last sound of his voice and the last tremble of his lyre. History relating outward events alone was an unmeaning gossip, with the world for a village. This life could only become other than phantasmagoric, could only become real, as it stood related to something that was higher and permanent. Hence the idea of Fate, of a higher power unseen—that shadow, as of an eagle circling to its swoop, which flits stealthily and swiftly across the windy plains of Troy. In the Odyssey we find pure allegory.

Now, under all these names—praiser, seer, soothsayer—we find the same idea lurking. The poet is he who can best see and best say what is ideal—what belongs to the world of soul and of beauty. Whether he celebrate the brave and good man, or the gods, or the beautiful as it appears in man or nature, something of a religious character still clings to him; he is the revealer of Deity. He may be unconscious of his mission; he may be false to it; but in proportion as he is a great poet, he rises to the level of it the more often. He does not always directly rebuke what is bad and base, but indirectly by making us feel what delight there is in the good and fair. If he besiege evil, it is with such beautiful engines of war (as Plutarch tells us of Demetrius) that the besieged themselves are charmed with them. Whoever reads the great poets cannot but be made better by it, for they always introduce him to a higher society, to a greater style of manners and of thinking. Whoever learns to love what is beautiful is made incapable of the low and mean and bad. If Plato excludes the poets from his Republic, it is expressly on the ground that they speak unworthy things of the gods; that is, that they have lost the secret of their art, and use artificial types instead of speaking the true universal language of imagination. He who translates the divine into the vulgar, the spiritual into the sensual, is the reverse of a poet.

The poet, under whatever name, always stands for the same thing—imagination. And imagination in its highest form gives him the power, as it were, of assuming the consciousness of whatever he speaks about, whether man or beast, or rock or tree. It is the ring of Canace, which whoso has on understands the language of all created things. And as regards expression, it seems to enable the poet to condense the whole of himself into a single word. Therefore, when a great poet has said a thing, it is finally and utterly expressed, and has as many meanings as there are men who read his verse. A great poet is something more than an interpreter between man and nature; he is also an interpreter between man and his own nature. It is he who gives us those key-words, the possession of which makes us masters of all the unsuspected treasure-caverns of thought, and feeling, and beauty which open under the dusty path of our daily life.

And it is not merely a dry lexicon that he compiles,—a thing which enables us to translate from one dead dialect into another as dead,—but all his verse is instinct with music, and his words open windows on every side to pictures of scenery and life. The difference between the dry fact and the poem is as great as that between reading the shipping news and seeing the actual coming and going of the crowd of stately ships,—"the city on the inconstant billows dancing,"—as there is between ten minutes of happiness and ten minutes by the clock. Everybody remembers the story of the little Montague who was stolen and sold to the chimney-sweep: how he could dimly remember lying in a beautiful chamber; how he carried with him in all his drudgery the vision of a fair, sad mother's face that sought him everywhere in vain; how he threw himself one day all sooty as he was from his toil, on a rich bed and fell asleep, and how a kind person woke him, questioned him, pieced together his broken recollections for him, and so at last made the visions of the beautiful chamber and the fair, sad countenance real to him again. It seems to me that the offices that the poet does for us are typified in this nursery-tale. We all of us have our vague reminiscences of the stately home of our childhood,—for we are all of us poets and geniuses in our youth, while earth is all new to us, and the chalice of every buttercup is brimming with the wine of poesy,—and we all remember the beautiful, motherly countenance which nature bent over us there. But somehow we all get stolen away thence; life becomes to us a sooty taskmaster, and we crawl through dark passages without end—till suddenly the word of some poet redeems us, makes us know who we are, and of helpless orphans makes us the heir to a great estate. It is to our true relations with the two great worlds of outward and inward nature that the poet reintroduces us.

But the imagination has a deeper use than merely to give poets a power of expression. It is the everlasting preserver of the world from blank materialism. It forever puts matter in the wrong, and compels it to show its title to existence. Wordsworth tells us that in his youth he was sometimes obliged to touch the walls to find if they were visionary or no, and such experiences are not uncommon with persons who converse much with their own thoughts. Dr. Johnson said that to kick one's foot against a stone was a sufficient confutation of Berkeley, and poor old Pyrrho has passed into a proverb because, denying the objectivity of matter, he was run over by a cart and killed. But all that he affirmed was that to the soul the cart was no more real than its own imaginative reproduction of it, and perhaps the shade of the philosopher ran up to the first of his deriders who crossed the Styx with a triumphant "I told you so! The cart did not run over *me,* for here I am without a bone broken."

And, in another sense also, do those poets who deal with human character, as all the greater do, continually suggest to us the purely phantasmal nature of life except as it is related to the world of ideas. For are not their personages more real than most of those in history? Is not Lear more authentic and permanent than Lord Raglan? Their realm is a purely spiritual one in which space and time and costume are nothing. What matters it that Shakspere puts a seaport in Bohemia, and knew less geography than Tommy who goes to the district school? He understood eternal boundaries, such as are laid down on no chart, and are not defined by such transitory affairs as mountain chains, rivers, and seas.

No great movement of the human mind takes place without the concurrent beat of those two wings, the imagination and the understanding. It is by the understanding that we are enabled to make the most of this world, and to use the collected material of experience in its condensed form of practical wisdom; and it is the imagination which forever beckons toward that other world which is always future, and makes us discontented with this. The one rests upon experience; the other leans forward and listens after the *in*experienced, and shapes the features of that future with which it is forever in travail. The imagination might be defined as the common sense of the invisible world, as the understanding is of the visible; and as those are the finest individual characters in which the two moderate and rectify each other, so those are the finest eras where the same may be said of society. In the voyage of life, not only do we depend on the needle, true to its earthly instincts, but upon observation of the fixed stars, those beacons lighted upon the eternal promontories of heaven above the stirs and shiftings of our lower system.

But it seems to be thought that we have come upon the earth too late, that there has been a feast of imagination formerly, and all that is left for us is to steal the scraps. We hear that there is no poetry in railroads and steamboats and telegraphs, and especially none in Brother Jonathan. If this be true, so much the worse for him. But because *he* is a materialist, shall there be no more poets? When we have said that we live in a materialistic age we have said something which meant more than we intended. If we say it in the way of blame, we have said a foolish thing, for probably one age is as good as another, and, at any rate, the worst is good enough company for us. The age of Shakspere was richer than our own, only

because it was lucky enough to have such a pair of eyes as his
to see it, and such a gift of speech as his to report it. And so
there is always room and occasion for the poet, who continues
to be, just as he was in the early time, nothing more nor less
than a "seer." He is always the man who is willing to take the
age he lives in on trust, as the very best that ever was. Shakspere did not sit down and cry for the water of Helicon to turn
the wheels of his little private mill at the Bankside. He appears to have gone more quietly about his business than any
other playwright in London, to have drawn off what water-
power he needed from the great prosy current of affairs that
flows alike for all and in spite of all, to have ground for the
public what grist they wanted, coarse or fine, and it seems a
mere piece of luck that the smooth stream of his activity reflected with such ravishing clearness every changing mood of
heaven and earth, every stick and stone, every dog and clown
and courtier that stood upon its brink. It is a curious illustration of the friendly manner in which Shakspere received everything that came along,—of what a *present* man he was,—that
in the very same year that the mulberry tree was brought into
England, he got one and planted it in his garden at Stratford.

It is perfectly true that this is a materialistic age, and for
that very reason we want our poets all the more. We find that
every generation contrives to catch its singing larks without
the sky's falling. When the poet comes, he always turns out to
be the man who discovers that the passing moment is the
inspired one, and that the secret of poetry is not to have lived
in Homer's day, or Dante's, but to be alive now. To be alive
now, that is the great art and mystery. They are dead men who
live in the past, and men yet unborn that live in the future.
We are like Hans in Luck, forever exchanging the burdensome
good we have for something else, till at last we come home
empty handed.

That pale-faced drudge of Time opposite me there, that
weariless sexton whose callous hands bury our rosy hours in
the irrevocable past, is even now reaching forward to a moment
as rich in life, in character, and thought, as full of oppor-

tunity, as any since Adam. This little isthmus that we are now standing on is the point to which martyrs in their triumphant pain, prophets in their fervor, and poets in their ecstasy, looked forward as the golden future, as the land too good for them to behold with mortal eyes; it is the point toward which the faint-hearted and desponding hereafter will look back as the priceless past when there was still some good and virtue and opportunity left in the world.

The people who feel their own age prosaic are those who see only its costume. And that is what makes it prosaic—that we have not faith enough in ourselves to think our own clothes good enough to be presented to posterity in. The artists fancy that the court dress of posterity is that of Van Dyck's time, or Caesar's. I have seen the model of a statue of Sir Robert Peel,—a statesman whose merit consisted in yielding gracefully to the present,—in which the sculptor had done his best to travesty the real man into a make-believe Roman. At the period when England produced its greatest poets, we find exactly the reverse of this, and we are thankful that the man who made the monument of Lord Bacon had genius to copy every button of his dress, everything down to the rosettes on his shoes, and then to write under his statue, "Thus sat Francis Bacon"—not "Cneius Pompeius"—"Viscount Verulam." Those men had faith even in their own shoe-strings.

After all, how is our poor scapegoat of a nineteenth century to blame? Why, for not being the seventeenth, to be sure! It is always raining opportunity, but it seems it was only the men two hundred years ago who were intelligent enough not to hold their cups bottom-up. We are like beggars who think if a piece of gold drop into their palm it must be counterfeit, and would rather change it for the smooth-worn piece of familiar copper. And so, as we stand in our mendicancy by the wayside, Time tosses carefully the great golden today into our hats, and we turn it over grumblingly and suspiciously, and are pleasantly surprised at finding that we can exchange it for beef and potatoes. Till Dante's time the Italian poets thought no language good enough to put their nothings into but Latin,

—and indeed a dead tongue was the best for dead thoughts,—but Dante found the common speech of Florence, in which men bargained and scolded and made love, good enough for him, and out of the world around him made a poem such as no Roman ever sang.

In our day, it is said despairingly, the understanding reigns triumphant: it is the age of common sense. If this be so, the wisest way would be to accept it manfully. But, after all, what is the meaning of it? Looking at the matter superficially, one would say that a striking difference between our science and that of the world's gray fathers is that there is every day less and less of the element of wonder in it. What they saw written in light upon the great arch of heaven, and, by a magnificent reach of sympathy, of which we are incapable, associated with the fall of monarchs and the fate of man, is for us only a professor, a piece of chalk, and a blackboard. The solemn and unapproachable skies we have vulgarized; we have peeped and botanized among the flowers of light, pulled off every petal, fumbled in every calyx, and reduced them to the bare stem of order and class. The stars can no longer maintain their divine reserves, but whenever there is a conjunction and congress of planets, every enterprising newspaper sends thither its special reporter with his telescope. Over those arcana of life where once a mysterious presence brooded, we behold scientific explorers skipping like so many incarnate notes of interrogation. We pry into the counsels of the great powers of nature, we keep our ears at the keyhole, and know everything that is going to happen. There is no longer any sacred inaccessibility, no longer any enchanting unexpectedness, and life turns to prose the moment there is nothing unattainable. It needs no more a voice out of the unknown proclaiming "Great Pan is dead!" We have found his tombstone, deciphered the arrowheaded inscription upon it, know his age to a day, and that he died universally regretted.

Formerly science was poetry. A mythology which broods over us in our cradle, which mingles with the lullaby of the nurse, which peoples the day with the possibility of divine encounters, and night with intimation of demonic ambushes, is some-thing quite other, as the material for thought and poetry, from one that we take down from our bookshelves, as sapless as the shelf it stood on, as remote from all present sympathy with man or nature as a town history with its genealogies of Mr. Nobody's great-grandparents.

We have utilized everything. The Egyptians found a hint of the solar system in the concentric circles of the onion, and revered it as a symbol, while we respect it as a condiment in cookery, and can pass through all Weathersfield without a thought of the stars. Our world is a museum of natural his-tory; that of our forefathers was a museum of supernatural history. And the rapidity with which the change has been going on is almost startling, when we consider that so modern and historical a personage as Queen Elizabeth was reigning at the time of the death of Dr. John Faustus, out of whose story the Teutonic imagination built up a mythus that may be set beside that of Prometheus.

Science, looked at scientifically, is bare and bleak enough. On those sublime heights the air is too thin for the lungs, and blinds the eyes. It is much better living down in the valleys, where one cannot see farther than the next farmhouse. Faith was never found in the bottom of a crucible, nor peace arrived at by analysis or synthesis. But all this is because science has become too grimly intellectual, has divorced itself from the moral and imaginative part of man. Our results are not arrived at in that spirit which led Kepler (who had his theory-traps set all along the tracks of the stars to catch a discovery) to say, "In my opinion the occasions of new discoveries have been no less wonderful than the discoveries themselves."

But we are led back continually to the fact that science can-not, if it would, disengage itself from human nature and from imagination. No two men have ever argued together without at least agreeing in this, that something more than proof is required to produce conviction, and that a logic which is capa-ble of grinding the stubbornest facts to powder (as every man's *own* logic always is) is powerless against so delicate a structure as the brain. Do what we will, we cannot contrive to bring together the yawning edges of proof and belief, to weld them into one. When Thor strikes Skrymir with his terrible hammer, the giant asks if a leaf has fallen. I need not appeal to the Thors of argument in the pulpit, the senate, and the mass-meeting, if they have not sometimes found the popular giant as provokingly insensible. The $\sqrt{-x}$ is nothing in comparison with the chance-caught smell of a single flower which by the magic of association recreates for us the unquestioning day of childhood. Demonstration may lead to the very gate of heaven, but there she makes us a civil bow, and leaves us to make our way back again to Faith, who has the key. That science which is of the intellect alone steps with indifferent foot upon the dead body of Belief, if only she may reach higher or see farther.

But we cannot get rid of our wonder—we who have brought down the wild lightning, from writing fiery doom upon the walls of heaven, to be our errand-boy and penny-postman. Wonder is crude imagination; and it is necessary to us, for man shall not live by bread alone, and exact knowledge is not enough. Do we get nearer the truth or farther from it that we have got a gas or an imponderable fluid instead of a spirit? We go on exorcising one thing after another, but what boots it? The evasive genius flits into something else, and defies us. The powers of the outer and inner world form hand in hand a magnetic circle for whose connection man is necessary. It is the imagination that takes his hand and clasps it with that other stretched to him in the dark, and for which he was vainly groping. It is that which renews the mystery in nature, makes it wonderful and beautiful again, and out of the gases of the man of science remakes the old spirit. But we seem to have created too many wonders to be capable of wondering any longer; as Coleridge said, when asked if he believed in ghosts, that he had seen too many of them. But nature all the more imperatively demands it, and science can at best scotch it, not kill it. In this day of newspapers and electric telegraphs, in which common sense and ridicule can magnetize a whole continent between dinner and tea, we say that such a phenomenon as Mahomet were impossible, and behold Joe Smith and the State of Deseret! Turning over the yellow leaves of the same copy of "Webster on Witchcraft" which Cotton Mather studied, I thought, "Well, that goblin is laid at last!"—and while I mused the tables were turning, and the chairs beating the devil's tattoo all over Christendom. I have a neighbor who dug down through tough strata of clay to a spring pointed out by a witch-hazel rod in the hands of a seventh son's seventh son, and the water is the sweeter to him for the wonder that is mixed with it. After all, it seems that our scientific gas, be it never so brilliant, is not equal to the dingy old Aladdin's lamp.

It is impossible for men to live in the world without poetry of some sort or other. If they cannot get the best they will get some substitute for it, and thus seem to verify Saint Augustine's slur that it is wine of devils. The mind bound down too closely to what is practical either becomes inert, or revenges itself by rushing into the savage wilderness of "isms." The insincerity of our civilization has disgusted some persons so much that they have sought refuge in Indian wigwams and found refreshment in taking a scalp now and then. Nature insists above all things upon balance. She contrives to maintain a harmony between the material and spiritual, nor allows the cerebrum an expansion at the cost of the cerebellum. If the character, for example, run on one side into religious enthusiasm, it is not unlikely to develop on the other a counterpoise of worldly prudence. Thus the Shaker and the Moravian are noted for thrift, and mystics are not always the worst managers. Through all changes of condition and experience man continues to be a citizen of the world of idea as well as the world of fact, and the tax-gatherers of both are punctual.

And these antitheses which we meet with in individual character we cannot help seeing on the larger stage of the world also, a moral accompanying a material development. History, the great satirist, brings together Alexander and the blower of peas to hint to us that the tube of the one and the sword of the other were equally transitory; but meanwhile Aristotle was conquering kingdoms out of the unknown, and establishing a dynasty of thought from whose hand the sceptre has not yet passed. So there are Charles V, and Luther; the expansion of trade resulting from the Spanish and Portuguese discoveries, and the Elizabethan literature; the Puritans seeking spiritual El Dorados while so much valor and thought were spent in finding mineral ones. It seems to be the purpose of God that a certain amount of genius shall go to each generation, particular quantities being represented by individuals, and while no *one* is complete in himself, all collectively make up a whole ideal figure of a man. Nature is not like certain varieties of the apple that cannot bear two years in succession. It is only that her expansions are uniform in all directions, that in every age she completes her circle, and like a tree adds a ring to her growth be it thinner or thicker.

Every man is conscious that he leads two lives, the one trivial and ordinary, the other sacred and recluse; the one which he carries to the dinner-table and to his daily work, which grows old with his body and dies with it, the other that which is made up of the few inspiring moments of his higher aspiration and attainment, and in which his youth survives for him, his dreams, his unquenchable longings for something nobler than success. It is this life which the poets nourish for him, and sustain with their immortalizing nectar. Through them he feels once more the white innocence of his youth. His faith in something nobler than gold and iron and cotton comes back to him, not as an upbraiding ghost that wrings its pale hands and is gone, but beautiful and inspiring as a first love that recognizes nothing in him that is not high and noble. The poets are nature's perpetual pleaders, and protest with us against what is worldly. Out of their own undying youth they speak to ours. "Wretched is the man," says Goethe, "who has learned to despise the dreams of his youth!" It is from this misery that the imagination and the poets, who are its spokesmen, rescue us. The world goes to church, kneels to the eternal Purity, and then contrives to sneer at innocence and ignorance of evil by calling it green. Let every man thank God for what little there may be left in him of his vernal sweetness. Let him thank God if he have still the capacity for feeling an unmarketable enthusiasm, for that will make him worthy of the society of the noble dead, of the companionship of the poets. And let him love the poets for keeping youth young, woman womanly, and beauty beautiful.

There is as much poetry as ever in the world if we only knew how to find it out; and as much imagination, perhaps, only that it takes a more prosaic direction. Every man who meets with misfortune, who is stripped of material prosperity, finds that he has a little outlying mountain-farm of imagination, which did not appear in the schedule of his effects, on which his spirit is able to keep itself alive, though he never thought of it while he was fortunate. Job turns out to be a great poet as soon as his flocks and herds are taken away from him.

There is no reason why our continent should not sing as well as the rest. We have had the practical forced upon us by our position. We have had a whole hemisphere to clear up and put to rights. And we are descended from men who were hardened and stiffened by a downright wrestle with necessity. There was no chance for poetry among the Puritans. And yet if any people have a right to imagination, it should be the descendants of these very Puritans. They had enough of it, or they could never have conceived the great epic they did, whose books are States, and which is written on this continent from Maine to California.

But there seems to be another reason why we should not become a poetical people. Formerly the poet embodied the hopes and desires of men in visible types. He gave them the shoes of swiftness, the cap of invisibility and the purse of Fortunatus. These were once stories for grown men, and not for the nursery as now. We are apt ignorantly to wonder how our forefathers could find satisfaction in fiction the absurdity of which any of our primary-school children could demonstrate. But we forget that the world's gray fathers were children themselves, and that in their little world, with its circle of the black unknown all about it, the imagination was as active as it is with people in the dark. Look at a child's toys, and we shall understand the matter well enough. Imagination is the fairy godmother (every child has one still), at the wave of whose wand sticks become heroes, the closet in which she has been shut fifty times for being naughty is turned into a palace, and a bit of lath acquires all the potency of Excalibur.

But nowadays it is the understanding itself that has turned poet. In her railroads she has given us the shoes of swiftness. Fine-ear herself could not hear so far as she, who in her magnetic telegraph can listen in Boston and hear what is going on in New Orleans. And what need of Aladdin's lamp when a man can build a palace with a patent pill? The office of the poet seems to be reversed, and he must give back these miracles of the understanding to poetry again, and find out what there is imaginative in steam and iron and telegraph-wires. After all, there is as much poetry in the iron horses that eat fire as in those of Diomed that fed on men. If you cut an apple across you may trace in it the lines of the blossom that the bee hummed around in May, and so the soul of poetry survives in things prosaic. Borrowing money on a bond does not seem the most promising subject in the world, but Shakspere found the "Merchant of Venice" in it. Themes of song are waiting everywhere for the right man to sing them, like those enchanted swords which no one can pull out of the rock till the hero comes, and he finds no more trouble than in plucking a violet.

John Quincy Adams, making a speech at New Bedford, many years ago, reckoned the number of whaleships (if I remember rightly) that sailed out of that port, and, comparing it with some former period, took it as a type of American success. But, alas! it is with quite other oil that those far-shining lamps of a nation's true glory which burn forever must be filled. It is not by any amount of material splendor or prosperity, but only by moral greatness, by ideas, by works of imagination, that a race can conquer the future. No voice comes to us from the once mighty Assyria but the hoot of the owl that nests amid her crumbling palaces. Of Carthage, whose merchant-fleets once furled their sails in every port of the known world, nothing is left but the deeds of Hannibal. She lies dead on the shore of her once subject sea, and the wind of the desert only flings its handfuls of burial-sand upon her corpse. A fog can blot Holland or Switzerland out of existence. But how large is the space occupied in the maps of the soul by little Athens and powerless Italy! They were great by the soul, and their vital force is as indestructible as the soul.

Till America has learned to love art, not as an amusement, not as the mere ornament of her cities, not as a superstition of what is *comme il faut* for a great nation, but for its humanizing and ennobling energy, for its power of making men better by arousing in them a perception of their own instincts for what is beautiful, and therefore sacred and religious, and an eternal rebuke of the base and worldly, she will not have succeeded in that high sense which alone makes a nation out of a people, and raises it from a dead name to a living power. Were our little mother-island sunk beneath the sea, or, worse, were she conquered by Scythian barbarians, yet Shakspere would be an immortal England, and would conquer countries, when the bones of her last sailor had kept their ghastly watch for ages in unhallowed ooze beside the quenched thunders of her navy.

Old Purchas in his "Pilgrims" tells of a sacred caste in India who, when they go out into the street cry out, "Poo! Poo!" to warn all the world out of their way lest they should be defiled by something unclean. And it is just so that the understanding in its pride of success thinks to pooh-pooh all that it considers unpractical and visionary. But whatever of life there is in man, except what comes of beef and pudding, is in the visionary and unpractical and if it be not encouraged to find its activity or its solace in the production or enjoyment of art and beauty, if it be bewildered or thwarted by an outward profession of faith covering up a practical unbelief in anything higher and holier than the world of sense, it will find vent in such wretched holes and corners as table-tippings and mediums who sell news from heaven at a quarter of a dollar the item. Imagination cannot be banished out of the world. She may be made a kitchen-drudge, a Cinderella, but there are powers that watch

over her. When her two proud sisters, the intellect and understanding, think her crouching over her ashes, she startles and
charms by her splendid apparition, and Prince Soul will put
up with no other bride.

The practical is a very good thing in its way—if it only be
not another name for the worldly. To be absorbed in it is to
eat of that insane root which the soldiers of Antonius found
in their retreat from Parthia—which whoso tasted kept gathering sticks and stones as if they were some great matter till he
died.

One is forced to listen, now and then, to a kind of talk
which makes him feel as if this were the after-dinner time of
the world, and mankind were doomed hereafter forever to that
kind of contented materialism which comes to good stomachs
with the nuts and raisins. The dozy old world has nothing to
do now but stretch its legs under the mahogany, talk about
stocks, and get rid of the hours as well as it can till bedtime.
The centuries before us have drained the goblet of wisdom
and beauty, and all we have left is to cast horoscopes in the
dregs. But divine beauty, and the love of it, will never be without apostles and messengers on earth, till Time flings his hour-
glass into the abyss as having no need to turn it longer to
number the indistinguishable ages of Annihilation. It was a favorite speculation with the learned men of the sixteenth century that they had come upon the old age and decrepit second
childhood of creation, and while they maundered, the soul
of Shakspere was just coming out of the eternal freshness of
Deity, "trailing" such "clouds of Glory" as would beggar a
Platonic year of sunsets.

No; morning and the dewy prime are born into the earth
again with every child. It is our fault if drought and dust
usurp the noon. Every age says to her poets, like the mistress
to her lover, "Tell me what I am like"; and, in proportion as
it brings forth anything worth seeing, has need of seers and
will have them. Our time is not an unpoetical one. We are in
our heroic age, still face to face with the shaggy forces of un-
subdued Nature, and we have our Theseuses and Perseuses,

though they may be named Israel Putnam and Daniel Boone. It is nothing against us that we are a commercial people. Athens was a trading community; Dante and Titian were the growth of great marts, and England was already commercial when she produced Shakspere.

This lesson I learn from the past: that grace and goodness, the fair, the noble, and the true, will never cease out of the world till the God from whom they emanate ceases out of it; that they manifest themselves in an eternal continuity of change to every generation of men, as new duties and occasions arise; that the sacred duty and noble office of the poet is to reveal and justify them to men; that so long as the soul endures, endures also the theme of new and unexampled song; that while there is grace in grace, love in love, and beauty in beauty, God will still send poets to find them and bear witness of them, and to hang their ideal portraitures in the gallery of memory. God with us is forever the mystical name of the hour that is passing. The lives of the great poets teach us that they were the men of their generation who felt most deeply the meaning of the present.

WALT WHITMAN

Walter Whitman (1819-1892) built himself into a legend which he spent most of his life proclaiming. Born at West Hills, Long Island, into a Quaker family, Whitman attended public schools until he was thirteen, then found employment in a law office and in a doctor's office before becoming a printer and an itinerant schoolteacher. He wrote for several newspapers and edited (1846-48) the Brooklyn *Eagle,* a Democratic paper which nourished his own convictions about an immediate and practicing democracy in the United States, but which could not tolerate Whitman's notions about immigration and the Free Soil movement. Discharged as editor, Whitman traveled for several months to New Orleans, then back to Manhattan via the Middle West. He began to read extensively in Hegel, Goethe, Emerson, Carlyle, the Bible, and Shakespeare. Most of his poetry after 1848 was an attempt to assimilate and literally reproduce his own cumulated experiences.

Both individualism and the democratic ideal found a place in his personal mysticism. Whitman never developed a logical system of ideas: he believed at the same time in the fullness of creation and in its progress; he acknowledged evil merely by asserting value in any state of being; and matter, to him, was both alive and spiritual. Out of these rationalizations of his own experiences grew his concept of the poet, the great ethical and social teacher unconfined by any mere social program.

The first statement of these views in verse was the 1855 edition of *Leaves of Grass,* which contained twelve poems and the Preface, published at his own expense, and reviewed by Whitman but by almost no one else. For the third edition of *Leaves* (1860) Whitman found a commercial publisher, and after the fifth edition his stature grew, particularly in Europe, where he was called the democratic epitome. His death occasioned a spate of biographies, which variously helped to fix the legend of this uncommon common man. Whitman himself had supervised both the *Complete Poems and Prose of Walt Whitman, 1855-1888* (1888-89) and the

Complete Prose Works (1892). His literary executors, Horace L. Traubel, Richard M. Bucke, and Thomas B. Harned, edited the first extensive collection of *The Complete Writings of Walt Whitman* (10 vols., 1902).

When Whitman revised the text of his 1855 Preface twenty-seven years later, for the seventh edition (and final revision) of *Leaves of Grass,* he omitted nearly a third of his original version, most of the omissions—the catalogues—having found their way into poems after the first edition. The 1882 document is a genteel and orderly distortion of the whole tone of Whitman's original declaration of independence. The suppressed passages are indicated by brackets.

PREFACE TO LEAVES OF GRASS

AMERICA does not repel the past or what it has produced under its forms or amid other politics or the idea of castes or the old religions . . . . accepts the lesson with calmness . . . is not so impatient as has been supposed that the slough still sticks to opinions and manners and literature while the life which served its requirements has passed into the new life of the new forms . . . perceives that the corpse is slowly borne from the eating and sleeping rooms of the house . . . perceives that it waits a little while in the door . . . that it was fittest for its days . . . that its action has descended to the stalwart and wellshaped heir who approaches . . . and that he shall be fittest for his days.

The Americans of all nations at any time upon the earth have probably the fullest poetical nature. The United States themselves are essentially the greatest poem. In the history of the earth hitherto the largest and most stirring appear tame and orderly to their ampler largeness and stir. Here at last is something in the doings of man that corresponds with the broadcast doing of the day and night. [Here is not merely a nation but a teeming nation of nations.] Here is action untied from strings necessarily blind to particulars and details magnificently moving in vast masses. Here is the hospitality which forever indicates heroes . . . . [Here are the roughs and beards

and space and ruggedness and nonchalance that the soul loves.]
Here the performance disdaining the trivial unapproached in
the tremendous audacity of its crowds and groupings and the
push of its perspective spreads with crampless and flowing
breadth and showers its prolific and splendid extravagance.
One sees it must indeed own the riches of the summer and
winter, and need never be bankrupt while corn grows from the
ground or the orchards drop apples or the bays contain fish or
men beget children upon women.

Other states indicate themselves in their deputies . . . . but
the genius of the United States is not best or most in its execu-
tives or legislatures, nor in its ambassadors or authors or colleges or churches or parlors, nor even in its newspapers or
inventors . . . but always most in the common people. [Their
manners speech dress friendships—the freshness and candor of
their physiognomy—the picturesque looseness of their carriage
. . . their deathless attachment to freedom—their aversion to
anything indecorous or soft or mean—the practical acknowledgment of the citizens of one state by the citizens of all other
states—the fierceness of their roused resentment—their curiosity
and welcome of novelty—their self-esteem and wonderful sympathy—their susceptibility to a slight—the air they have of persons who never knew how it felt to stand in the presence of
superiors—the fluency of their speech—their delight in music,
the sure symptom of manly tenderness and native elegance of
soul . . . their good temper and openhandedness—the terrible
significance of their elections—the President's taking off his hat
to them not they to him—these too are unrhymed poetry. It
awaits the gigantic and generous treatment worthy of it.]

The largeness of nature or of the nation were monstrous
without a corresponding largeness and generosity of the spirit
of the citizen. Not native nor swarming states nor streets and
steamships nor prosperous business nor farms nor capital nor
learning may suffice for the ideal of man . . . nor suffice the
poet. No reminiscences may suffice either. A live nation can
always cut a deep mark and can have the best authority the
cheapest . . . namely, from its own soul. This is the sum of

the profitable uses of individuals or states and of present action and grandeur and of the subjects of poets.—As if it were necessary to trot back generation after generation to the eastern records! As if the beauty and sacredness of the demonstrable must fall behind that of the mythical! As if men do not make their mark out of any times! As if the opening of the western continent by discovery and what has transpired since in North and South America were less than the small theatre of the antique or the aimless sleep-walking of the middle ages! The pride of the United States leaves the wealth and finesse of the cities and all returns of commerce and agriculture and all the magnitude of geography or shows of exterior victory to enjoy the breed of fullsized men or one fullsized man unconquerable and simple.

The American poets are to enclose old and new for America is the race of races. [Of them a bard is to be commensurate with a people. To him the other continents arrive as contribution . . . he gives them reception for their sake and his own sake. His spirit responds to his country's spirit . . . he incarnates its geography and natural life and rivers and lakes. Mississippi with annual freshets and changing chutes, Missouri and Columbia and Ohio and Saint Lawrence with the falls and beautiful masculine Hudson, do not embouchure where they spend themselves more than they embouchure into him. The blue breadth over the inland sea of Virginia and Maryland and the sea off Massachusetts and Maine and over Manhattan Bay and over Champlain and Erie and over Ontario and Huron and Michigan and Superior, and over the Texan and Mexican and Floridian and Cuban seas and over the seas off California and Oregon, is not tallied by the blue breadth of the waters below more than the breadth of above and below is tallied by him. When the long Atlantic coast stretches longer and the Pacific coast stretches longer he easily stretches with them north or south. He spans between them also from east to west and reflects what is between them. On him rise solid growths that offset the growths of pine and cedar and hemlock and liveoak and locust and chestnut and cypress and hickory and limetree and cottonwood and tuliptree and cactus and wildvine and tamarind and persimmon . . . and tangles as tangled as any canebrake or swamp . . . and forests coated with transparent ice and icicles hanging from the boughs and crackling in the wind . . . and sides and peaks of mountains . . . and pasturage sweet and free as savannah or upland or prairie . . . with flights and songs and screams that answer those of the wildpigeon and highhole and orchard-oriole and coot and surf-duck and redshouldered-hawk and fish-hawk and white-ibis and indian-hen and cat-owl and water-pheasant and qua-bird and pied-sheldrake and blackbird and mockingbird and buzzard and condor and night-heron and eagle. To him the hereditary countenance descends both mother's and father's. To him enter the essences of the real things and past and present events—of the enormous diversity of temperature and agriculture and mines—the tribes of red aborigines—the weather-beaten vessels entering new ports or making landings on rocky coasts—the first settlements north or south—the rapid stature and muscle—the haughty defiance of '76 and the war and peace and formation of the constitution . . . the union always surrounded by blatherers and always calm and impregnable—the perpetual coming of immigrants—the wharfhem'd cities and superior marine—the unsurveyed interior—the loghouses and clearings and wild animals and hunters and trappers . . . . the free commerce the fisheries and whaling and gold-digging—the endless gestation of new states—the convening of Congress every December, the members duly coming up from all climates and the uttermost parts . . . . the noble character of the young mechanics and of all free American workmen and work women . . . . the general ardor and friendliness and enterprise—the perfect equality of the female with the male . . . . the large amativeness—the fluid movement of the population—the factories and mercantile life and laborsaving machinery—the Yankee swap—the New York firemen and the target excursion—the southern plantation life—the character of the northeast and of the northwest and southwest—slavery and the tremulous spreading of hands to protect it, and the stern oppo-

sition to it which shall never cease till it ceases or the speaking
of tongues and the moving of lips cease.] For such the expression of the American poet is to be transcendent and new. It is
to be indirect and not direct or descriptive or epic. Its quality
goes through these to much more. Let the age and wars of
other nations be chanted and their eras and characters be illustrated and that finish the verse. Not so the great psalm of the
republic. Here the theme is creative and has vista. [Here comes
one among the wellbeloved stonecutters and plans with decision and science and sees the solid and beautiful forms of the
future where there are now no solid forms.]

[Of all nations the United States with veins full of poetical
stuff most need poets and will doubtless have the greatest and
use them the greatest. Their Presidents shall not be their common referee so much as their poets shall. Of all mankind the
great poet is the equable man. Not in him but off from him
things are grotesque or eccentric or fail of their sanity. Nothing
out of its place is good and nothing in its place is bad. He
bestows on every object or quality its fit proportions neither
more nor less. He is the arbiter of the diverse and he is the
key. He is the equalizer of his age and land . . . . he supplies
what wants supplying and checks what wants checking. If
peace is the routine out of him speaks the spirit of peace, large,
rich, thrifty, building vast and populous cities, encouraging
agriculture and the arts and commerce—lighting the study of
man, the soul, immortality—federal, state or municipal government, marriage, health, freetrade, intertravel by land and sea
. . . . nothing too close, nothing too far off . . . the stars not too
far off. In war he is the most deadly force of the war. Who
recruits him recruits horse and foot . . . he fetches parks of
artillery the best that engineer ever knew. If the time becomes
slothful and heavy he knows how to arouse it . . . he can make
every word he speaks draw blood.] Whatever stagnates in the
flat of custom or obedience or legislation he never stagnates.
Obedience does not master him, he masters it. High up out of
reach he stands turning a concentrated light . . . he turns the
pivot with his finger . . . he baffles the swiftest runners as he

stands and easily overtakes and envelops them. The time stray-
ing toward infidelity and confections and persiflage he with-
holds by his steady faith ... [he spreads out his dishes ... he
offers the sweet firmfibred meat that grows men and women.
His brain is the ultimate brain. He is no arguer ... he is judgment. He judges not as the judge judges but as the sun falling
around a helpless thing. As he sees the farthest he has the most
faith. His thoughts are the hymns of the praise of things. In
the talk on the soul and eternity and God off of his equal
plane he is silent. He sees eternity less like a play with a pro-
logue and denouement ... he sees eternity in men and women
... he does not see men and women as dreams or dots.] Faith
is the antiseptic of the soul ... it pervades the common people
and preserves them ... they never give up believing and expect-
ing and trusting. There is that indescribable freshness and un-
consciousness about an illiterate person that humbles and
mocks the power of the noblest expressive genius. The poet
sees for a certainty how one not a great artist may be just as
sacred and perfect as the greatest artist ...... The power to
destroy or remould is freely used by him but never the power
of attack. What is past is past. If he does not expose superior
models and prove himself by every step he takes he is not what
is wanted. The presence of the greatest poet conquers ... not
parleying or struggling or any prepared attempts. Now he has
passed that way see after him! there is not left any vestige of
despair or misanthropy or cunning or exclusiveness or the
ignominy of a nativity or color or delusion of hell or the
necessity of hell ... and no man thenceforward shall be de-
graded for ignorance or weakness or sin.

The greatest poet hardly knows pettiness or triviality. If he
breathes into any thing that was before thought small it dilates
with the grandeur and life of the universe. He is a seer ... he
is individual ... he is complete in himself ... the others are
as good as he, only he sees it and they do not. He is not one of
the chorus .... he does not stop for any regulations ... he is
the president of regulation. What the eyesight does to the rest
he does to the rest. Who knows the curious mystery of the eye-

sight? The other senses corroborate themselves, but this is removed from any proof but its own and foreruns the identities of the spiritual world. A single glance of it mocks all the investigations of man and all the instruments and books of the earth and all reasoning. What is marvelous? what is unlikely? what is impossible or baseless or vague? after you have once just opened the space of a peachpit and given audience to far and near and to the sunset and had all things enter with electric swiftness softly and duly without confusion or jostling or jam.

The land and sea, the animals fishes and birds, the sky of heaven and the orbs, the forests mountains and rivers, are not small themes . . . but folks expect of the poet to indicate more than the beauty and dignity which always attaches to dumb real objects . . . they expect him to indicate the path between reality and their souls. Men and women perceive the beauty well enough . . . probably as well as he. The passionate tenacity of hunters, woodmen, early risers, cultivators of gardens and orchards and fields, the love of healthy women for the manly form, seafaring persons, drivers of horses, the passion for light and the open air, all is an old varied sign of the unfailing perception of beauty and of a residence of the poetic in outdoor people. They can never be assisted by poets to perceive . . . some may but they never can. The poetic quality is not marshalled in rhyme or uniformity or abstract addresses to things nor in melancholy complaints or good precepts, but is the life of these and much else and is in the soul. The profit of rhyme is that it drops seeds of a sweeter and more luxuriant rhyme, and of uniformity that it conveys itself into its own roots in the ground out of sight. The rhyme and uniformity of perfect poems show the free growth of metrical laws and bud from them as unerringly and loosely as lilacs or roses on a bush, and take shapes as compact as the shapes of chestnuts and oranges and melons and pears, and shed the perfume impalpable to form. The fluency and ornaments of the finest poems or music or orations or recitations are not independent but dependent. All beauty comes from beautiful blood and a

beautiful brain. If the greatnesses are in conjunction in a man
or woman it is enough . . . . the fact will prevail through the
universe . . . . but the gaggery and gilt of a million years will
not prevail. Who troubles himself about his ornaments or
fluency is lost. This is what you shall do: Love the earth and
sun and the animals, despise riches, give alms to everyone that
asks, stand up for the stupid and crazy, devote your income
and labor to others, hate tyrants, argue not concerning God,
have patience and indulgence toward the people, take off your
hat to nothing known or unknown or to any man or number
of men, go freely with powerful uneducated persons and with
the young and with the mothers of families, [read these leaves
in the open air every season of every year of your life,] re-
examine all you have been told at school or church or in any
book, dismiss whatever insults your own soul, and your very
flesh shall be a great poem and have the richest fluency not
only in its words but in the silent lines of its lips and face and
between the lashes of your eyes and in every motion and joint
of your body . . . . The poet shall not spend his time in
unneeded work. He shall know that the ground is always ready
plowed and manured . . . others may not know it but he shall.
He shall go directly to the creation. His trust shall master
the trust of everything he touches . . . . and shall master all
attachment.

The known universe has one complete lover and that is the
greatest poet. He consumes an eternal passion and is indifferent which chance happens and which possible contingency of
fortune or misfortune and persuades daily and hourly his delicious pay. What balks or breaks others is fuel for his burning
progress to contact and amorous joy. Other proportions of the
reception of pleasure dwindle to nothing to his proportions.
All expected from heaven or from the highest he is rapport
with in the sight of the daybreak or a scene of the winter
woods or the presence of children playing or with his
arm round the neck of a man or woman. His love above all
love has leisure and expanse . . . . he leaves room ahead of himself. He is no irresolute or suspicious lover . . . he is sure . . .

he scorns intervals. His experience and the showers and thrills are not for nothing. Nothing can jar him . . . . suffering and darkness cannot—death and fear cannot. To him complaint and jealousy and envy are corpses buried and rotten in the earth . . . . he saw them buried. The sea is not surer of the shore or the shore of the sea than he is of the fruition of his love and of all perfection and beauty.

The fruition of beauty is no chance of hit or miss . . . it is inevitable of life . . . . it is exact and plumb as gravitation. From the eyesight proceeds another eyesight and from the hearing proceeds another hearing and from the voice proceeds another voice eternally curious of the harmony of things with man. [To these respond perfections not only in the committees that were supposed to stand for the rest but in the rest themselves just the same.] These understand the law of perfection in masses and floods . . . [that its finish is to each for itself and onward from itself] . . . that it is profuse and impartial . . . that there is not a minute of the light or dark nor an acre of the earth or sea without it—nor any direction of the sky nor any trade or employment nor any turn of events. This is the reason that about the proper expression of beauty there is precision and balance . . . one part does not need to be thrust above another. The best singer is not the one who has the most lithe and powerful organ . . . the pleasure of poems is not in them that take the handsomest measure [and similes] and sound.

Without effort and without exposing in the least how it is done the greatest poet brings the spirit of any or all events and passions and scenes and persons some more and some less to bear on your individual character as you hear or read. To do this well is to compete with the laws that pursue and follow time. What is the purpose must surely be there and the clue of it must be there . . . and the faintest indication is the indication of the best and then becomes the clearest indication. Past and present and future are not disjoined but joined. The greatest poet forms the consistence of what is to be from what has been and is. He drags the dead out of their coffins and stands them again on their feet . . . he says to the past, Rise and walk before me that I may realize you. He learns the lesson . . . . he places himself where the future becomes present. The greatest poet does not only dazzle his rays over character and scenes and passions . . . he finally ascends and finishes all . . . he exhibits the pinnacles that no man can tell what they are for or what is beyond . . . . he glows a moment on the extremest verge. He is most wonderful in his last half-hidden smile or frown . . . by that flash of the moment of parting the one that sees it shall be encouraged or terrified afterward for many years. The greatest poet does not moralize or make applications of morals . . . he knows the soul. The soul has that measureless pride which consists in never acknowledging any lessons but its own. But it has sympathy as measureless as its pride and the one balances the other and neither can stretch too far while it stretches in company with the other. The inmost secrets of art sleep with the twain. The greatest poet has lain close betwixt both and they are vital in his style and thoughts.

The art of art, the glory of expression and the sunshine of the light of letters, is simplicity. Nothing is better than simplicity . . . . nothing can make up for excess or for lack of definiteness. To carry on the heave of impulse and pierce intellectual depths and give all subjects their articulations are powers neither common nor very uncommon. But to speak in literature with the perfect rectitude and insouciance of the movements of animals and the unimpeachableness of the sentiment of trees in the woods and grass by the roadside is the flawless triumph of art. If you have looked on him who has achieved it you have looked on one of the masters of the artists of all nations and times. You shall not contemplate the flight of the graygull over the bay or the mettlesome action of the blood horse or the tall leaning of sunflowers on their stalk or the appearance of the sun journeying through heaven or the appearance of the moon afterward with any more satisfaction than you shall contemplate him. The greatest poet has less a marked style and is more the channel of thoughts and things without increase or diminution, and is the free channel of himself. He swears to his art, I will not be meddlesome, I will not have in my writing any elegance or effect or originality to hang in the way between me and the rest like curtains. I will have nothing hang in the way, not the richest curtains. What I tell I tell for precisely what it is. Let who may exalt or startle or fascinate or sooth, I will have purposes as health or heat or snow has and be as regardless of observation. What I experience or portray shall go from my composition [without a shred of my composition]. You shall stand by my side and look in the mirror with me.

The old red blood and stainless gentility of great poets will be proved by their unconstraint. A heroic person walks at his ease through and out of that custom or precedent or authority that suits him not. Of the traits of the brotherhood of writers savants musicians inventors and artists nothing is finer than silent defiance advancing from new free forms. In the need of poems philosophy politics mechanism science behavior, the craft of art, an appropriate native grand-opera, shipcraft, or any craft, he is greatest forever and forever who contributes the greatest original practical example. The cleanest expression is that which finds no sphere worthy of itself and makes one.

The message of great poets to each man and woman is, Come to us on equal terms, Only then can you understand us, We are no better than you, What we enclose you enclose. What we enjoy you may enjoy. Did you suppose there could be only one Supreme? We affirm there can be unnumbered Supremes, and that one does not countervail another any more than one eyesight countervails another . . and that men can be good or grand only of the consciousness of their supremacy within them. What do you think is the grandeur of storms and dismemberments and the deadliest battles and wrecks and the wildest fury of the elements, and the power of the sea and the motion of nature and of the throes of human desires and dignity and hate and love? It is that something in the soul which says, Rage on, Whirl on, I tread master here and everywhere, Master of the spasms of the sky and of the shatter of the sea, Master of nature and passion and death, And of all terror and all pain.

The American bards shall be marked for generosity and affection and for encouraging competitors . . . They shall be kosmos . . without monopoly or secrecy . . . glad to pass any thing to any one . . hungry for equals night and day. They shall not be careful of riches and privilege . . . . they shall be riches and privilege . . . . they shall perceive who the most affluent man is. The most affluent man is he that confronts all the shows he sees by equivalents out of the stronger wealth of himself. The American bard shall delineate no class of persons nor one or two out of the strata of interests nor love most nor truth most nor the soul most nor the body most . . . . and not be for the eastern states more than the western or the northern states more than the southern.

Exact science and its practical movements are no checks on the greatest poet but always his encouragement and support. The outset and remembrance are there . . there the arms that lifted him first and brace him best . . . . there he returns after all his goings and comings. The sailor and traveler . . the anatomist chemist astronomer geologist phrenologist spiritualist mathematician historian and lexicographer are not poets, but they are the lawgivers of poets and their construction underlies the structure of every perfect poem. No matter what rises or is uttered they sent the seed of the conception of it . . . of them and by them stand the visible proofs of souls . . . . . [always of their fatherstuff must be begotten the sinewy races of bards.] If there shall be love and content between the father and the son and if the greatness of the son is the exuding of the greatness of the father there shall be love between the poet and the man of demonstrable science. In the beauty of poems are the tuft and final applause of science.

Great is the faith of the flush of knowledge and of the investigation of the depths of qualities and things. Cleaving and circling here swells the soul of the poet yet is president of itself always. The depths are fathomless and therefore calm. The innocence and nakedness are resumed . . . they are neither modest nor immodest. The whole theory of the [special and] supernatural and all that was twined with it or educed out of it departs as a dream. What has ever happened . . . what happens and whatever may or shall happen, the vital laws enclose all . . . . they are sufficient for any case and for all cases . . . none to be hurried or retarded . . . . any miracle of affairs or persons inadmissible in the vast clear scheme where every motion and every spear of grass and the frames and spirits of men and women and all that concerns them are unspeakably perfect miracles all referring to all and each distinct and in its place. It is also not consistent with the reality of the soul to admit that there is anything in the known universe more divine than men and women.

Men and women and the earth and all upon it are simply to be taken as they are, and the investigation of their past and present and future shall be unintermitted and shall be done with perfect candor. Upon this basis philosophy speculates ever looking toward the poet, ever regarding the eternal tendencies of all toward happiness never inconsistent with what is clear to the senses and to the soul. For the eternal tendencies of all toward happiness make the only point of sane philosophy. Whatever comprehends less than that . . . whatever is less than the laws of light and of astronomical motion . . . or less than the laws that follow the thief the liar the glutton and the drunkard through this life and doubtless afterward . . . . . . or less than vast stretches of time or the slow formation of density or the patient upheaving of strata—is of no account. Whatever would put God in a poem or system of philosophy as contending against some being or influence is also of no account. Sanity and ensemble characterize the great master . . . spoilt in one principle all is spoilt. The great master has nothing to do with miracles. He sees health for himself in being one of the mass . . . he sees the hiatus in singular eminence. To the perfect shape comes common ground. To be under the general law is great for that is to correspond with it. The master knows that he is unspeakably great and that all are unspeakably great . . . . that nothing for instance is greater than to conceive children and bring them up well . . . that to be is just as great as to perceive or tell.

In the make of the great masters the idea of political liberty is indispensable. Liberty takes the adherence of heroes wherever men and women exist . . . but never takes any adherence or welcome from the rest more than from poets. They are the voice and exposition of liberty. They out of ages are worthy the grand idea . . . . to them it is confided and they must sustain it. Nothing has precedence of it and nothing can warp or degrade it. [The attitude of great poets is to cheer up slaves and horrify despots. The turn of their necks, the sound of their feet, the motions of their wrists, are full of hazard to the one and hope to the other. Come nigh them awhile and though they neither speak or advise you shall learn the faithful American lesson. Liberty is poorly served by men whose good intent is quelled from one failure or two failures or any number of failures, or from the casual indifference or ingratitude of the people, or from the sharp show of the tushes of power, or the bringing to bear soldiers and cannon or any penal statutes. Liberty relies upon itself, invites no one, promises nothing, sits in calmness and light, is positive and composed, and knows no discouragement. The battle rages with many a loud alarm and frequent advance and retreat . . . . the enemy triumphs . . . . the prison, the handcuffs, the iron necklace and anklet, the scaffold, garrote and leadballs do their work . . . . the cause is asleep . . . . the strong throats are choked with their own blood . . . . the young men drop their eyelashes toward the ground when they pass each other . . . . and is liberty gone out of that place? No never. When liberty goes it is not the first to go nor the second or third to go . . . it is the last . . When the memories of the old martyrs are faded utterly away . . . . when the large names of patriots are laughed at in the public halls from the lips of the orators . . . . when the boys are no more christened after the same but christened after tyrants and traitors instead . . . . when the laws of the free are grudgingly permitted and laws for informers and blood money are sweet to the taste of the people . . . . when I and you walk abroad upon the earth stung with compassion at the sight of numberless brothers answering our equal friendship and calling no man master—and when we are elated with noble joy at the sight of slaves . . . when the soul retires in the cool communion of the night and surveys its experience and has much ecstasy over the word and deed that put back a helpless innocent person into the gripe of the gripers or into any cruel inferiority . . . . when those in all parts of these states who could easier realize the true American character but do not yet—when the swarms of cringers, suckers, doughfaces, lice of politics, planners of sly involutions for their own preferment to city offices or state legislatures or the judiciary or congress or the presidency, obtain a response of love and natural deference from the people whether they get the offices or no . . . . when it is better to be a bound booby and rogue in office at a high salary than the poorest free mechanic or farmer with his hat unmoved from his head and firm eyes and a candid and generous heart . . . and when servility by town or state or the federal government or any oppression on a large scale or small scale can be tried on without its own punishment following duly after in exact proportion against the smallest chance of escape . . . or rather when all life and all the souls of men and women are discharged from any part of the earth—then only shall the instinct of liberty be discharged from that part of the earth.]

As the attributes of the poets of the kosmos concentre in the real body [and soul] and in the pleasure of things they possess the superiority of genuineness over all fiction and romance. As they emit themselves facts are showered over with light . . . . the daylight is lit with more volatile light . . . . also the deep between the setting and rising sun goes deeper many fold. Each precise object or condition or combination or process exhibits a beauty . . . . the multiplication table its—old age its—the carpenter's trade its—the grand opera its . . . the huge-hulled cleanshaped New-York clipper at sea under steam or full sail gleams with unmatched beauty . . . . the American circles and large harmonies of government gleam with theirs . . . .

and the commonest definite intentions and actions with theirs.
The poets of the kosmos advance through all interpositions
and coverings and turmoils and stratagems to first principles.
They are of use . . . . they dissolve poverty from its need and
riches from its conceit. You large proprietor they say shall not
realize or perceive more than any one else. The owner of the
library is not he who holds a legal title to it having bought
and paid for it. Any one and every one is owner of the library
who can read the same through all the varieties of tongues
and subjects and styles, and in whom they enter with ease [and
take residence and force toward paternity and maternity,] and
make supple and powerful and rich and large . . . . These
American states strong and healthy and accomplished shall
receive no pleasure from violations of natural models and must
not permit them. In paintings or mouldings or carvings in
mineral or wood, or in the illustrations of books or newspapers, or in any comic or tragic prints, or in the patterns of
woven stuffs or anything to beautify rooms or furniture or
costumes, or to put upon cornices or monuments or on the
prows or sterns of ships, or to put anywhere before the human
eye indoors or out, that which distorts honest shapes or which
creates unearthly beings or places or contingencies is a nui-
sance and revolt. Of the human form especially it is so great
it must never be made ridiculous. Of ornaments to a work
nothing outre can be allowed . . . but those ornaments can be
allowed that conform to the perfect facts of the open air and
that flow out of the nature of the work and come irrepressibly
from it and are necessary to the completion of the work. Most
works are most beautiful without ornament . . . . Exaggerations will be revenged in human physiology. Clean and vigorous children are jetted and conceived only in those communities where the models of natural forms are public every day.
. . . . . Great genius and the people of these states must never
be demeaned to romances. As soon as histories are properly
told there is no more need of romances.

The great poets are also to be known by the absence in
them of tricks and by the justification of perfect personal can-

dor. [Then folks echo a new cheap joy and a divine voice
leaping from their brains: How beautiful is candor!] All
faults may be forgiven of him who has perfect candor. Hence-
forth let no man of us lie, for we have seen that openness wins
the inner and outer world and that there is no single exception, and that never since our earth gathered itself in a mass
have deceit or subterfuge or prevarication attracted its smallest particle or the faintest tinge of a shade—and that through
the enveloping wealth and rank of a state or the whole republic of states a sneak or sly person shall be discovered and despised . . . . and that the soul has never been once fooled and
never can be fooled . . . . and thrift without the loving nod of
the soul is only a fetid puff . . . . and there never grew up in
any of the continents of the globe nor upon any planet or
satellite [or star, nor upon the asteroids, nor in any part of
ethereal space, nor in the midst of density, nor under the
fluid wet of the sea,] nor in that condition which precedes the
birth of babes, nor at any time during the changes of life, [nor
in that condition that follows what we term death,] nor in
any stretch of abeyance or action afterward of vitality, nor in
any process of formation or reformation anywhere, a being
whose instinct hated the truth.

Extreme caution or prudence, the soundest organic health,
large hope and comparison and fondness for women and children, large alimentiveness and destructiveness and causality,
with a perfect sense of the oneness of nature and the propriety
of the same spirit applied to human affairs . . these are called
up of the float of the brain of the world to be parts of the
greatest poet from his birth out of his mother's womb and
from her birth out of her mother's. Caution seldom goes far
enough. It has been thought that the prudent citizen was the
citizen who applied himself to solid gains and did well for
himself and his family and completed a lawful life without
debt or crime. The greatest poet sees and admits these economies as he sees the economies of food and sleep, but has
higher notions of prudence than to think he gives much when
he gives a few slight attentions at the latch of the gate. The

premises of the prudence of life are not the hospitality of it or
the ripeness and harvest of it. Beyond the independence of a
little sum laid aside for burial-money, and of a few clapboards
around and shingles overhead on a lot of American soil
owned, and the easy dollars that supply the year's plain cloth-
ing and meals, the melancholy prudence of the abandonment
of such a great being as a man is to the toss and pallor of
years of moneymaking with all their scorching days and icy
nights and all their stifling deceits and underhanded dodgings,
or infinitesimals of parlors, or shameless stuffing while others
starve . . . and all the loss of the bloom and odor of the earth
and of the flowers and atmosphere and of the sea and of the
true taste of the women and men you pass or have to do with
in youth or middle age, and the issuing sickness and desperate
revolt at the close of a life without elevation or naivete, and
the ghastly chatter of a death without serenity or majesty, is
the great fraud upon modern civilization and forethought,
blotching the surface and system which civilization undeni-
ably drafts, and moistening with tears the immense features it
spreads and spreads with such velocity before the reached
kisses of the soul . . . Still the right explanation remains to
be made about prudence. The prudence of the mere wealth
and respectability of the most esteemed life appears too faint
for the eye to observe at all when little and large alike drop
quietly aside at the thought of the prudence suitable for immortality. What is wisdom that fills the thinness of a year or
seventy or eighty years to wisdom spaced out by ages and
coming back at a certain time with strong reinforcements and
rich presents and the clear faces of wedding-guests as far as
you can look in every direction running gaily towards you?
Only the soul is of itself . . . . all else has reference to what ensues. All that a person does or thinks is of consequence. [Not
a move can a man or woman make that affects him or her in a
day or a month or any part of the direct lifetime or the hour
of death but the same affects him or her onward afterward
through the indirect lifetime. The indirect is always as great
and real as the direct. The spirit received from the body just

as much as it gives to the body. Not one name of word or deed
. . . not of venereal sores or discolorations . . not the privacy
of the onanist . . . not of the putrid veins of gluttons or rum-
drinkers . . . not peculation or cunning or betrayal or murder
. . not serpentine poison of those that seduce women . . . not
the foolish yielding of women . . not prostitution . . not of
any depravity of young men . . not of the attainment of gain
by discreditable means . . not any nastiness of appetite . .
not any harshness of officers to men or judges to prisoners or
fathers to sons or sons to fathers or of husbands to wives or
bosses to their boys . . not of greedy looks or malignant
wishes . . . nor any of the wiles practiced by people upon
themselves . . . ever is or ever can be stamped on the programme but it is duly realized and returned, and that returned in further performances . . . and they returned again.]
Nor can the push of charity or personal force ever be anything
else than the profoundest reason, whether it bring arguments
to hand or no. No specification is necessary . . to add or sub-
tract or divide is in vain. Little or big, learned or unlearned,
white or black, legal or illegal, sick or well, from the first inspiration down the windpipe to the last expiration out of it,
all that a male or female does that is vigorous and benevolent
and clean is so much sure profit to him or her in the unshak-
able order of the universe and through the whole scope of it
forever. [If the savage or felon is wise it is well . . . . if the greatest poet or savant is wise it is simply the same . . if the President or chief justice is wise it is the same . . . if the young
mechanic or farmer is wise it is no more or less . . . if the pros-
titute is wise it is no more or less. The interest will come
round . . all will come round. All the best actions of war and
peace . . . all help given to relatives and strangers and the
poor and old and sorrowful and young children and widows
and the sick, and to all shunned persons . . all furtherance of
fugitives and of the escape of slaves . . all the self-denial that
stood steady and aloof on wrecks and saw others take the seats
of the boats . . . all offering of substance or life for the good
old cause, or for a friend's sake or opinion's sake . . . all pains

of enthusiasts scoffed at by their neighbors . . all the vast
sweet love and precious suffering of mothers . . . all honest
men baffled in strifes recorded or unrecorded . . . all the grandeur and good of the few ancient nations whose fragments of
annals we inherit . . and all the good of the hundreds of far
mightier and more ancient nations unknown to us by name or
date or location . . . . all that was ever manfully begun,
whether it succeeded or not . . . all that has at any time been
well suggested out of the divine heart of men or by the divinity of his mouth or by the shaping of his great hands . . and
all that is well thought or done this day on any part of the
surface of the globe . . or on any of the wandering stars or
fixed stars by those there as we are here . . or that is hence-
forth to be well thought or done by you whoever you are, or
by anyone—these singly and wholly inured at their time and
inure now and will inure always to the identities from which
they sprung or shall spring . . . . Did you guess any of them
lived only its moment? The world does not so exist . . . no
parts palpable or impalpable so exist . . . no result exists now
without being from its long antecedent result, and that from
its antecedent, and so backward without the farthest mention-
able spot coming a bit nearer to the beginning than any other
spot . . . . . Whatever satisfies the soul is truth.] The prudence
of the greatest poet answers at last the craving and glut of the
soul, [is not contemptuous of less ways of prudence if they
conform to its ways,] puts off nothing, permits no let-up for its
own case or any case, has no particular sabbath or judgment-
day, divides not the living from the dead or the righteous
from the unrighteous, is satisfied with the present, matches
every thought or act by its correlative, knows no possible for-
giveness or deputed atonement . . [knows that the young
man who composedly periled his life and lost it has done exceedingly well for himself, while the man who has not periled
his life and retains it to old age in riches and ease has perhaps
achieved nothing for himself worth mentioning . . and that
only that person has no great prudence to learn who has
learnt to prefer real longlived things, and favors body and

soul the same, and perceives the indirect assuredly following the direct, and what evil or good he does leaping onward and waiting to meet him again—and who in his spirit in any emergency whatever neither hurries or avoids death.]

The direct trial of him who would be the greatest poet is today. If he does not flood himself with the immediate age as with vast oceanic tides . . . . . [and if he does not attract his own land body and soul to himself and hang on its neck with incomparable love and plunge his semitic muscle into its merits and demerits . . .] and if he be not himself the age transfigured . . . and if to him is not opened the eternity which gives similitude to all periods and locations and processes and animate and inanimate forms, and which is the bond of time, and rises up from its inconceivable vagueness and infiniteness in the swimming shape of today, and is held by the ductile anchors of life, and makes the present spot the passage from what was to what shall be, and commits itself to the representation of this wave of an hour and this one of the sixty beautiful children of the wave—let him merge in the general run and wait his development . . . . Still the final test of poems or any character or work remains. The prescient poet projects himself centuries ahead and judges performer or performance after the changes of time. Does it live through them? Does it still hold on untired? Will the same style and the direction of genius to similar points be satisfactory now? [Has no new discovery in science or arrival at superior planes of thought and judgment and behavior fixed him or his so that either can be looked down upon?] Have the marches of tens and hundreds and thousands of years made willing detours to the right hand and the left hand for his sake? Is he beloved long and long after he is buried? Does the young man think often of him? and the young woman think often of him? and do the middle-aged and the old think of him?

A great poem is for ages and ages in common and for all degrees and complexions and all departments and sects and for a woman as much as a man and a man as much as a woman. [A great poem is no finish to a man or woman] but rather a beginning. Has any one fancied he could sit at last under some due authority and rest satisfied with explanations and realize and be content and full? To no such terminus does the greatest poet bring . . . he brings neither cessation or sheltered fatness and ease. The touch of him tells in action. Whom he takes he takes with firm sure grasp into live regions previously unattained . . . thenceforward is no rest . . . . they see the space and ineffable sheen that turn the old spots and lights into dead vacuums. [The companion of him beholds the birth and progress of stars and learns one of the meanings.] Now there shall be a man cohered out of tumult and chaos . . . . the elder encourages the younger and shows him how . . . they two shall launch off fearlessly together till the new world fits an orbit for itself and looks unabashed on the lesser orbits of the stars and sweeps through the ceaseless rings and shall never be quiet again.

There will soon be no more priests. Their work is done. [They may wait awhile . . perhaps a generation or two . . dropping off by degrees. A superior breed shall take their place . . . . the gangs of kosmos and prophets en masse shall take their place.] A new order shall arise and they shall be the priests of man, and every man shall be his own priest. [The churches built under their umbrage shall be the churches of men and women. Through the divinity of themselves shall the kosmos and the new breed of poets be interpreters of men and women and of all events and things.] They shall find their inspiration in real objects today, symptoms of the past and future . . . . They shall not deign to defend immortality or God or the perfection of things or liberty or the exquisite beauty and reality of the soul. They shall arise in America and be responded to from the remainder of the earth.

The English language befriends the grand American expression . . . . it is brawny enough and limber and full enough. On the tough stock of a race through all change of circumstance was never without the idea of political liberty, which is the animus of all liberty, it has attracted the terms of daintier and gayer and subtler and more elegant tongues. It is the powerful language of resistance . . . it is the dialect of common sense. It is the speech of the proud and melancholy races and of all who aspire. It is the chosen tongue to express growth faith self-esteem freedom justice equality friendliness amplitude prudence decision and courage. It is the medium that shall well nigh express the inexpressible.

No great literature nor any like style of behaviour or oratory or social intercourse or household arrangements or public institutions or the treatment by bosses of employed people, nor executive detail or detail of the army or navy, nor spirit of legislation or courts or police or tuition or architecture or songs or amusements [or the costumes of young men,] can long elude the jealous and passionate instinct of American standards. Whether or no the sign appears from the mouths of the people, it throbs a live interrogation in every freeman's and freewoman's heart after that which passes by or this built to remain. Is it uniform with my country? Are its disposals without ignominious distinctions? Is it for the evergrowing communes of brothers and lovers, large well-united, proud beyond the old models, generous beyond all models? Is it something grown fresh out of the fields or drawn from the sea for use to me today here? I know that what answers for me an American must answer for any individual or nation that serves for a part of my materials. Does this answer? [or is it without reference to universal needs? or sprung of the needs of the less modern science and forms? Does this acknowledge liberty with audible and absolute acknowledgement, and set slavery at naught for life and death? Will it help breed one good shaped and well-hung man, and a woman to be his perfect and independent mate? Does it improve manners?] Is it for the nursing of the young of the republic? Does it solve readily with the sweet milk of the nipples of the breasts of the mother of many children? [Has it too the old ever-fresh forbearance and impartiality? Does it look with the same love on the last born and those hardening toward stature, and on the errant, and on those who disdain all strength of assault outside of their own.

[The poems distilled from other poems will probably pass

away. The coward will surely pass away. The expectation of the vital and great can only be satisfied by the demeanor of the vital and great. The swarms of the polished deprecating and reflectors and the polite float off and leave no remembrance.] America prepares with composure and good will for the visitors that have sent word. It is not intellect that is to be their warrant and welcome. The talented, the artist, the ingenious, the editor, the statesman, the erudite . . they are not unappreciated . . they fall in their place and do their work. The soul of the nation also does its work. [No disguise can pass on it . . no disguise can conceal from it.] It rejects none, it permits all. Only [toward as good as itself and] toward the like of itself will it advance half-way. An individual is as superb as a nation when he has the qualities which make a superb nation. The soul of the largest and wealthiest and proudest nation may well go half-way to meet that of its poets. [The signs are effectual. There is no fear of mistake. If the one is true the other is true. The proof of a poet is that his country absorbs him as affectionately as he has absorbed it.]

HENRY JAMES

Henry James (1843-1916) was born in New York City, one of four sons of Henry James senior, student of theology, lecturer, and writer, who determined to give his children cosmopolitan educations. The boy attended schools in Geneva, Paris, Bonn, and Newport before attending the Harvard Law School. After four more years (1864-68) of residence in Cambridge, Massachusetts, during which he wrote critical reviews and short stories, James began a series of visits to Europe, settling in England in 1876, after which he made occasional visits to America. The year before his death he became a naturalized British citizen.

Commuting between Europe and America cultivated James's acute moral sense, and the predominant theme of his fiction and of his plays develops an awareness of manners as symptoms of morals in two societies. This awareness developed, in his later fiction, into moral and psychological studies of individuals in a society marked by intelligence and precise ritual. Among these individuals, in James's fictional world, were artists, whose relations with society and with their art became another definable theme in his fiction.

James's concern for the technique of fiction, his objective self-appraisal, and his analyses of the performances of others in this art form helped make him an extraordinary literary critic. Among his critical writings are *French Poets and Novelists* (1878), *Hawthorne* (1879), *Partial Portraits* (1888), *Picture and Text* (1893), *Essays in London and Elsewhere* (1893), and *Notes on Novelists* (1914). A revision (1918) of *Within the Rim and Other Essays* (1914-15), *Notes and Reviews by Henry James* (1921), along with *The Notebooks of Henry James* (1947), were posthumously published. His major critical work—which R. P. Blackmur, one of James's later editors, calls the most sustained, eloquent, and original piece of literary criticism in existence—is the collection of prefaces to his writing, which James prepared for Scribner's New York Edition: *The Novels and Tales of Henry James* (26 vols., 1907-17). His preoccupation, in these prefaces, and in his earlier and comparable essay, "The Art of Fiction,"

James in a way explained, in his preface to the novel, *What Maisie Knew*, where he wrote, "The effort really to see and really to represent is no idle business in face of the *constant* force that makes for muddlement."

"The Art of Fiction" was first published in *Longman's Magazine*, September 1884, and reprinted (1885) with Walter Besant's "The Art of Fiction." It again appeared, with James's minor revisions, in *Partial Portraits* (1888), from which this text is taken.

THE ART OF FICTION

I SHOULD not have affixed so comprehensive a title to these few remarks, necessarily wanting in any completeness, upon a subject the full consideration of which would carry us far, did I not seem to discover a pretext for my temerity in the interesting pamphlet lately published under this name by Mr. Walter Besant. Mr. Besant's lecture at the Royal Institution—the original form of his pamphlet—appears to indicate that many persons are interested in the art of fiction, and are not indifferent to such remarks, as those who practice it may attempt to make about it. I am therefore anxious not to lose the benefit of this favourable association, and to edge in a few words under cover of the attention which Mr. Besant is sure to have excited. There is something very encouraging in his having put into form certain of his ideas on the mystery of story-telling.

It is a proof of life and curiosity—curiosity on the part of the brotherhood of novelists as well as on the part of their readers. Only a short time ago it might have been supposed that the English novel was not what the French call *discutable*. It had no air of having a theory, a conviction, a consciousness of itself behind it—of being the expression of an artistic faith, the result of choice and comparison. I do not say it was necessarily the worse for that; it would take much more courage than I possess to intimate that the form of the novel as Dickens and Thackeray (for instance) saw it had any taint of incompleteness. It was, however, *naïf* (if I may help myself out with another French word); and evidently, if it be destined to suffer in any way for having lost its *naïveté,* it has now an idea of making sure of the corresponding advantages. During the period I have alluded to there was a comfortable, good-humoured feeling abroad that a novel is a novel, as a pudding is a pudding, and that our only business with it could be to swallow it. But within a year or two, for some reason or other, there have been signs of returning animation—the era of discussion would appear to have been to a certain extent opened. Art lives upon discussion, upon experiment, upon curiosity, upon variety of attempt, upon the exchange of views and the comparison of standpoints; and there is a presumption that those times when no one has anything particular to say about it, and has no reason to give for practice or preference, though they may be times of honour, are not times of development—are times possibly, even a little of dulness. The successful application of any art is a delightful spectacle, but the theory too is interesting; and though there is a great deal of the latter without the former I suspect there has never been a genuine success that has not had a latent core of conviction. Discussion, suggestion, formulation, these things are fertilizing when they are frank and sincere. Mr. Besant has set an excellent example in saying what he thinks, for his part, about the way in which fiction should be written, as well as about the way in which it should be published; for his view of the "art," carried on into an appendix, covers that too. Other labourers in the same field will doubtless take up the argument, they will give it the light of their experience, and the effect will surely be to make our interest in the novel a little more what it had for some time threatened to fail to be—a serious, active, inquiring interest, under protection of which this delightful study may, in moments of confidence, venture to say a little more what it thinks of itself.

It must take itself seriously for the public to take it so. The old superstition about fiction being "wicked" has doubtless died out in England; but the spirit of it lingers in a certain

oblique regard directed toward any story which does not more
or less admit that it is only a joke. Even the most jocular novel
feels in some degree the weight of the proscription that was
formerly directed against literary levity: the jocularity does
not always succeed in passing for orthodoxy. It is still expected, though perhaps people are ashamed to say it, that a
production which is after all only a "make-believe" (for what
else is a "story"?) shall be in some degree apologetic—shall
renounce the pretension of attempting really to represent life.
This, of course, any sensible, wide-awake story declines to do,
for it quickly perceives that the tolerance granted to it on such
a condition is only an attempt to stifle it disguised in the form
of generosity. The old evangelical hostility to the novel, which
was as explicit as it was narrow, and which regarded it as little
less favourable to our immortal part than a stage-play, was in
reality far less insulting. The only reason for the existence of
a novel is that it does attempt to represent life. When it re-
linquishes this attempt, the same attempt that we see on the
canvas of the painter, it will have arrived at a very strange
pass. It is not expected of the picture that it will make itself
humble in order to be forgiven; and the analogy between the
art of the painter and the art of the novelist is, so far as I am
able to see, complete. Their inspiration is the same, their process (allowing for the different quality of the vehicle) is the
same, their success is the same. They may learn from each
other, they may explain and sustain each other. Their cause
is the same, and the honour of one is the honour of another.
The Mahometans think a picture an unholy thing, but it is a
long time since any Christian did, and it is therefore the more
odd that in the Christian mind the traces (dissimulated though
they may be) of a suspicion of the sister art should linger to
this day. The only effectual way to lay it to rest is to emphasize
the analogy to which I just alluded—to insist on the fact that
as the picture is reality, so the novel is history. That is the only
general description (which does it justice) that we may give of
the novel. But history also is allowed to represent life; it is not,
any more than painting, expected to apologize. The subject-

matter of fiction is stored up likewise in documents and records, and if it will not give itself away, as they say in California, it must speak with assurance, with the tone of the historian.
Certain accomplished novelists have a habit of giving themselves away which must often bring tears to the eyes of people
who take their fiction seriously. I was lately struck, in reading
over many pages of Anthony Trollope, with his want of dis-
cretion in this particular. In a digression, a parenthesis or an
aside, he concedes to the reader that he and this trusting
friend are only "making believe." He admits that the events he
narrates have not really happened, and that he can give his
narrative any turn the reader may like best. Such a betrayal of
a sacred office seems to me, I confess, a terrible crime; it is
what I mean by the attitude of apology, and it shocks me every
whit as much in Trollope as it would have shocked me in
Gibbon or Macaulay. It implies that the novelist is less occupied in looking for the truth (the truth, of course I mean, that
he assumes, the premises that we must grant him, whatever
they may be) than the historian, and in doing so it deprives
him at a stroke of all his standing-room. To represent and
illustrate the past, the actions of men, is the task of either
writer, and the only difference that I can see is, in proportion
as he succeeds, to the honour of the novelist, consisting as it
does in his having more difficulty in collecting his evidence,
which is so far from being purely literary. It seems to me to
give him a great character, the fact that he has at once so much
in common with the philosopher and the painter; this double
analogy is a magnificent heritage.

It is of all this evidently that Mr. Besant is full when he
insists upon the fact that fiction is one of the *fine* arts, deserv-
ing in its turn of all the honours and emoluments that have
hitherto been reserved for the successful profession of music,
poetry, painting, architecture. It is impossible to insist too
much on so important a truth, and the place that Mr. Besant
demands for the work of the novelist may be represented, a
trifle less abstractly, by saying that he demands not only that
it shall be reputed artistic, but that it shall be reputed very

artistic indeed. It is excellent that he should have struck this note, for his doing so indicates that there was need of it, that his proposition may be to many people a novelty. One rubs one's eyes at the thought; but the rest of Mr. Besant's essay confirms the revelation. I suspect in truth that it would be possible to confirm it still further, and that one would not be far wrong in saying that in addition to the people to whom it has never occurred that a novel ought to be artistic, there are a great many others who, if this principle were urged upon them, would be filled with an indefinable mistrust. They would find it difficult to explain their repugnance, but it would operate strongly to put them on their guard. "Art," in our Protestant communities, where so many things have got so strangely twisted about, is supposed in certain circles to have some vague injurious effect upon those who make it an important consideration, who let it weigh in the balance. It is assumed to be opposed in some mysterious manner to morality, to amusement, to instruction. When it is embodied in the work of the painter (the sculptor is another affair!) you know what it is: it stands there before you, in the honesty of pink and green and a gilt frame; you can see the worst of it at a glance, and you can be on your guard. But when it is introduced into literature it becomes more insidious—there is danger of its hurting you before you know it. Literature should be either instructive or amusing, and there is in many minds an impression that these artistic preoccupations, the search for form, contribute to neither end, interfere indeed with both. They are too frivolous to be edifying, and too serious to be diverting; and they are moreover priggish and paradoxical and superfluous. That, I think, represents the manner in which the latent thought of many people who read novels as an exercise in skipping, would explain itself if it were to become articulate. They would argue, of course, that a novel ought to be "good," but they would interpret this term in a fashion of their own, which indeed would vary considerably from one critic to another. One would say that being good means representing virtuous and aspiring characters placed in prominent positions; another would say that it depends on a "happy ending," on a distribution at the last of prizes, pensions, husbands, wives, babies, millions, appended paragraphs, and cheerful remarks. Another still would say that it means being full of incident and movement, so that we shall wish to jump ahead, to see who was the mysterious stranger, and if the stolen will was ever found, and shall not be distracted from this pleasure by any tiresome analysis or "description." But they would all agree that the "artistic" idea would spoil some of their fun. One would hold it accountable for all the description, another would see it revealed in the absence of sympathy. Its hostility to a happy ending would be evident, and it might even in some cases render any ending at all impossible. The "ending" of a novel is, for many persons, like that of a good dinner, a course of dessert and ices, and the artist in fiction is regarded as a sort of meddlesome doctor who forbids agreeable aftertastes. It is therefore true that this conception of Mr. Besant's of the novel as a superior form encounters not only a negative but a positive indifference. It matters little that as a work of art it should really be as little or as much of its essence to supply happy endings, sympathetic characters, and an objective tone, as if it were a work of mechanics: the association of ideas, however incongruous, might easily be too much for it if an eloquent voice were not sometimes raised to call attention to the fact that it is at once as free and as serious a branch of literature as any other.

Certainly this might sometimes be doubted in presence of the enormous number of works of fiction that appeal to the credulity of our generation, for it might easily seem that there could be no great character in a commodity so quickly and easily produced. It must be admitted that good novels are much compromised by bad ones, and that the field at large suffers discredit from overcrowding. I think, however, that this injury is only superficial, and that the superabundance of written fiction proves nothing against the principle itself. It has been vulgarised, like all other kinds of literature, like everything else today, and it has proved more than some kinds accessible to vulgarisation. But there is as much difference as there ever was between a good novel and a bad one: the bad is swept with all the daubed canvases and spoiled marble into some unvisited limbo, or infinite rubbish-yard beneath the back-windows of the world, and the good subsists and emits its light and stimulates our desire for perfection. As I shall take the liberty of making but a single criticism of Mr. Besant, whose tone is so full of love of his art, I may as well have done with it at once. He seems to me to mistake, in attempting to say so definitely beforehand, what sort of an affair the good novel will be. To indicate the danger of such an error as that has been the purpose of these few pages; to suggest that certain traditions on the subject, applied *a priori,* have already had much to answer for, and that the good health of an art which undertakes so immediately to reproduce life must demand that it be perfectly free. It lives upon exercise, and the very meaning of exercise is freedom. The only obligation to which in advance we may hold a novel, without incurring the accusation of being arbitrary, is that it be interesting. That general responsibility rests upon it, but it is the only one I can think of. The ways in which it is at liberty to accomplish this result (of interesting us) strike me as innumerable, and such as can only suffer from being marked out or fenced in by prescription. They are as various as the temperament of man, and they are successful in proportion as they reveal a particular mind, different from others. A novel is in its broadest definition a personal, a direct impression of life: that, to begin with, constitutes its value, which is greater or less according to the intensity of the impression. But there will be no intensity at all, and therefore no value, unless there is freedom to feel and say. The tracing of a line to be followed, of a tone to be taken, of a form to be filled out, is a limitation of that freedom and a suppression of the very thing that we are most curious about. The form, it seems to me, is to be appreciated after the fact: then the author's choice has been made, his standard has been indicated; then we can follow lines and directions and compare tones and resemblances. Then in a word we can enjoy one of the most charming of pleasures, we can estimate quality, we can apply the test of execution. The execution belongs to the author alone; it is what is most personal to him, and we measure him by that. The advantage, the luxury, as well as the torment and responsibility of the novelist, is that there is no limit to what he may attempt as an executant—no limit to his possible experiments, efforts, discoveries, successes. Here it is especially that he works, step by step, like his brother of the brush, of whom we may always say that he has painted his picture in a manner best known to himself. His manner is his secret, not necessarily a jealous one. He cannot disclose it as a general thing if he would; he would be at a loss to teach it to others. I say this with a due recollection of having insisted on the community of method of the artist who paints a picture and the artist who writes a novel. The painter *is* able to teach the rudiments of his practice, and it is possible, from the study of good work (granted the aptitude), both to learn how to paint and to learn how to write. Yet it remains true, without injury to the *rapprochement,* that the literary artist would be obliged to say to his pupil much more than the other, "Ah, well, you must do it as you can." It is a question of degree, a matter of delicacy. If there are exact sciences, there are also exact arts, and the grammar of painting is so much more definite that it makes the difference.

I ought to add, however, that if Mr. Besant says at the beginning of his essay that the "laws of fiction may be laid down and taught with as much precision and exactness as the laws of harmony, perspective, and proportion," he mitigates what might appear to be an extravagance by applying his remark to "general" laws, and by expressing most of these rules in a manner with which it would certainly be unaccommodating to disagree. That the novelist must write from his experience, that his "characters must be real and such as might be met with in actual life"; that "a young lady brought up in a quiet country village should avoid descriptions of garrison life," and "a writer whose friends and personal experiences belong to the lower middle-class should carefully avoid introducing his characters into society"; that one should enter one's notes in a common-place book; that one's figures should be clear in outline; that making them clear by some trick of speech or of carriage is a bad method, and "describing them at length" is a worse one; that English Fiction should have a "conscious moral purpose"; that "it is almost impossible to estimate too highly the value of careful workmanship—that is, of style"; that "the most important point of all is the story," that "the story is everything": these are principles with most of which it is surely impossible not to sympathise. That remark about the lower middle-class writer and his knowing his place is perhaps rather chilling; but for the rest I should find it difficult to dissent from any one of these recommendations. At the same time, I should find it difficult positively to assent to them, with the exception, perhaps, of the injunction as to entering one's notes in a common-place book. They scarcely seem to me to have the quality that Mr. Besant attributes to the rules of the novelist—the "precision and exactness" of "the laws of harmony, perspective, and proportion." They are suggestive, they are even inspiring, but they are not exact, though they are doubtless as much so as the case admits of: which is a proof of that liberty of interpretation for which I just contended. For the value of these different injunctions—so beautiful and so vague—is wholly in the meaning one attaches to them. The characters, the situation, which strike one as real will be those that touch and interest one most, but the measure of reality is very difficult to fix. The reality of Don Quixote or of Mr. Micawber is a very delicate shade; it is a reality so coloured by the author's vision that, vivid as it may be, one would hesitate to propose it as a model: one would expose one's self to some very embarrassing questions on the part of a pupil. It goes without saying that you will not write a good novel unless you possess the sense of reality; but it will be difficult to give you a recipe for calling that sense into being. Humanity is immense, and reality has a myriad forms; the most one can affirm is that some of the flowers of fiction have the odour of it, and others have not; as for telling you in advance how your nosegay should be com-

posed, that is another affair. It is equally excellent and incon-
clusive to say that one must write from experience; to our
supposititious aspirant such a declaration might savour of
mockery. What kind of experience is intended, and where does it
begin and end? Experience is never limited, and it is never
complete; it is an immense sensibility, a kind of huge spider-
web of the finest silken threads suspended in the chamber of
consciousness, and catching every air-borne particle in its tis-
sue. It is the very atmosphere of the mind; and when the mind
is imaginative—much more when it happens to be that of a
man of genius—it takes to itself the faintest hints of life, it converts the very pulses of the air into revelations. The young
lady living in a village has only to be a damsel upon whom
nothing is lost to make it quite unfair (as it seems to me) to
declare to her that she shall have nothing to say about the
military. Greater miracles have been seen than that, imagination assisting, she should speak the truth about some of these
gentlemen. I remember an English novelist, a woman of genius,
telling me that she was much commended for the impression
she had managed to give in one of her tales of the nature and
way of life of the French Protestant youth. She had been asked
where she learned so much about this recondite being, she had
been congratulated on her peculiar opportunities. These opportunities consisted in her having once, in Paris, as she ascended
a staircase, passed an open door where, in the household of a
pasteur, some of the young Protestants were seated at table
round a finished meal. The glimpse made a picture; it lasted
only a moment, but that moment was experience. She had got
her direct personal impression, and she turned out her type.
She knew what youth was, and what Protestantism; she also
had the advantage of having seen what it was to be French, so
that she converted these ideas into a concrete image and produced a reality. Above all, however, she was blessed with the
faculty which when you give it an inch takes an ell, and which
for the artist is a much greater source of strength than any
accident of residence or of place in the social scale. The power
to guess the unseen from the seen, to trace the implication of

things, to judge the whole piece by the pattern, the condition of feeling life in general so completely that you are well on your way to knowing any particular corner of it—this cluster of gifts may almost be said to constitute experience, and they occur in country and in town, and in the most differing stages of education. If experience consists of impressions, it may be said that impressions *are* experience, just as (have we not seen it?) they are the very air we breathe. Therefore, if I should certainly say to a novice, "Write from experience and experience only," I should feel that this was rather a tantalising monition if I were not careful immediately to add, "Try to be one of the people on whom nothing is lost!"

I am far from intending by this to minimise the importance of exactness—of truth of detail. One can speak best from one's own taste, and I may therefore venture to say that the air of reality (solidity of specification) seems to me to be the supreme virtue of a novel—the merit on which all its other merits (including that conscious moral purpose of which Mr. Besant speaks) helplessly and submissively depend. If it be not there they are all as nothing, and if these be there, they owe their effect to the success with which the author has produced the illusion of life. The cultivation of this success, the study of this exquisite process, form, to my taste, the beginning and the end of the art of the novelist. They are his inspiration, his despair, his reward, his torment, his delight. It is here in very truth that he competes with life; it is here that he competes with his brother the painter in *his* attempt to render the look of things, the look that conveys their meaning, to catch the colour, the relief, the expression, the surface, the substance of the human spectacle. It is in regard to this that Mr. Besant is well inspired when he bids him take notes. He cannot possibly take too many, he cannot possibly take enough. All life solicits him, and to "render" the simplest surface, to produce the most momentary illusion, is a very complicated business. His case would be easier, and the rule would be more exact, if Mr. Besant had been able to tell him what notes to take. But this, I fear, he can never learn in any manual; it is the business of

his life. He has to take a great many in order to select a few,
he has to work them up as he can, and even the guides and
philosophers who might have most to say to him must leave
him alone when it comes to the application of precepts, as we
leave the painter in communion with his palette. That his
characters "must be clear in outline," as Mr. Besant says—he
feels that down to his boots; but how he shall make them so is
a secret between his good angel and himself. It would be ab-
surdly simple if he could be taught that a great deal of "description" would make them so, or that on the contrary the
absence of description and the cultivation of dialogue, or the
absence of dialogue and the multiplication of "incident,"
would rescue him from his difficulties. Nothing, for instance,
is more possible than that he be of a turn of mind for which
this odd, literal opposition of description and dialogue, incident and description, has little meaning and light. People
often talk of these things as if they had a kind of internecine
distinctness, instead of melting into each other at every breath,
and being intimately associated parts of one general effort of
expression. I cannot imagine composition existing in a series
of blocks, nor conceive, in any novel worth discussing at all, of
a passage of description that is not in its intention narrative, a
passage of dialogue that is not in its intention descriptive,
a touch of truth of any sort that does not partake of the nature
of incident, or an incident that derives its interest from any
other source than the general and only source of the success
of a work of art—that of being illustrative. A novel is a living
thing, all one and continuous, like any other organism, and in
proportion as it lives will it be found, I think, that in each
of the parts there is something of each of the other parts. The
critic who over the close texture of a finished work shall pretend to trace a geography of items will mark some frontiers as
artificial, I fear, as any that have been known to history. There
is an old-fashioned distinction between the novel of character
and the novel of incident which must have cost many a smile
to the intending fabulist who was keen about his work. It
appears to me as little to the point as the equally celebrated

distinction between the novel and the romance—to answer as little to any reality. There are bad novels and good novels, as there are bad pictures and good pictures; but that is the only distinction in which I see any meaning, and I can as little imagine speaking of a novel of character as I can imagine speaking of a picture of character. When one says picture one says of character, when one says novel one says of incident, and the terms may be transposed at will. What is character but the determination of incident? What is incident but the illustration of character? What is either a picture or a novel that is *not* of character? What else do we seek in it and find in it? It is an incident for a woman to stand up with her hand resting on a table and look out at you in a certain way; or if it be not an incident I think it will be hard to say what it is. At the same time it is an expression of character. If you say you don't see it (character in *that*—*allons donc!*), that is exactly what the artist who has reasons of his own for thinking he *does* see it undertakes to show you. When a young man makes up his mind that he has not faith enough after all to enter the church as he intended, that is an incident, though you may not hurry to the end of the chapter to see whether perhaps he doesn't change once more. I do not say that these are extraordinary or startling incidents. I do not pretend to estimate the degree of interest proceeding from them, for this will depend upon the skill of the painter. It sounds almost puerile to say that some incidents are intrinsically much more important than others, and I need not take this precaution after having professed my sympathy for the major ones in remarking that the only classification of the novel that I can understand is into that which has life and that which has it not.

The novel and the romance, the novel of incident and that of character—these clumsy separations appear to me to have been made by critics and readers for their own convenience, and to help them out of some of their occasional queer predicaments, but to have little reality or interest for the producer, from whose point of view it is of course that we are attempting to consider the art of fiction. The case is the same with another shadowy category which Mr. Besant apparently is disposed to set up—that of the "modern English novel"; unless indeed it be that in this matter he has fallen into an accidental confusion of standpoints. It is not quite clear whether he intends the remarks in which he alludes to it to be didactic or historical. It is as difficult to suppose a person intending to write a modern English as to suppose him writing an ancient English novel: that is a label which begs the question. One writes the novel, one paints the picture, of one's language and of one's time, and calling it modern English will not, alas! make the difficult task any easier. No more, unfortunately, will calling this or that work of one's fellow-artist a romance—unless it be, of course, simply for the pleasantness of the thing, as for instance when Hawthorne gave this heading to his story of *Blithedale*. The French, who have brought the theory of fiction to remarkable completeness, have but one name for the novel, and have not attempted smaller things in it, that I can see, for that. I can think of no obligation to which the "romancer" would not be held equally with the novelist; the standard of execution is equally high for each. Of course it is of execution that we are talking—that being the only point of a novel that is open to contention. This is perhaps too often lost sight of, only to produce interminable confusions and cross-purposes. We must grant the artist his subject, his idea, his *donnée:* our criticism is applied only to what he makes of it. Naturally I do not mean that we are bound to like it or find it interesting: in case we do not our course is perfectly simple—to let it alone. We may believe that of a certain idea even the most sincere novelist can make nothing at all, and the event may perfectly justify our belief; but the failure will have been a failure to execute, and it is in the execution that the fatal weakness is recorded. If we pretend to respect the artist at all, we must allow him his freedom of choice, in the face, in particular cases, of innumerable presumptions that the choice will not fructify. Art derives a considerable part of its beneficial exercise from flying in the face of presumptions, and some of the most interesting experiments of which it is capable are hidden in the bosom of common things. Gustave Flaubert has written a story about the devotion of a servant-girl to a parrot, and the production, highly finished as it is, cannot on the whole be called a success. We are perfectly free to find it flat, but I think it might have been interesting; and I, for my part, am extremely glad he should have written it; it is a contribution to our knowledge of what can be done—or what cannot. Ivan Turgénieff has written a tale about a deaf and dumb serf and a lap-dog, and the thing is touching, loving, a little masterpiece. He struck the note of life where Gustave Flaubert missed it—he flew in the face of a presumption and achieved a victory.

Nothing, of course, will ever take the place of the good old fashion of "liking" a work of art or not liking it: the most improved criticism will not abolish that primitive, that ultimate test. I mention this to guard myself from the accusation of intimating that the idea, the subject, of a novel or a picture, does not matter. It matters, to my sense, in the highest degree, and if I might put up a prayer it would be that artists should select none but the richest. Some, as I have already hastened to admit, are much more remunerative than others, and it would be a world happily arranged in which persons intending to treat them should be exempt from confusions and mistakes. This fortunate condition will arrive only, I fear, on the same day that critics become purged from error. Meanwhile, I repeat, we do not judge the artist with fairness unless we say to him, "Oh, I grant you your starting-point, because if I did not I should seem to prescribe to you, and heaven forbid I should take that responsibility. If I pretend to tell you what you must not take, you will call upon me to tell you then what you must take; in which case I shall be prettily caught. Moreover, it isn't till I have accepted your data that I can begin to measure you. I have the standard, the pitch; I have no right to tamper with your flute and then criticize your music. Of course I may not care for your idea at all; I may think it silly, or stale, or unclean; in which case I wash my hands of you altogether. I may content myself with believing that you will not have succeeded in being interesting, but I shall, of course, not attempt to demonstrate it, and you will be as indifferent to me as I am to you. I needn't remind you that there are all sorts of tastes: who can know it better? Some people, for excellent reasons, don't like to read about carpenters; others, for reasons even better, don't like to read about courtesans. Many object to Americans. Others (I believe they are mainly editors and publishers) won't look at Italians. Some readers don't like quiet subjects; others don't like bustling ones. Some enjoy a complete illusion, others the consciousness of large concessions. They choose their novels accordingly, and if they don't care about your idea they won't, *a fortiori,* care about your treatment."

So that it comes back very quickly, as I have said, to the liking: in spite of M. Zola, who reasons less powerfully than he represents, and who will not reconcile himself to this absoluteness of taste, thinking that there are certain things that people *ought* to like, and that they can be made to like. I am quite at a loss to imagine anything (at any rate in this matter of fiction) that people *ought* to like or to dislike. Selection will be sure to take care of itself, for it has a constant motive behind it. That motive is simply experience. As people feel life, so they will feel the art that is most closely related to it. This closeness of relation is what we should never forget in talking of the effort of the novel. Many people speak of it as a factitious, artificial form, a product of ingenuity, the business of which it is to alter and arrange the things that surround us, to translate them into conventional, traditional moulds. This, however, is a view of the matter which carries us but a very short way, condemns the art to an eternal repetition of a few familiar *clichés,* cuts short its development, and leads us straight up to a dead wall. Catching the very note and trick, the strange irregular rhythm of life, that is the attempt whose strenuous force keeps Fiction on her feet. In proportion as in what she offers us we see life *without* rearrangement do we feel that we are touching the truth; in proportion as we see it *with* rearrangement do we feel that we are being put off with a substitute, a compromise and convention. It is not uncommon to hear an extraordinary assurance of remark in regard to this matter of rearranging, which is often spoken of as if it were the last word of art. Mr. Besant seems to me in danger of falling into the great error with his rather unguarded talk about "selection." Art is essentially selection, but it is a selection whose main care is to be typical, to be inclusive. For many people art means rose-coloured window-panes, and selection means picking a bouquet for Mrs. Grundy. They will tell you glibly that artistic considerations have nothing to do with the disagreeable, with the ugly; they will rattle off shallow commonplaces about the province of art and the limits of art till you are moved to some wonder in return as to the province and the limits of ignorance. It appears to me that no one can ever have made a seriously artistic attempt without becoming conscious of an immense increase—a kind of revelation—of freedom. One perceives in that case—by the light of a heavenly ray—that the province of art is all life, all feeling, all observation, all vision. As Mr. Besant so justly intimates, it is all experience. That is a sufficient answer to those who maintain that it must not touch the sad things of life, who stick into its divine unconscious bosom little prohibitory inscriptions on the end of sticks, such as we see in public gardens—"It is forbidden to walk on the grass; it is forbidden to touch the flowers; it is not allowed to introduce dogs or to remain after dark; it is requested to keep to the right." The young aspirant in the line of fiction whom we continue to imagine will do nothing without taste, for in that case his freedom would be of little use to him; but the first advantage of his taste will be to reveal to him the absurdity of the little sticks and tickets. If he have taste, I must add, of course, he will have ingenuity, and my disrespectful reference to that quality just now was not meant to imply that it is useless in fiction. But it is only a secondary aid; the first is a capacity for receiving straight impressions.

Mr. Besant has some remarks on the question of "the story" which I shall not attempt to criticise, though they seem to me to contain a singular ambiguity, because I do not think I understand them. I cannot see what is meant by talking as if there were a part of a novel which is the story and part of it which for mystical reasons is not—unless indeed the distinction be made in a sense in which it is difficult to suppose that any-one should attempt to convey anything. "The story," if it repre-sents anything, represents the subject, the idea, the *donnée* of the novel; and there is surely no "school"—Mr. Besant speaks of a school—which urges that a novel should be all treatment and no subject. There must assuredly be something to treat; every school is intimately conscious of that. This sense of the story being the idea, the starting-point, of the novel, is the only one that I see in which it can be spoken of as something different from its organic whole; and since in proportion as the work is successful the idea permeates and penetrates it, informs and animates it, so that every word and every punctu-ation-point contribute directly to the expression, in that pro-portion do we lose our sense of the story being a blade which may be drawn more or less out of its sheath. The story and the novel, the idea and the form, are the needle and thread, and I never heard of a guild of tailors who recommended the use of the thread without the needle, or the needle without the thread. Mr. Besant is not the only critic, who may be observed to have spoken as if there were certain things in life which constitute stories, and certain others which do not. I find the same odd implication in an entertaining article in the *Pall Mall Gazette,* devoted, as it happens, to Mr. Besant's lecture. "The story is the thing!" says this graceful writer, as if with a tone of opposition to some other idea. I should think it was, as every painter who, as the time for "sending in" his picture looms in the distance, finds himself still in quest of a subject— as every belated artist not fixed about his theme will heartily agree. There are some subjects which speak to us and others which do not, but he would be a clever man who should undertake to give a rule—an index expurgatorius—by which the story and the no-story should be known apart. It is impos-sible (to me at least) to imagine any such rule which shall not be altogether arbitrary. The writer in the *Pall Mall* opposes the delightful (as I suppose) novel of *Margot la Balafrée* to certain tales in which "Bostonian nymphs" appear to have "rejected English dukes for psychological reasons." I am not acquainted with the romance just designated, and can scarcely forgive the *Pall Mall* critic for not mentioning the name of the author, but the title appears to refer to a lady who may have received a scar in some heroic adventure. I am inconsolable at not being acquainted with this episode, but am utterly at a loss to see why it is a story when the rejection (or acceptance) of a duke is not, and why a reason, psychological or other, is not a subject when a cicatrix is. They are all particles of the multitudinous life with which the novel deals, and surely no dogma which pretends to make it lawful to touch the one and unlawful to touch the other will stand for a moment on its feet. It is the special picture that must stand or fall, according as it seems to possess truth or to lack it. Mr. Besant does not, to my sense, light up the subject by intimating that a story must, under penalty of not being a story, consist of "adventures." Why of adventures more than of green spectacles? He mentions a category of impossible things, and among them he places "fiction without adventure." Why without adventure, more than without matrimony, or celibacy, or parturition, or cholera, or hydropathy, or Jansenism? This seems to me to bring the novel back to the hapless little *rôle* of being an artificial, ingenious thing—bring it down from its large, free character of an immense and exquisite correspondence with life. And what *is* adventure when it comes to that, and by what sign is the listening pupil to recognize it? It is an adventure—an immense one—for me to write this little article; and for a Bostonian nymph to reject an English duke is an adventure only less stirring, I should say, than for an English duke to be rejected by a Bostonian nymph. I see dramas within dramas in that, and innumerable points of view. A psychological reason is, to my imagination, an object adorably pictorial; to catch the tint of its complexion—I feel as if that idea might inspire one to Titianesque efforts. There are few things more exciting to me, in short, than a psychological reason, and yet, I protest, the novel seems to me the most magnificent form of art. I have just been reading, at the same time, the delightful story of *Treasure Island,* by Mr. Robert Louis Stevenson and, in a manner less consecutive, the last tale from M. Edmond de Goncourt, which is entitled *Chérie.* One of these works treats of murders, mysteries, islands of dreadful renown, hair-breadth escapes, miraculous coincidences, and buried doubloons. The other treats of a little French girl who lived in a fine house in Paris, and died of wounded sensibility because no one would marry her. I call *Treasure Island* delightful, because it appears to me to have succeeded wonderfully in what it attempts; and I venture to bestow no epithet upon *Chérie,* which strikes me as having failed deplorably in what it attempts—that is, in tracing the development of the moral consciousness of a child. But one of these productions strikes me as exactly as much of a novel as the other, and as having a "story" quite as much. The moral consciousness of a child is as much a part of life as the islands of the Spanish Main, and the one sort of geography seems to me to have those "surprises" of which Mr. Besant speaks quite as much as the other. For myself (since it comes back in the last resort, as I say, to the preference of the individual), the picture of the child's experience has the advantage that I can at successive steps (an immense luxury, near to the "sensual pleasure" of which Mr. Besant's critic in the *Pall Mall* speaks) say Yes or No, as it may be, to what the artist puts before me. I have been a child in fact, but I have been on a quest for a buried treasure only in supposition, and it is a simple accident that with M. de Goncourt I should have for the most part to say No. With George Eliot, when she painted that country with a far other intelligence, I always said Yes.

The most interesting part of Mr. Besant's lecture is unfortunately the briefest passage—his very cursory allusion to the "conscious moral purpose" of the novel. Here again it is not very clear whether he be recording a fact or laying down a principle; it is a great pity that in the latter case he should not have developed his idea. This branch of the subject is of immense importance, and Mr. Besant's few words point to considerations of the widest reach, not to be lightly disposed of. He will have treated the art of fiction but superficially who is not prepared to go every inch of the way that these considerations will carry him. It is for this reason that at the beginning of these remarks I was careful to notify the reader that my reflections on so large a theme have no pretension to be exhaustive. Like Mr. Besant, I have left the question of the morality of the novel till the last, and at the last I find I have used up my space. It is a question surrounded with difficulties, as witness the very first that meets us, in the form of a definite question, on the threshold. Vagueness, in such a discussion, is fatal, and what is the meaning of your morality and your conscious moral purpose? Will you not define your terms and explain how (a novel being a picture) a picture can be either moral or immoral? You wish to paint a moral picture or carve a moral statue: will you not tell us how you would set about it? We are discussing the Art of Fiction: questions of art are questions (in the widest sense) of execution; questions of morality are quite another affair, and will you not let us see how it is that you find it so easy to mix them up? These things are so clear to Mr. Besant that he has deduced from them a law which he sees embodied in English Fiction, and which is "a truly admirable thing and a great cause for congratulation." It is a great cause for congratulation indeed when such thorny problems become as smooth as silk. I may add that in so far as Mr. Besant perceives that in point of fact English Fiction has addressed itself preponderantly to these delicate questions he will appear to many people to have made a vain discovery. They will have been positively struck, on the contrary, with the moral timidity of the usual English novelist; with his (or with her) aversion to face the difficulties with which on every side the treatment of reality bristles. He is apt to be extremely shy (whereas the picture that Mr. Besant draws is a picture of boldness), and the sign of his work, for the most part, is a cautious silence on certain subjects. In the English novel (by which of course I mean the American as well), more than in any other, there is a traditional difference between that which people know and that which they agree to admit that they know, that which they see and that which they speak of, that which they feel to be a part of life and that which they allow to enter into literature. There is the great difference, in short, between what they talk of in conversation and what they talk of in print. The essence of moral energy is to survey the whole field, and I should directly reverse Mr. Besant's remark and say not that the English novel has a purpose, but that it has a diffidence. To what degree a purpose in a work of art is a source of corruption I shall not attempt to inquire; the one that seems to me least dangerous is the purpose of making a perfect work. As for our novel, I may say lastly on this score that as we find it in England today it strikes me as addressed in a large degree to "young people," and that this in itself constitutes a presumption that it will be rather shy. There are certain things which it is generally agreed not to discuss, not even to mention, before young people. This is very well, but the absence of discussion is not a symptom of the moral passion. The purpose of the English novel—"a truly admirable thing, and a great cause for congratulation"—strikes me therefore as rather negative.

There is one point at which the moral sense and the artistic sense lie very near together; that is in the light of the very obvious truth that the deepest quality of a work of art will always be the quality of the mind of the producer. In the proportion as that intelligence is fine will the novel, the picture, the statue partake of the substance of beauty and truth. To be constituted of such elements is, to my vision, to have purpose enough. No good novel will ever proceed from a superficial mind; that seems to me an axiom which, for the artist in fiction, will cover all needful moral ground: if the youthful aspirant take it to heart it will illuminate for him many of the mysteries of "purpose." There are many other useful things that might be said to him, but I have come to the end of my article, and can only touch them as I pass. The critic in the *Pall Mall Gazette,* whom I have already quoted, draws atten-

tion to the danger, in speaking of the art of fiction, of general-
ising. The danger that he has in mind is rather, I imagine,
that of particularising, for there are some comprehensive remarks which, in addition to those embodied in Mr. Besant's
suggestive lecture, might without fear of misleading him be
addressed to the ingenuous student. I should remind him first
of the magnificence of the form that is open to him, which
offers to sight so few restrictions and such innumerable opportunities. The other arts, in comparison, appear confined and
hampered; the various conditions under which they are exercised are so rigid and definite. But the only condition that I
can think of attaching to the composition of the novel is, as
I have already said, that it be sincere. This freedom is a splendid privilege, and the first lesson of the young novelist is to
learn to be worthy of it. "Enjoy it as it deserves," I should say
to him, "take possession of it, explore it to its utmost extent,
publish it, rejoice in it. All life belongs to you, and do not
listen either to those who would shut you up into corners of
it and tell you that it is only here and there that art inhabits,
or to those who would persuade you that this heavenly messenger wings her way outside of life altogether, breathing a
superfine air, and turning away her head from the truth of
things. There is no impression of life, no manner of seeing it
and feeling it, to which the plan of the novelist may not offer
a place; you have only to remember that talents so dissimilar
as those of Alexandre Dumas and Jane Austen, Charles Dickens
and Gustave Flaubert, have worked in this field with equal
glory. Do not think too much about optimism and pessimism;
try and catch the colour of life itself. In France today we see a
prodigious effort (that of Emile Zola, to whose solid and serious work no explorer of the capacity of the novel can allude
without respect), we see an extraordinary effort, vitiated by a
spirit of pessimism on a narrow basis. M. Zola is magnificent,
but he strikes an English reader as ignorant; he has an air of
working in the dark; if he had as much light as energy, his
results would be of the highest value. As for the aberrations

of a shallow optimism, the ground (of English fiction especially) is strewn with their brittle particles as with broken glass. If you must indulge in conclusions, let them have the taste of a wide knowledge. Remember that your first duty is to be as complete as possible—to make as perfect a work. Be generous and delicate and pursue the prize."

WILLIAM DEAN HOWELLS

William Dean Howells (1837-1920) was born in Ohio and grew up in small Middle Western towns until he journeyed to Boston, at the age of twenty-three, and, within a year—following his campaign biography of Lincoln—continued to Venice, where he was United States consul. Upon his return, in 1865, Howells became successively an editorial assistant on the staff of the *Nation,* assistant editor and editor (1871-81) of the *Atlantic Monthly;* during his tenure as editor he published his own fiction. After four more years in Europe he returned and settled in New York, and resumed his activities as professional author, and as editor, on the staff of *Harper's New Monthly Magazine.*

In the sixty years between his first volume of poems, in 1860, and his death, in 1920, he wrote five volumes of poems, twenty plays, forty-three volumes of prose fiction—novels, short novels, and short stories—thirty-three volumes of essays, variously about travel, autobiography, and biography, and a half-dozen volumes of literary criticism which comprised a gospel of realism in American fiction. There is no collected edition of Howells' writing. Moreover, all the patterns and developments suggested by this canon have not yet been discovered, although the change from his earlier novels of manners, through *Indian Summer* (1886), to the social consciousness of his later novels, from *The Rise of Silas Lapham* (1885), is generally considered—with Howells concurring—the decisive development of his literary career. The change took time and reflected as much his early Swedenborgian training as it did his growing commitment to the literary philosophy of the French realists, of Turgenev and of George Eliot, discovery of Tolstoi and of socialism, and his move to New York City. What evolved, in the 1880s, was an understanding of literary realism which denied both the inherited sentimental conventions and the new social determinism. In his criticism and his fiction Howells spoke for a faithful authenticity in dramatizing average and ordinary experience; the modesty of his realism grew partly out of his understanding of the inhibitions imposed on fiction by the commercial process of publishing.

For nearly fifty years, as editor, novelist, and literary critic, and as a friend and guide to his colleagues, Howells was more influential than any other man of letters in establishing a public for imaginative writing in America.

Criticism and Fiction (1891) is a reprinting of selections from Howells' column, "The Editor's Easy Chair," in *Harper's New Monthly Magazine.* Its twenty-eight chapters draw upon material which appeared in the magazine between 1886 and 1890. Number IX is drawn primarily from Howells' column in June 1887; XVI, primarily from the issue of November 1889; XVIII, primarily from the issue of April 1887; XIX, primarily from the issue of September 1887; and XXV, from June 1889. But there was much rearrangement, the final form of an essay sometimes compassing as many as a half-dozen fragments. A detailed collation is in: William M. Gibson and George Arms, *A Bibliography of William Dean Howells* (1948). This text is from the 1891 edition.

"The What and the How in Art" was first printed under the standing title, "Life and Letters," in *Harper's Weekly,* March 21, 1896, and was collected in *Literature and Life* (1902), with thirty other essays which had appeared variously in *Harper's Weekly, Scribner's, Atlantic Monthly, North American Review, Harper's New Monthly Magazine,* and *Literature* from 1893 to 1901. The text here is drawn from *Literature and Life.*

FROM CRITICISM AND FICTION

IX

I WOULD have my fellow-critics consider what they are really in the world for. It is not, apparently, for a great deal, because their only excuse for being is that somebody else has been. The critic exists because the author first existed. If books failed to appear, the critic must disappear, like the poor aphis or the lowly caterpillar in the absence of vegetation. These insects may both suppose that they have something to do with the creation of vegetation; and the critic may suppose that he has something to do with the creation of literature; but a very little reasoning ought to convince alike the aphis, caterpillar, and critic that they are mistaken. The critic—to drop the others—must perceive, if he will question himself more carefully, that his office is mainly to ascertain facts and traits of literature, not to invent or denounce them; to discover principles, not to establish them; to report, not to create.

It is so much easier to say that you like this or dislike that, than to tell why one thing is, or where another thing comes from, that many flourishing critics will have to go out of business altogether if the scientific method comes in, for then the critic will have to know something besides his own mind, which is often but a narrow field. He will have to know something of the laws of that mind, and of its generic history.

The history of all literature shows that even with the youngest and weakest author criticism is quite powerless against his will to do his own work in his own way; and if this is the case in the green wood, how much more in the dry! It has been thought by the sentimentalist that criticism, if it cannot cure, can at least kill, and Keats was long alleged in proof of its efficacy in this sort. But criticism neither cured nor killed Keats, as we all now very well know. It wounded, it cruelly hurt him, no doubt; and it is always in the power of the critic to give pain to the author—the meanest critic to the greatest author—for no one can help feeling a rudeness. But every literary movement has been violently opposed at the start, and yet never stayed in the least, or arrested, by criticism; every author has been condemned for his virtues, but in no wise changed by it. In the beginning he reads the critics; but presently perceiving that he alone makes or mars himself, and that they have no instruction for him, he mostly leaves off reading them, though he is always glad of their kindness or grieved by their harshness when he chances upon it. This, I believe, is the general experience, modified, of course, by exceptions.

Then, are we critics of no use in the world? I should not like to think that, though I am not quite ready to define our use. More than one sober thinker is inclining at present to suspect that aesthetically or specifically we are of no use, and that we are only useful historically; that we may register laws, but not enact them. I am not quite prepared to admit that aesthetic criticism is useless, though in view of its futility in any given instance it is hard to deny that it is so. It certainly seems as useless against a book that strikes the popular fancy, and prospers on in spite of condemnation by the best critics, as it is against a book which does not generally please, and which no critical favor can make acceptable. This is so common a phenomenon that I wonder it has never hitherto suggested to criticism that its point of view was altogether mistaken, and that it was really necessary to judge books not as dead things, but as living things—things which have an influence and a power irrespective of beauty and wisdom, and merely as expressions of actuality in thought and feeling. Perhaps criticism has a cumulative and final effect; perhaps it does some good we do not know of. It apparently does not affect the author directly, but it may reach him through the reader. It may in some cases enlarge or diminish his audience for a while, until he has thoroughly measured and tested his own powers. If criticism is to affect literature at all, it must be through the writers who have newly left the starting-point, and are reasonably uncertain of the race, not with those who have won it again and again in their own way. I doubt if it can do more than that; but if it can do that I will admit that it may be the toad of adversity, ugly and venomous, from whose unpleasant brow he is to snatch the precious jewel of lasting fame.

I employ this figure in all humility, and I conjure our fraternity to ask themselves, without rancor or offence, whether I am right or not. In this quest let us get together all the modesty and candor and impartiality we can; for if we should happen to discover a good reason for continuing to exist, these qualities will be of more use to us than any others in examining the work of people who really produce something.

XVI

"How few materials," says Emerson, "are yet used by our arts! The mass of creatures and of qualities are still hid and expectant," and to break new ground is still one of the uncommonest and most heroic of the virtues. The artists are not alone to blame for the timidity that keeps them in the old furrows of the worn-out fields; most of those whom they live to please, or live by pleasing, prefer to have them remain there; it wants rare virtue to appreciate what is new, as well as to invent it; and the "easy things to understand" are the conventional things. This is why the ordinary English novel, with its hackneyed plot, scenes, and figures, is more comfortable to the ordinary American than an American novel, which deals, at its worst, with comparatively new interests and motives. To adjust one's self to the enjoyment of these costs an intellectual effort, and an intellectual effort is what no ordinary person likes to make. It is only the extraordinary person who can say, with Emerson: "I ask not for the great, the remote, the romantic . . . . I embrace the common; I sit at the feet of the familiar and the low . . . . Man is surprised to find that things near are not less beautiful and wondrous than things remote . . . . The perception of the worth of the vulgar is fruitful in discoveries . . . . The foolish man wonders at the unusual, but the wise man at the usual . . . . Today always looks mean to the thoughtless; but today is a king in disguise . . . . Banks and tariffs, the newspapers and caucus, Methodism and Unitarianism, are flat and dull to dull people, but rest on the same foundations of wonder as the town of Troy and the temple of Delphos."

Perhaps we ought not to deny their town of Troy and their temple of Delphos to the dull people; but if we ought, and if we did, they would still insist upon having them. An English novel, full of titles and rank, is apparently essential to the happiness of such people; their weak and childish imagination is at home in its familiar environment; they know what they are reading; the fact that it is hash many times warmed over reassures them; whereas a story of our own life, honestly studied and faithfully represented, troubles them with varied misgiving. They are not sure that it is literature; they do not feel that it is good society; its characters, so like their own, strike them as commonplace; they say they do not wish to know such people.

Everything in England is appreciable to the literary sense, while the sense of the literary worth of things in America is still faint and weak with most people, with the vast majority who "ask for the great, the remote, the romantic," who cannot "embrace the common," cannot "sit at the feet of the familiar and the low," in the good company of Emerson. We are all, or nearly all, struggling to be distinguished from the mass, and to be set apart in select circles and upper classes like the fine people we have read about. We are really a mixture of the plebeian ingredients of the whole world; but that is not bad; our vulgarity consists in trying to ignore "the worth of the vulgar," in believing that the superfine is better.

XVIII

In General Grant's confession of novel-reading there is a sort of inference that he had wasted his time, or else the guilty conscience of the novelist in me imagines such an inference. But however this may be, there is certainly no question concerning the intention of a correspondent who once wrote to me after reading some rather bragging claims I had made for fiction as a mental and moral means. "I have very grave doubts," he said, "as to the whole list of magnificent things that you seem to think novels have done for the race, and can witness in myself many evil things which they have done for me. Whatever in my mental make-up is wild and visionary, whatever is untrue, whatever is injurious, I can trace to the perusal of some work of fiction. Worse than that, they beget such high-strung and supersensitive ideas of life that plain industry and plodding perseverance are despised, and matter-of-fact poverty, or every-day, commonplace distress, meets with no sympathy, if indeed noticed at all, by one who has wept over the impossibly accumulated sufferings of some gaudy hero or heroine."

I am not sure that I had the controversy with this correspondent that he seemed to suppose; but novels are now so fully accepted by everyone pretending to cultivated taste—and they really form the whole intellectual life of such immense numbers of people, without question of their influence, good or bad, upon the mind—that it is refreshing to have them frankly denounced, and to be invited to revise one's ideas and feelings in regard to them. A little honesty, or a great deal of honesty, in this quest will do the novel, as we hope yet to have it, and as we have already begun to have it, no harm; and for my own part I will confess that I believe fiction in the past to have been largely injurious, as I believe the stage play to be still almost wholly injurious, through its falsehood, its folly, its wantonness, and its aimlessness. It may be safely assumed that most of the novel-reading which people fancy an intellectual pastime is the emptiest dissipation, hardly more related to thought or the wholesome exercise of the mental faculties than opium-eating; in either case the brain is drugged, and left weaker and crazier for the debauch. If this may be called the negative result of the fiction habit, the positive injury that most novels work is by no means so easily to be measured in the case of young men whose character they help so much to form or deform, and the women of all ages whom they keep so much in ignorance of the world they misrepresent. Grown men have little harm from them, but in the other cases, which are the vast majority, they hurt because they are not true—not because they are malevolent, but because they are idle lies about human nature and the social fabric, which it behooves us to know and to understand, that we may deal with ourselves and with one another. One need not go so far as our correspondent, and trace to the fiction habit "whatever is wild and visionary, whatever is untrue, whatever is injurious," in one's life; bad as the fiction habit is it is probably not responsible

for the whole sum of evil in its victims, and I believe that if
the reader will use care in choosing from this fungus-growth
with which the fields of literature teem every day, he may
nourish himself as with the true mushroom, at no risk from
the poisonous species.

The tests are very plain and simple, and they are perfectly
infallible. If a novel flatters the passions, and exalts them
above the principles, it is poisonous; it may not kill, but it will
certainly injure; and this test will alone exclude an entire class
of fiction, of which eminent examples will occur to all. Then
the whole spawn of so-called unmoral romances, which imagine a world where the sins of sense are unvisited by the
penalties following, swift or slow, but inexorably sure, in the
real world, are deadly poison: these do kill. The novels that
merely tickle our prejudices and lull our judgment, or that
coddle our sensibilities or pamper our gross appetite for the
marvellous, are not so fatal, but they are innutritious, and clog
the soul with unwholesome vapors of all kinds. No doubt they
too help to weaken the moral fibre, and make their readers
indifferent to "plodding perseverance and plain industry," and
to "matter-of-fact poverty and commonplace distress."

Without taking them too seriously, it still must be owned
that the "gaudy hero and heroine" are to blame for a great
deal of harm in the world. That heroine long taught by example, if not precept, that Love, or the passion or fancy she
mistook for it, was the chief interest of a life, which is really
concerned with a great many other things; that it was lasting
in the way she knew it; that it was worthy of every sacrifice,
and was altogether a finer thing than prudence, obedience,
reason; that love alone was glorious and beautiful, and these
were mean and ugly in comparison with it. More lately she has
begun to idolize and illustrate Duty, and she is hardly less
mischievous in this new role, opposing duty, as she did love,
to prudence, obedience, and reason. The stock hero, whom, if
we met him, we could not fail to see was a most deplorable
person, has undoubtedly imposed himself upon the victims of

the fiction habit as admirable. With him, too, love was and is the great affair, whether in its old romantic phase of chivalrous achievement or manifold suffering for love's sake, or its more recent development of the "virile," the bullying, and the brutal, or its still more recent agonies of self-sacrifice, as idle and useless as the moral experiences of the insane asylums. With his vain posturings and his ridiculous splendor he is really a painted barbarian, the prey of his passions and his delusions, full of obsolete ideals, and the motives and ethics of a savage, which the guilty author of his being does his best— or his worst—in spite of his own light and knowledge, to foist upon the reader as something generous and noble. I am not merely bringing this charge against that sort of fiction which is beneath literature and outside of it, "the shoreless lakes of ditch-water," whose miasmas fill the air below the empyrean where the great ones sit; but I am accusing the work of some of the most famous, who have, in this instance or in that, sinned against the truth, which can alone exalt and purify men. I do not say that they have constantly done so, or even commonly done so; but that they have done so at all marks them as of the past, to be read with the due historical allowance for their epoch and their conditions. For I believe that, while inferior writers will and must continue to imitate them in their foibles and their errors, no one hereafter will be able to achieve greatness who is false to humanity, either in its facts or its duties. The light of civilization has already broken even upon the novel, and no conscientious man can now set about painting an image of life without perpetual questions of the verity of his work, and without feeling bound to distinguish so clearly that no reader of his may be misled, between what is right and what is wrong, what is noble and what is base, what is health and what is perdition, in the actions and the characters he portrays.

The fiction that aims merely to entertain—the fiction that is to serious fiction as the opera-bouffe, the ballet, and the pantomime are to the true drama—need not feel the burden of this obligation so deeply; but even such fiction will not be gay or trivial to any reader's hurt, and criticism will hold it to account if it passes from painting to teaching folly.

More and more not only the criticism which prints its opinions, but the infinitely vaster and powerfuler criticism which thinks and feels them merely, will make this demand. I confess that I do not care to judge any work of the imagination without first of all applying this test to it. We must ask ourselves before we ask anything else, Is it true?—true to the motives, the impulses, the principles that shape the life of actual men and women? This truth, which necessarily includes the highest morality and the highest artistry—this truth given, the book cannot be wicked and cannot be weak; and without it all graces of style and feats of invention and cunning of construction are so many superfluities of naughtiness. It is well for the truth to have all these, and shine in them, but for falsehood they are merely meretricious, the bedizenment of the wanton; they atone for nothing, they count for nothing. But in fact they come naturally of truth, and grace it without solicitation; they are added unto it. In the whole range of fiction I know of no true picture of life—that is, of human nature—which is not also a masterpiece of literature, full of divine and natural beauty. It may have no touch or tint of this special civilization or of that; it had better have this local color well ascertained; but the truth is deeper and finer than aspects, and if the book is true to what men and women know of one another's souls it will be true enough, and it will be great and beautiful. It is the conception of literature as something apart from life, superfinely aloof, which makes it really unimportant to the great mass of mankind, without a message or a meaning for them; and it is the notion that a novel may be false in its portrayal of causes and effects that makes literary art contemptible even to those whom it amuses, that forbids them to regard the novelist as a serious or right-minded person. If they do not in some moment of indignation cry out against all novels, as my correspondent does, they remain besotted in the fume of the delusions purveyed to them, with no higher feeling for the author than such maudlin affection as the habitué of an opium-joint perhaps knows for the attendant who fills his pipe with the drug.

Or, as is the case of another correspondent who writes that in his youth he "read a great many novels, but always regarded it as an amusement, like horse-racing and card-playing," for which he had no time when he entered upon the serious business of life, it renders them merely contemptuous. His view of the matter may be commended to the brotherhood and sisterhood of novelists as full of wholesome if bitter suggestion; and we urge them not to dismiss it with high literary scorn as that of some Boeotian dull to the beauty of art. Refuse it as we may, it is still the feeling of the vast majority of people, for whom life is earnest, and who find only a distorted and misleading likeness of it in our books. We may fold ourselves in our scholars' gowns, and close the doors of our studies, and affect to despise this rude voice; but we cannot shut it out. It comes to us from wherever men are at work, from wherever they are truly living, and accuses us of unfaithfulness, of triviality, of mere stage-play; and none of us can escape conviction except he prove himself worthy of his time—a time in which the great masters have brought literature back to life, and filled its ebbing veins with the red tides of reality. We cannot all equal them; we need not copy them; but we can all go to the sources of their inspiration and their power; and to draw from these no one need go far—no one need really go out of himself.

Fifty years ago, Carlyle, in whom the truth was always alive, but in whom it was then unperverted by suffering, by celebrity, and by despair, wrote in his study of Diderot: "Were it not reasonable to prophesy that this exceeding great multitude of novel-writers and such like must, in a new generation, gradually do one of two things: either retire into the nurseries, and work for children, minors, and semi-fatuous persons of both sexes, or else, what were far better, sweep their novel-fabric into the dust-cart, and betake themselves with such faculty as they have to understand and record what is true, of which

surely there is, and will forever be, a whole infinitude unknown to us of infinite importance to us? Poetry, it will more
and more come to be understood, is nothing but higher knowledge; and the only genuine Romance (for grown persons),
Reality."

If, after half a century, fiction still mainly works for "children, minors, and semi-fatuous persons of both sexes," it is
nevertheless one of the hopefulest signs of the world's progress
that it has begun to work for "grown persons," and if not
exactly in the way that Carlyle might have solely intended in
urging its writers to compile memoirs instead of building the
"novel-fabric," still it has, in the highest and widest sense,
already made Reality its Romance. I cannot judge it, I do not
even care for it, except as it has done this; and I can hardly
conceive of a literary self-respect in these days compatible with
the old trade of make-believe, with the production of the kind
of fiction which is too much honored by classification with
card-playing and horse-racing. But let fiction cease to lie about
life; let it portray men and women as they are, actuated by the
motives and the passions in the measure we all know; let it
leave off painting dolls and working them by springs and
wires; let it show the different interests in their true proportions; let it forbear to preach pride and revenge, folly and
insanity, egotism and prejudice, but frankly own these for
what they are, in whatever figures and occasions they appear;
let it not put on fine literary airs; let it speak the dialect, the
language, that most Americans know—the language of unaffected people everywhere—and there can be no doubt of an
unlimited future, not only of delightfulness but of usefulness,
for it.

XIX

This is what I say in my severer moods, but at other times
I know that, of course, no one is going to hold all fiction to
such strict account. There is a great deal of it which may be
very well left to amuse us, if it can, when we are sick or when

we are silly, and I am not inclined to despise it in the performance of this office. Or, if people find pleasure in having their
blood curdled for the sake of having it uncurdled again at the
end of the book, I would not interfere with their amusement,
though I do not desire it. There is a certain demand in primitive natures for the kind of fiction that does this, and the
author of it is usually very proud of it. The kind of novels he
likes, and likes to write, are intended to take his reader's mind,
or what that reader would probably call his mind, off himself;
they make one forget life and all its cares and duties; they are
not in the least like the novels which make you think of these,
and shame you into at least wishing to be a helpfuler and
wholesomer creature than you are. No sordid details of verity
here, if you please; no wretched being humbly and weakly
struggling to do right and to be true, suffering for his follies
and his sins, tasting joy only through the mortification of self,
and in the help of others; nothing of all this, but a great whirl-
ing splendor of peril and achievement, a wild scene of heroic
adventure and of emotional ground and lofty tumbling, with a
stage "picture" at the fall of the curtain, and all the good
characters in a row, their left hands pressed upon their hearts,
and kissing their right hands to the audience, in the good old
way that has always charmed and always will charm, Heaven
bless it!

In a world which loves the spectacular drama and the practically bloodless sports of the modern amphitheatre the author
of this sort of fiction has his place, and we must not seek to
destroy him because he fancies it the first place. In fact, it is a
condition of his doing well the kind of work he does that he
should think it important, that he should believe in himself;
and I would not take away this faith of his, even if I could. As
I say, he has his place. The world often likes to forget itself,
and he brings on his heroes, his goblins, his feats, his hair-
breadth escapes, his imminent deadly breaches, and the poor,
foolish, childish old world renews the excitements of its nonage.
Perhaps this is a work of beneficence; and perhaps our brave
conjurer in his cabalistic robe is a philanthropist in disguise.

Within the last four or five years there has been throughout
the whole English-speaking world what Mr. Grant Allen happily calls the "recrudescence" of taste in fiction. The effect is
less noticeable in America than in England, where effete Philistinism, conscious of the dry-rot of its conventionality, is
casting about for cure in anything that is wild and strange and
unlike itself. But the recrudescence has been evident enough
here, too; and a writer in one of our periodicals has put into
convenient shape some common errors concerning popularity
as a test of merit in a book. He seems to think, for instance,
that the love of the marvellous and impossible in fiction,
which is shown not only by "the unthinking multitude clamoring about the book counters" for fiction of that sort, but by
the "literary elect" also, is proof of some principle in human
nature which ought to be respected as well as tolerated. He
seems to believe that the ebullition of this passion forms a
sufficient answer to those who say that art should represent
life, and that the art which misrepresents life is feeble art and
false art. But it appears to me that a little carefuller reasoning
from a little closer inspection of the facts would not have
brought him to these conclusions. In the first place, I doubt
very much whether the "literary elect" have been fascinated in
great numbers by the fiction in question; but if I supposed
them to have really fallen under that spell, I should still be
able to account for their fondness and that of the "unthinking
multitude" upon the same grounds, without honoring either
very much. It is the habit of hasty casuists to regard civilization as inclusive of all the members of a civilized community;
but this is a palpable error. Many persons in every civilized
community live in a state of more or less evident savagery with
respect to their habits, their morals, and their propensities;
and they are held in check only by the law. Many more yet are
savage in their tastes, as they show by the decoration of their
houses and persons, and by their choice of books and pictures;
and these are left to the restraints of public opinion. In fact,
no man can be said to be thoroughly civilized or always civilized; the most refined, the most enlightened person has his

moods, his moments of barbarism, in which the best, or even the second best, shall not please him. At these times the lettered and the unlettered are alike primitive and their gratifications are of the same simple sort; the highly cultivated person may then like melodrama, impossible fiction, and the trapeze as sincerely and thoroughly as a boy of thirteen or a barbarian of any age.

I do not blame him for these moods; I find something instructive and interesting in them; but if they lastingly established themselves in him, I could not help deploring the state of that person. No one can really think that the "literary elect," who are said to have joined the "unthinking multitude" in clamoring about the book counters for the romances of no-man's land, take the same kind of pleasure in them as they do in a novel of Tolstoï, Tourguéneff, George Eliot, Thackeray, Balzac, Manzoni, Hawthorne, Henry James, Thomas Hardy, Palacio Valdés, or even Walter Scott. They have joined the "unthinking multitude," perhaps because they are tired of thinking, and expect to find relaxation in feeling—feeling crudely, grossly, merely. For once in a way there is no great harm in this; perhaps no harm at all. It is perfectly natural; let them have their innocent debauch. But let us distinguish, for our own sake and guidance, between the different kinds of things that please the same kind of people; between the things that please them habitually and those that please them occasionally; between the pleasures that edify them and those that amuse them. Otherwise we shall be in danger of becoming permanently part of the "unthinking multitude," and of remaining puerile, primitive, savage. We shall be so in moods and at moments; but let us not fancy that those are high moods or fortunate moments. If they are harmless, that is the most that can be said for them. They are lapses from which we can perhaps go forward more vigorously; but even this is not certain.

My own philosophy of the matter, however, would not bring me to prohibition of such literary amusements as the writer quoted seems to find significant of a growing indifference to truth and sanity in fiction. Once more, I say, these amusements have their place, as the circus has, and the burlesque and negro minstrelsy, and the ballet, and prestidigitation. No one of these is to be despised in its place; but we had better understand that it is not the highest place, and that it is hardly an intellectual delight. The lapse of all the "literary elect" in the world could not dignify unreality; and their present mood, if it exists, is of no more weight against that beauty in literature which comes from truth alone, and never can come from anything else, than the permanent state of the "unthinking multitude."

Yet even as regards the "unthinking multitude," I believe I am not able to take the attitude of the writer I have quoted. I am afraid that I respect them more than he would like to have me, though I cannot always respect their taste, any more than that of the "literary elect." I respect them for their good sense in most practical matters; for their laborious, honest lives; for their kindness, their good-will; for that aspiration towards something better than themselves which seems to stir, however dumbly, in every human breast not abandoned to literary pride or other forms of self-righteousness. I find every man interesting, whether he thinks or unthinks, whether he is savage or civilized; for this reason I cannot thank the novelist who teaches us not to know but to unknow our kind. Yet I should by no means hold him to such strict account as Emerson, who felt the absence of the best motive, even in the greatest of the masters, when he said of Shakespeare that, after all, he was only master of the revels. The judgment is so severe, even with the praise which precedes it, that one winces under it; and if one is still young, with the world gay before him, and life full of joyous promise, one is apt to ask, defiantly, Well, what is better than being such a master of the revels as Shakespeare was? Let each judge for himself. To the heart again of serious youth, uncontaminate and exigent of ideal good, it must always be a grief that the great masters seem so often to have been willing to amuse the leisure and vacancy of meaner men, and leave their mission to the soul but partially fulfilled. This, perhaps, was what Emerson had in mind; and

if he had it in mind of Shakespeare, who gave us, with his histories and comedies and problems, such a searching homily as
"Macbeth" one feels that he scarcely recognized the limitations
of the dramatist's art. Few consciences, at times, seem so enlightened as that of this personally unknown person, so with-
drawn into his work, and so lost to the intensest curiosity of
after-time; at other times he seems merely Elizabethan in his
coarseness, his courtliness, his imperfect sympathy.

XXV

Who can deny that fiction would be incomparably stronger,
incomparably truer, if once it could tear off the habit which
enslaves it to the celebration chiefly of a single passion, in one
phase or another, and could frankly dedicate itself to the service of all the passions, all the interests, all the facts? Every novelist who has thought about his art knows that it would, and I
think that upon reflection he must doubt whether his sphere
would be greatly enlarged if he were allowed to treat freely the
darker aspects of the favorite passion. But, as I have shown,
the privilege, the right to do this, is already perfectly recognized. This is proved again by the fact that serious criticism
recognizes as master-works (I will not push the question of supremacy) the two great novels which above all others have
moved the world by their study of guilty love. If by any chance,
if by some prodigious miracle, any American should now arise
to treat it on the level of *Anna Karenina* and *Madame Bovary,*
he would be absolutely sure of success, and of fame and grati-
tude as great as those books have won for their authors.

But what editor of what American magazine would print
such a story?

Certainly I do not think anyone would; and here our novelist
must again submit to conditions. If he wishes to publish such a
story (supposing him to have once written it), he must publish
it as a book. A book is something by itself, responsible for its
character, which becomes quickly known, and it does not necessarily penetrate to every member of the household. The

father or the mother may say to the child, "I would rather you wouldn't read that book"; if the child cannot be trusted, the book may be locked up. But with the magazine and its serial the affair is different. Between the editor of a reputable English or American magazine and the families which receive it there is a tacit agreement that he will print nothing which a father may not read to his daughter, or safely leave her to read herself.

After all, it is a matter of business; and the insurgent novelist should consider the situation with coolness and common sense. The editor did not create the situation; but it exists, and he could not even attempt to change it without many sorts of disaster. He respects it, therefore, with the good faith of an honest man. Even when he is himself a novelist, with ardor for his art and impatience of the limitations put upon it, he interposes his veto, as Thackeray did in the case of Trollope, when a contributor approaches forbidden ground.

It does not avail to say that the daily papers teem with facts far fouler and deadlier than any which fiction could imagine. That is true, but it is true also that the sex which reads the most novels reads the fewest newspapers; and, besides, the reporter does not command the novelist's skill to fix impressions in a young girl's mind or to suggest conjecture. The magazine is a little despotic, a little arbitrary; but unquestionably its favor is essential to success, and its conditions are not such narrow ones. You cannot deal with Tolstoï's and Flaubert's subjects in the absolutely artistic freedom of Tolstoï and Flaubert; since De Foe, that is unknown among us; but if you deal with them in the manner of George Eliot, of Thackeray, of Dickens, of society, you may deal with them even in the magazines. There is no other restriction upon you. All the horrors and miseries and tortures are open to you; your pages may drop blood; sometimes it may happen that the editor will even exact such strong material from you. But probably he will require nothing but the observance of the convention in question; and if you do not yourself prefer bloodshed he will leave you free to use all sweet and peaceable means of interesting his readers.

Believe me, it is no narrow field he throws open to you, with that little sign to keep off the grass up at one point only. Its vastness is still almost unexplored, and whole regions in it are unknown to the fictionist. Dig anywhere, and do but dig deep enough, and you strike riches; or, if you are of the mind to range, the gentler climes, the softer temperatures, the serener skies, are all free to you, and are so little visited that the chance of novelty is greater among them.

THE WHAT AND THE HOW IN ART

ONE of the things always enforcing itself upon the consciousness of the artist of any sort is the fact that those whom artists work for rarely care for their work artistically. They care for it morally, personally, partially. I suspect that criticism itself has rather a muddled preference for the what over the how, and that it is always haunted by a philistine question of the material when it should, aesthetically speaking, be concerned solely with the form.

I

The other night at the theatre I was witness of a curious and amusing illustration of my point. They were playing a most soul-filling melodrama, of the sort which gives you assurance from the very first that there will be no trouble in the end, but everything will come out just as it should, no matter what obstacles oppose themselves in the course of the action. An over-ruling Providence, long accustomed to the exigencies of the stage, could not fail to intervene at the critical moment in behalf of innocence and virtue, and the spectator never had the least occasion for anxiety. Not unnaturally there was a

black-hearted villain in the piece; so very black-hearted that he
seemed not to have a single good impulse from first to last.
Yet he was, in the keeping of the stage Providence, as harmless
as a blank cartridge, in spite of his deadly aims. He accomplished no more mischief, in fact, than if all his intents had
been of the best; except for the satisfaction afforded by the edifying spectacle of his defeat and shame, he need not have been
in the play at all; and one might almost have felt sorry for
him, he was so continually baffled. But this was not enough for
the audience, or for that part of it which filled the gallery to
the roof. Perhaps he was such an uncommonly black-hearted
villain, so very, very cold-blooded in his wickedness that the
justice unsparingly dealt out to him by the dramatist could
not suffice. At any rate, the gallery took such a vivid interest in
his punishment that it had out the actor who impersonated the
wretch between all the acts, and hissed him throughout his
deliberate passage across the stage before the curtain. The
hisses were not at all for the actor, but altogether for the character. The performance was fairly good, quite as good as the
performance of any virtuous part in the piece, and easily up to
the level of other villainous performances (I never find much
nature in them, perhaps because there is not much nature in
villainy itself; that is, villainy pure and simple); but the mere
conception of the wickedness this bad man had attempted was
too much for an audience of the average popular goodness. It
was only after he had taken poison, and fallen dead before
their eyes, that the spectators forbore to visit him with a lively
proof of their abhorrence; apparently they did not care to
"give him a realizing sense that there was a punishment after
death," as the man in Lincoln's story did with the dead dog.

II

The whole affair was very amusing at first, but it has since
put me thinking (I like to be put upon thinking; the eight-
eenth-century essayists were) that the attitude of the audience
towards this deplorable reprobate is really the attitude of most

readers of books, lookers at pictures and statues, listeners to music, and so on through the whole list of the arts. It is absolutely different from the artist's attitude, from the connoisseur's attitude; it is quite irreconcilable with their attitude, and yet I wonder if in the end it is not what the artist works for. Art is not produced for artists, or even for connoisseurs; it is produced for the general, who can never view it otherwise than morally, personally, partially, from their associations and preconceptions.

Whether the effect with the general is what the artist works for or not, he does not succeed without it. Their brute liking or misliking is the final test; it is universal suffrage, that elects, after all. Only, in some cases of this sort the polls do not close at four o'clock on the first Tuesday after the first Monday of November, but remain open forever, and the voting goes on. Still, even the first day's canvass is important, or at least significant. It will not do for the artist to electioneer, but if he is beaten, he ought to ponder the causes of his defeat, and question how he has failed to touch the chord of universal interest. He is in the world to make beauty and truth evident to his fellow-men, who are as a rule incredibly stupid and ignorant of both, but whose judgment he must nevertheless not despise. If he can make something that they will cheer, or something that they will hiss, he may not have done any great thing, but if he has made something that they will neither cheer nor hiss, he may well have his misgivings, no matter how well, how finely, how truly he has done the thing.

This is very humiliating, but a tacit snub to one's artist-pride such as one gets from public silence is not a bad thing for one. Not long ago I was talking about pictures with a painter, a very great painter, to my thinking; one whose pieces give me the same feeling I have from reading poetry; and I was excusing myself to him with respect to art, and perhaps putting on a little more modesty than I felt. I said that I could enjoy pictures only on the literary side, and could get no answer from my soul to those excellences of handling and execution which seemed chiefly to interest painters. He replied that it was a confession of weakness in a painter if he appealed merely or mainly to technical knowledge in the spectator; that he narrowed his field and dwarfed his work by it; and that if he painted for painters merely, or for the connoisseurs of painting, he was denying his office, which was to say something clear and appreciable to all sorts of men in the terms of art. He even insisted that a picture ought to tell a story.

The difficulty in humbling one's self to this view of art is in the ease with which one may please the general by art which is no art. Neither the play nor the playing that I saw at the theatre when the actor was hissed for the wickedness of the villain he was personating, was at all fine; and yet I perceived, on reflection, that they had achieved a supreme effect. If I may be so confidential, I will say that I should be very sorry to have written that piece; yet I should be very proud if, on the level I chose and with the quality I cared for, I could invent a villain that the populace would have out and hiss for his surpassing wickedness. In other words, I think it a thousand pities whenever an artist gets so far away from the general, so far within himself or a little circle of amateurs, that his highest and best work awakens no response in the multitude. I am afraid this is rather the danger of the arts among us, and how to escape it is not so very plain. It makes one sick and sorry often to see how cheaply the applause of the common people is won. It is not an infallible test of merit, but if it is wanting to any performance, we may be pretty sure it is not the greatest performance.

III

The paradox lies in wait here, as in most other human affairs, to confound us, and we try to baffle it, in this way and in that. We talk, for instance, of poetry for poets, and we fondly imagine that this is different from talking of cookery for cooks. Poetry is not made for poets; they have enough poetry of their own, but it is made for people who are not poets. If it does not please these, it may still be poetry, but it is poetry which has failed of its truest office. It is none the less its truest office because some very wretched verse seems often to do it.

The logic of such a fact is not that the poet should try to achieve this truest office of his art by means of doggerel, but that he should study how and where and why the beauty and the truth he has made manifest are wanting in universal interest, in human appeal. Leaving the drama out of the question, and the theatre which seems now to be seeking only the favor of the dull rich, I believe that there never was a time or a race more open to the impressions of beauty and of truth than ours. The artist who feels their divine charm, and longs to impart it, has now and here a chance to impart it more widely than ever artist had in the world before. Of course, the means of reaching the widest range of humanity are the simple and the elementary, but there is no telling when the complex and the recondite may not universally please. The art is to make them plain to everyone, for everyone has them in him. Lowell used to say that Shakespeare was subtle, but in letters a foot high.

The painter, sculptor, or author who pleases the polite only has a success to be proud of as far as it goes, and to be ashamed of that it goes no further. He need not shrink from giving pleasure to the vulgar because bad art pleases them. It is part of his reason for being that he should please them, too; and if he does not it is a proof that he is wanting in force, however much he abounds in fineness. Who would not wish his picture to draw a crowd about it? Who would not wish his novel to sell five hundred thousand copies, for reasons besides the sordid love of gain which I am told governs novelists? One should not really wish it any the less because chromos and historical romances are popular.

Sometime, I believe, the artist and his public will draw nearer together in a mutual understanding, though perhaps not in our present conditions. I put that understanding off till the good time when life shall be more than living, more even than the question of getting a living; but in the meantime I think that the artist might very well study the springs of feeling in others; and if I were a dramatist I think I should quite humbly go to that play where they hiss the villain for his villainy, and inquire how his wickedness had been made so appreciable, so vital, so personal. Not being a dramatist, I still cannot indulge the greatest contempt of that play and its public.

GEORGE SANTAYANA

George Santayana (1863–1952) was born in Madrid, Spain, and, at the age of nine, was brought to America. He grew up as a Bostonian, from the time he attended a private kindergarten, through his years at Boston Latin School, to his graduation from Harvard. After two years of graduate study in Berlin, Santayana returned to America in 1899, and, except for leaves of absence during which he taught at the Sorbonne and at Oxford, he was a professor of philosophy at Harvard until 1912. Tiring of academic scholarship, he resigned his professorship and traveled to Oxford and then to Paris before settling in Rome for the rest of his life.

The Works of George Santayana (14 vols., 1936–37), a limited edition, is the most complete collection of his writing. It is comprised primarily of his philosophical writings, and his prefaces to many of the volumes record his development as a philosopher. A Platonist who, nevertheless, came to believe in the reality of matter, Santayana defined what he called intuitive essences, which were engendered by material events, and which made the substance of art. He believed in the synthesis of a kind of intuitive experience. In his philosophy of art, Santayana disregarded arbitrary distinctions between morals and aesthetics and he described the arts as simultaneously useful and expressive acts.

Santayana also wrote a best-selling novel about the decaying inheritance of Calvinism in America, *The Last Puritan* (1935), and a verse drama (1899, 1924); and he published a collection of his poems (1922). The literary significance of his philosophical writings, apart from his aesthetics, lies in the writing itself, in its wit and vitality, and in the way Santayana could fertilize an intelligent idea with a metaphor.

"The Elements and Function of Poetry" is the final chapter of *Poetry and Religion* (1900), in the preface to which Santayana explained the governing idea of his volume: "This idea is that religion and poetry are identical in essence, and differ merely in the way in which they are attached to practical affairs. Poetry is called religion when it intervenes in life, and religion, when it merely supervenes upon life, is seen to be nothing but poetry."

THE ELEMENTS AND FUNCTION
OF POETRY

IF a critic, in despair of giving a serious definition of poetry, should be satisfied with saying that poetry is metrical discourse, he would no doubt be giving an inadequate account of the matter, yet not one of which he need be ashamed or which he should regard as superficial. Although a poem be not made by counting of syllables upon the fingers, yet "numbers" is the most poetical synonym we have for verse, and "measure" the most significant equivalent for beauty, for goodness, and perhaps even for truth. Those early and profound philosophers, the followers of Pythagoras, saw the essence of all things in number, and it was by weight, measure, and number, as we read in the Bible, that the Creator first brought Nature out of the void. Every human architect must do likewise with his edifice; he must mould his bricks or hew his stones into symmetrical solids and lay them over one another in regular strata, like a poet's lines.

Measure is a condition of perfection, for perfection requires that order should be pervasive, that not only the whole before us should have a form, but that every part in turn should have a form of its own, and that those parts should be co-ordinated among themselves as the whole is co-ordinated with the other parts of some greater cosmos. Leibnitz lighted in his speculations upon a conception of organic nature which may be false as a fact, but which is excellent as an ideal; he tells us that the difference between living and dead matter, between animals and machines, is that the former are composed of parts that are themselves organic, every portion of the body being itself a machine, and every portion of that machine still a machine, and so *ad infinitum;* whereas, in artificial bodies the organization is not in this manner infinitely deep. Fine Art, in this as in all things, imitates the method of Nature and makes its most beautiful works out of materials that are themselves beautiful. So that even if the difference between verse and prose consisted only in measure, that difference would already be analogous to that between jewels and clay.

The stuff of language is words, and the sensuous material of words is sound; if language therefore is to be made perfect, its materials must be made beautiful by being themselves subjected to a measure, and endowed with a form. It is true that language is a symbol for intelligence rather than a stimulus to sense, and accordingly the beauties of discourse which commonly attract attention are merely the beauties of the objects and ideas signified; yet the symbols have a sensible reality of their own, a euphony which appeals to our senses if we keep them open. The tongue will choose those forms of utterance which have a natural grace as mere sound and sensation; the memory will retain these catches, and they will pass and repass through the mind until they become types of instinctive speech and standards of pleasing expression.

The highest form of such euphony is song; the singing voice gives to the sounds it utters the thrill of tonality,—a thrill itself dependent, as we know, on the numerical proportions of the vibrations that it includes. But this kind of euphony and sensuous beauty, the deepest that sounds can have, we have almost wholly surrendered in our speech. Our intelligence has become complex, and language, to express our thoughts, must commonly be more rapid, copious, and abstract than is compatible with singing. Music at the same time has become complex also, and when united with words, at one time disfigures them in the elaboration of its melody, and at another overpowers them in the volume of its sound. So that the art of singing is now in the same plight as that of sculpture,—an abstract and conventional thing surviving by force of tradition and of an innate but now impotent impulse, which under simpler conditions would work itself out into the proper forms of those arts. The truest kind of euphony is thus denied to our poetry. If any verses are still set to music, they are commonly

the worst only, chosen for the purpose of musicians of special-
ized sensibility and inferior intelligence, who seem to be attracted only by tawdry effects of rhetoric and sentiment.

When song is given up, there still remains in speech a certain sensuous quality, due to the nature and order of the
vowels and consonants that compose the sounds. This kind of
euphony is not neglected by the more dulcet poets, and is now
so studied in some quarters that I have heard it maintained by
a critic of relative authority that the beauty of poetry consists
entirely in the frequent utterance of the sound of "j" and "sh,"
and the consequent copius flow of saliva in the mouth. But
even if saliva is not the whole essence of poetry, there is an unmistakable and fundamental diversity of effect in the various
vocalization of different poets, which becomes all the more
evident when we compare those who use different languages.
One man's speech, or one nation's, is compact, crowded with
consonants, rugged, broken with emphatic beats; another
man's, or nation's, is open, tripping, rapid, and even. So Byron,
mingling in his boyish fashion burlesque with exquisite sentiment, contrasts English with Italian speech:—

> I love the language, that soft bastard Latin
> Which melts like kisses from a female mouth
> And sounds as if it should be writ on satin
> With syllables which breathe of the sweet South,
> And gentle liquids gliding all so pat in
> That not a single accent seems uncouth,
> Like our harsh Northern whistling, grunting guttural
> Which we're obliged to hiss and spit and sputter all.

And yet these contrasts, strong when we compare extreme
cases, fade from our consciousness in the actual use of a
mother-tongue. The function makes us unconscious of the instrument, all the more as it is an indispensable and almost
invariable one. The sense of euphony accordingly attaches itself rather to another and more variable quality; the tune, or
measure, or rhythm of speech. The elementary sounds are prescribed by the language we use, and the selection we may make
among those sounds is limited; but the arrangement of words

is still undetermined, and by casting our speech into the moulds of metre and rhyme we can give it a heightened power, apart from its significance. A tolerable definition of poetry, on its formal side, might be found in this: that poetry is speech in which the instrument counts as well as the meaning—poetry is speech for its own sake and for its own sweetness. As common windows are intended only to admit the light, but painted windows also to dye it, and to be an object of attention in themselves as well as a cause of visibility in other things, so, while the purest prose is a mere vehicle of thought, verse, like stained glass, arrests attention in its own intricacies, confuses it in its own glories, and is even at times allowed to darken and puzzle in the hope of casting over us a supernatural spell.

Long passages in Shelley's "Revolt of Islam" and Keats's "Endymion" are poetical in this sense; the reader gathers, probably, no definite meaning, but is conscious of a poetic medium, of speech euphonious and measured, and redolent of a kind of objectless passion which is little more than the sensation of the movement and sensuous richness of the lines. Such poetry is not great; it has, in fact, a tedious vacuity, and is unworthy of a mature mind; but it is poetical, and could be produced only by a legitimate child of the Muse. It belongs to an apprenticeship, but in this case the apprenticeship of genius. It bears that relation to great poems which scales and aimless warblings bear to great singing—they test the essential endowment and fineness of the organ which is to be employed in the art. Without this sensuous background and ingrained predisposition to beauty, no art can reach the deepest and most exquisite effects; and even without an intelligible superstructure these sensuous qualities suffice to give that thrill of exaltation, that suggestion of an ideal world, which we feel in the presence of any true beauty.

The sensuous beauty of words and their utterance in measure suffice, therefore, for poetry of one sort—where these are there is something unmistakably poetical, although the whole of poetry, or the best of poetry, be not yet there. Indeed, in such works as "The Revolt of Islam" or "Endymion" there is already more than mere metre and sound; there is the colour and choice of words, the fanciful, rich, or exquisite juxtaposition of phrases. The vocabulary and the texture of the style are precious; affected, perhaps, but at any rate refined.

This quality, which is that almost exclusively exploited by the Symbolist, we may call euphuism—the choice of coloured words and rare and elliptical phrases. If great poets are like architects and sculptors, the euphuists are like goldsmiths and jewellers; their work is filigree in precious metals, encrusted with glowing stones. Now euphuism contributes not a little to the poetic effect of the tirades of Keats and Shelley; if we wish to see the power of versification without euphuism we may turn to the tirades of Pope, where metre and euphony are displayed alone, and we have the outline or skeleton of poetry without the filling.

> In spite of pride, in erring reason's spite,
> One truth is clear, Whatever is, is right.

We should hesitate to say that such writing was truly poetical; so that some euphuism would seem to be necessary as well as metre, to the formal essence of poetry.

An example of this sort, however, takes us out of the merely verbal into the imaginative region; the reason that Pope is hardly poetical to us is not that he is inharmonious,—not a defect of euphony,—but that he is too intellectual and has an excess of mentality. It is easier for words to be poetical without any thought, when they are felt merely as sensuous and musical, than for them to remain so when they convey an abstract notion,—especially if that notion be a tart and frigid sophism, like that of the couplet just quoted. The pyrotechnics of the intellect then take the place of the glow of sense, and the artifice of thought chills the pleasure we might have taken in the grace of expression.

If poetry in its higher reaches is more philosophical than history, because it presents the memorable types of men and things apart from unmeaning circumstances, so in its primary substance and texture poetry is more philosophical than prose because it is nearer to our immediate experience. Poetry breaks up the trite conceptions designated by current words into the sensuous qualities out of which those conceptions were originally put together. We name what we conceive and believe in, not what we see; things, not images; souls, not voices and silhouettes. This naming, with the whole education of the senses which it accompanies, subserves the uses of life; in order to thread our way through the labyrinth of objects which assault us, we must make a great selection in our sensuous experience; half of what we see and hear we must pass over as insignificant, while we piece out the other half with such an ideal complement as is necessary to turn it into a fixed and well-ordered world. This labour of perception and understanding, this spelling of the material meaning of experience is enshrined in our work-a-day language and ideas; ideas which are literally poetic in the sense that they are "made" (for every conception in an adult mind is a fiction), but which are at the same time prosaic because they are made economically, by abstraction, and for use.

When the child of poetic genius, who has learned this intellectual and utilitarian language in the cradle, goes afield and gathers for himself the aspects of Nature, he begins to encumber his mind with the many living impressions which the intellect rejected, and which the language of the intellect can hardly convey; he labours with his nameless burden of perception, and wastes himself in aimless impulses of emotion and revery, until finally the method of some art offers a vent to his inspiration, or to such part of it as can survive the test of time and the discipline of expression.

The poet retains by nature the innocence of the eye, or recovers it easily; he disintegrates the fictions of common perception into their sensuous elements, gathers these together again into chance groups as the accidents of his environment or the affinities of his temperament may conjoin them; and this wealth of sensation and this freedom of fancy, which make an extraordinary ferment in his ignorant heart, presently bubble over into some kind of utterance.

The fulness and sensuousness of such effusions bring them nearer to our actual perceptions than common discourse could come; yet they may easily seem remote, overloaded, and obscure to those accustomed to think entirely in symbols, and never to be interrupted in the algebraic rapidity of their thinking by a moment's pause and examination of heart, nor ever to plunge for a moment into that torrent of sensation and imagery over which the bridge of prosaic associations habitually carries us safe and dry to some conventional act. How slight that bridge commonly is, how much an affair of trestles and wire, we can hardly conceive until we have trained ourselves to an extreme sharpness of introspection. But psychologists have discovered, what laymen generally will confess, that we hurry by the procession of our mental images as we do by the traffic of the street, intent on business, gladly forgetting the noise and movement of the scene and looking only for the corner we would turn or the door we would enter. Yet in our alertest moment the depths of the soul are still dreaming; the real world stands drawn in bare outline against a background of chaos and unrest. Our logical thoughts dominate experience only as the parallels and meridians make a checker-board of the sea. They guide our voyage without controlling the waves, which toss for ever in spite of our ability to ride over them to our chosen ends. Sanity is a madness put to good uses; waking life is a dream controlled.

Out of the neglected riches of this dream the poet fetches his wares. He dips into the chaos that underlies the rational shell of the world and brings up some superfluous image, some emotion dropped by the way, and reattaches it to the present object; he reinstates things unnecessary, he emphasizes things ignored, he paints in again into the landscape the tints which the intellect has allowed to fade from it. If he seems sometimes to obscure a fact, it is only because he is restoring an experience. We may observe this process in the simplest cases. When Ossian, mentioning the sun, says it is round as the shield of his fathers, the expression is poetical. Why? Because he has added to the word sun, in itself sufficient and unequivocal, other words, unnecessary for practical clearness, but serving to restore the individuality of his perception and its associations in his mind. There is no square sun with which the sun he is speaking of could be confused; to stop and call it round is a luxury, a halting in the sensation for the love of its form. And to go on to tell us, what is wholly impertinent, that the shield of his fathers was round also, is to invite us to follow the chance wanderings of his fancy, to give us a little glimpse of the stuffing of his own brain, or, we might almost say, to turn over the pattern of his embroidery and show us the loose threads hanging on the wrong side. Such an escapade disturbs and interrupts the true vision of the object, and a great poet, rising to a perfect conception of the sun and forgetting himself, would have disdained to make it; but it has a romantic and pathological interest, it restores an experience, and is in that measure poetical. We have been made to halt at the sensation, and to penetrate for a moment into its background of dream.

But it is not only thoughts or images that the poet draws in this way from the store of his experience, to clothe the bare form of conventional objects: he often adds to these objects a more subtle ornament, drawn from the same source. For the first element which the intellect rejects in forming its ideas of things is the emotion which accompanies perception; and this emotion is the first thing the poet restores. He stops at the image, because he stops to enjoy. He wanders into the by-paths of association because the by-paths are delightful. The love of beauty which made him give measure and cadence to his words, the love of harmony which made him rhyme them, reappear in his imagination and make him select there also the material that is itself beautiful, or capable of assuming beautiful forms. The link that binds together the ideas, sometimes so wide apart, which his wit assimilates, is most often the link of emotion; they have in common some element of beauty or of horror.

The poet's art is to a great extent the art of intensifying emotions by assembling the scattered objects that naturally arouse them. He sees the affinities of things by seeing their common affinities with passion. As the guiding principle of practical thinking is some interest, so that only what is pertinent to that interest is selected by the attention; as the guiding principle of scientific thinking is some connection of things in time or space, or some identity of law; so in poetic thinking the guiding principle is often a mood or a quality of sentiment. By this union of disparate things having a common overtone of feeling, the feeling is itself evoked in all its strength; nay, it is often created for the first time, much as by a new mixture of old pigments Perugino could produce the unprecedented limpidity of his colour, or Titian the unprecedented glow of his. Poets can thus arouse sentiments finer than any which they have known, and in the act of composition become discoverers of new realms of delightfulness and grief. Expression is a misleading term which suggests that something previously known is rendered or imitated; whereas the expression is itself an original fact, the values of which are then referred to the thing expressed, much as the honours of a Chinese mandarin are attributed retroactively to his parents. So the charm which a poet, by his art of combining images and shades of emotion, casts over a scene or an action, is attached to the principal actor in it, who gets the benefit of the setting furnished him by a well-stocked mind.

The poet is himself subject to this illusion, and a great part of what is called poetry, although by no means the best part of it, consists in this sort of idealization by proxy. We dye the world of our own colour; by a pathetic fallacy, by a false projection of sentiment, we soak Nature with our own feeling, and then celebrate her tender sympathy with our moral being. This aberration, as we see in the case of Wordsworth, is not inconsistent with a high development of both the faculties which it confuses,—I mean vision and feeling. On the contrary, vision and feeling, when most abundant and original, most easily present themselves in this undivided form. There would be need of a force of intellect which poets rarely possess to rationalize their inspiration without diminishing its volume:

and if, as is commonly the case, the energy of the dream and the passion in them is greater than that of the reason, and they cannot attain true propriety, and supreme beauty in their works, they can, nevertheless, fill them with lovely images and a fine moral spirit.

The pouring forth of both perceptive and emotional elements in their mixed and indiscriminate form gives to this kind of imagination the directness and truth which sensuous poetry possesses on a lower level. The outer world bathed in the hues of human feeling, the inner world expressed in the forms of things,—that is the primitive condition of both before intelligence and the prosaic classification of objects have abstracted them and assigned them to their respective spheres. Such identifications, on which a certain kind of metaphysics prides itself also, are not discoveries of profound genius; they are exactly like the observation of Ossian that the sun is round and that the shield of his fathers was round too; they are disintegrations of conventional objects, so that the original associates of our perceptions reappear; then the thing and the emotion which chanced to be simultaneous are said to be one, and we return, unless a better principle of organization is substituted for the principle abandoned, to the chaos of a passive animal consciousness, where all is mixed together, projected together, and felt as an unutterable whole.

The pathetic fallacy is a return to that early habit of thought by which our ancestors peopled the world with benevolent and malevolent spirits; what they felt in the presence of objects they took to be a part of the objects themselves. In returning to this natural confusion, poetry does us a service in that she recalls and consecrates those phases of our experience which, as useless to the understanding of material reality, we are in danger of forgetting altogether. Therein is her vitality, for she pierces to the quick and shakes us out of our servile speech and imaginative poverty; she reminds us of all we have felt, she invites us even to dream a little, to nurse the wonderful spontaneous creations which at every waking moment we are snuffing out in our brain. And the indulgence is no mere momentary pleasure; much of its exuberance clings afterward to our ideas; we see the more and feel the more for that exercise; we are capable of finding greater entertainment in the common aspects of Nature and life. When the veil of convention is once removed from our eyes by the poet, we are better able to dominate any particular experience and, as it were, to change its scale, now losing ourselves in its infinitesimal texture, now in its infinite ramifications.

If the function of poetry, however, did not go beyond this recovery of sensuous and imaginative freedom, at the expense of disrupting our useful habits of thought, we might be grateful to it for occasionally relieving our numbness, but we should have to admit that it was nothing but a relaxation; that spiritual discipline was not to be gained from it in any degree, but must be sought wholly in that intellectual system that builds the science of Nature with the categories of prose. So conceived, poetry would deserve the judgment passed by Plato on all the arts of flattery and entertainment; it might be crowned as delightful, but must be either banished altogether as meretricious or at least confined to a few forms and occasions where it might do little harm. The judgment of Plato has been generally condemned by philosophers, although it is eminently rational, and justified by the simplest principles of morals. It has been adopted instead, although unwittingly, by the practical and secular part of mankind, who look upon artists and poets as inefficient and brainsick people under whose spell it would be a serious calamity to fall, although they may be called in on feast days as an ornament and luxury together with the cooks, hairdressers, and florists.

Several circumstances, however, might suggest to us the possibility that the greatest function of poetry may be still to find. Plato, while condemning Homer, was a kind of poet himself; his quarrel with the followers of the Muse was not a quarrel with the goddess; and the good people of Philistia, distrustful as they may be of profane art, pay undoubting honour to religion, which is a kind of poetry as much removed from their sphere as the midnight revels upon Mount Citheron, which, to be sure, were also religious in their inspiration. Why, we may ask, these apparent inconsistencies? Why do our practical men make room for religion in the background of their world? Why did Plato, after banishing the poets, poetize the universe in his prose? Because the abstraction by which the world of science and of practice is drawn out of our experience, is too violent to satisfy even the thoughtless and vulgar; the ideality of the machine we call Nature, the conventionality of the drama we call the world, are too glaring not to be somehow perceived by all. Each must sometimes fall back upon the soul; he must challenge this apparition with the thought of death; he must ask himself for the mainspring and value of his life. He will then remember his stifled loves; he will feel that only his illusions have ever given him a sense of reality, only his passions the hope and the vision of peace. He will read himself through and almost gather a meaning from his experience; at least he will half believe that all he has been dealing with was a dream and a symbol, and raise his eyes toward the truth beyond.

This plastic moment of the mind, when we become aware of the artificiality and inadequacy of what common sense perceives, is the true moment of poetic opportunity,—an opportunity, we may hasten to confess, which is generally missed. The strain of attention, the concentration and focussing of thought on the unfamiliar immediacy of things, usually brings about nothing but confusion. We are dazed, we are filled with a sense of unutterable things, luminous yet indistinguishable, many yet one. Instead of rising to imagination, we sink into mysticism.

To accomplish a mystical disintegration is not the function of any art; if any art seems to accomplish it, the effect is only incidental, being involved, perhaps, in the process of constructing the proper object of that art, as we might cut down trees and dig them up by the roots to lay the foundations of a temple. For every art looks to the building up of something. And just because the world built up by common sense and natural science is an inadequate world (a skeleton which needs the filling of sensation before it can live), therefore the moment when we realize its inadequacy is the moment when the higher arts find their opportunity. When the world is shattered to bits they can come and "build it nearer to the heart's desire."

The great function of poetry, which we have not yet directly mentioned, is precisely this: to repair to the material of experience, seizing hold of the reality of sensation and fancy beneath the surface of conventional ideas, and then out of that living but indefinite material to build new structures, richer, finer, fitter to the primary tendencies of our nature, truer to the ultimate possibilities of the soul. Our descent into the elements of our being is then justified by our subsequent freer ascent toward its goal; we revert to sense only to find food for reason; we destroy conventions only to construct ideals.

Such analysis for the sake of creation is the essence of all great poetry. Science and common sense are themselves in their way poets of no mean order, since they take the material of experience and make out of it a clear, symmetrical, and beautiful world; the very propriety of this art, however, has made it common. Its figures have become mere rhetoric and its metaphors prose. Yet, even as it is, a scientific and mathematical vision has a higher beauty than the irrational poetry of sensation and impulse, which merely tickles the brain, like liquor, and plays upon our random, imaginative lusts. The imagination of a great poet, on the contrary, is as orderly as that of an astronomer, and as large; he has the naturalist's patience, the naturalist's love of detail and eye trained to see fine gradations and essential lines; he knows no hurry; he has no pose, no sense of originality; he finds his effects in his subject, and his subject in his inevitable world. Resembling the naturalist in all this, he differs from him in the balance of his interests; the poet has the concreter mind; his visible world wears all its colours and retains its indwelling passion and life. Instead of studying in experience its calculable elements, he studies its moral values, its beauty, the openings it offers to the soul: and the cosmos he constructs is accordingly an ideal theatre for the spirit in which its noblest potential drama is enacted and its destiny resolved.

This supreme function of poetry is only the consummation of the method by which words and imagery are transformed into verse. As verse breaks up the prosaic order of syllables and subjects them to a recognizable and pleasing measure, so poetry breaks up the whole prosaic picture of experience to introduce into it a rhythm more congenial and intelligible to the mind. And in both these cases the operation is essentially the same as that by which, in an intermediate sphere, the images rejected by practical thought, and the emotions ignored by it, are so marshalled as to fill the mind with a truer and intenser consciousness of its memorable experience. The poetry of fancy, of observation, and of passion moves on this intermediate level; the poetry of mere sound and virtuosity is confined to the lower sphere; and the highest is reserved for the poetry of the creative reason. But one principle is present throughout,—the principle of Beauty,—the art of assimilating phenomena, whether works, images, emotions, or systems of ideas, to the deeper innate cravings of the mind.

Let us now dwell a little on this higher function of poetry and try to distinguish some of its phases.

The creation of characters is what many of us might at first be tempted to regard as the supreme triumph of the imagination. If we abstract, however, from our personal tastes and look at the matter in its human and logical relations, we shall see, I think, that the construction of characters is not the ultimate task of poetic fiction. A character can never be exhaustive of our materials: for it exists by its idiosyncrasy, by its contrast with other natures, by its development of one side, and one side only, of our native capacities. It is, therefore, not by characterization as such that the ultimate message can be rendered. The poet can put only a part of himself into any of his heroes, but he must put the whole into his noblest work. A character is accordingly only a fragmentary unity; fragmentary in respect to its origin,—since it is conceived by enlargement, so to speak, of a part of our own being to the exclusion of the rest,—and fragmentary in respect to the object it presents, since a character must live in an environment and be appreciated by contrast and by the sense of derivation. Not the character, but its effects and causes, is the truly interesting thing. Thus in master poets, like Homer and Dante, the characters, although well drawn, are subordinate to the total movement and meaning of the scene. There is indeed something pitiful, something comic, in any comprehended soul; souls, like other things, are only definable by their limitations. We feel instinctively that it would be insulting to speak of any man to his face as we should speak of him in his absence, even if what we say is in the way of praise: for absent he is a character understood, but present he is a force respected.

In the construction of ideal characters, then, the imagination is busy with material,—particular actions and thoughts,— which suggest their unification in persons; but the characters thus conceived can hardly be adequate to the profusion of our observations, nor exhaustive, when all personalities are taken together, of the interest of our lives. Characters are initially imbedded in life, as the gods themselves are originally imbedded in Nature. Poetry must, therefore, to render all reality, render also the background of its figures, and the events that condition their acts. We must place them in that indispensable environment which the landscape furnishes to the eye and the social medium to the emotions.

The visible landscape is not a proper object for poetry. Its elements, and especially the emotional stimulation which it gives, may be suggested or expressed in verse; but landscape is not thereby represented in its proper form; it appears only as an element and associate of moral unities. Painting, architecture, and gardening, with the art of stage setting, have the visible landscape for their object, and to those arts we may leave it. But there is a sort of landscape larger than the visible, which escapes the synthesis of the eye; it is present to that topographical sense by which we always live in the consciousness that there is a sea, that there are mountains, that the sky is above us, even when we do not see it, and that the tribes of men, with their different degrees of blamelessness, are scattered over the broad-backed earth. This cosmic landscape poetry alone can render, and it is no small part of the art to awaken the sense of it at the right moment, so that the object that occupies the centre of vision may be seen in its true lights, coloured by its wider associations, and dignified by its felt affinities to things permanent and great. As the Italian masters were wont not to paint their groups of saints about the Virgin without enlarging the canvas, so as to render a broad piece of sky, some mountains and rivers, and nearer, perhaps, some decorative pile; so the poet of larger mind envelops his characters in the atmosphere of Nature and history, and keeps us constantly aware of the world in which they move.

The distinction of a poet—the dignity and humanity of his thought—can be measured by nothing, perhaps, so well as by the diameter of the world in which he lives; if he is supreme, his vision, like Dante's, always stretches to the stars. And Virgil, a supreme poet sometimes unjustly belittled, shows us the same thing in another form; his landscape is the Roman universe, his theme the sacred springs of Roman greatness in piety, constance, and law. He has not written a line in forgetfulness that he was a Roman; he loves country life and its labours because he sees in it the origin and bulwark of civic greatness; he honours tradition because it gives perspective and momentum to the history that ensues; he invokes the gods, because they are symbols of the physical and moral forces by which Rome struggled to dominion.

Almost every classic poet has the topographical sense; he swarms with proper names and allusions to history and fable; if an epithet is to be thrown in anywhere to fill up the measure of a line, he chooses instinctively an appellation of place or family; his wine is not red, but Samian; his gorges are not deep, but are the gorges of Haemus; his songs are not sweet, but Pierian. We may deride their practice as conventional, but they could far more justly deride ours as insignificant. Conventions do not arise without some reason, and genius will know how to rise above them by a fresh appreciation of their rightness, and will feel no temptation to overturn them in favour of personal whimsies. The ancients found poetry not so much in sensible accidents as in essential forms and noble associations; and this fact marks very clearly their superior education. They dominated the world as we no longer dominate it, and lived, as we are too distracted to live, in the presence of the rational and the important.

A physical and historical background, however, is of little moment to the poet in comparison with that other environment of his characters,— the dramatic situations in which they are involved. The substance of poetry is, after all, emotion; and if the intellectual emotion of comprehension and the mimetic one of impersonation are massive, they are not so intense as the appetites and other transitive emotions of life; the passions are the chief basis of all interests, even the most ideal, and the passions are seldom brought into play except by the contact of man with man. The various forms of love and hate are only possible in society, and to imagine occasions in which these feelings may manifest all their inward vitality is the poet's function,—one in which he follows the fancy of every child, who puffs himself out in his day-dreams into an endless variety of heroes and lovers. The thrilling adventures which he craves demand an appropriate theatre; the glorious emotions with which he bubbles over must at all hazards find or feign their correlative objects.

But the passions are naturally blind, and the poverty of the imagination, when left alone, is absolute. The passions may ferment as they will, they never can breed an idea out of their own energy. This idea must be furnished by the senses, by outward experience, else the hunger of the soul will gnaw its own emptiness for ever. Where the seed of sensation has once fallen, however, the growth, variations, and exuberance of fancy may be unlimited. Only we still observe (as in the child, in dreams, and in the poetry of ignorant or mystical poets) that the intensity of inwardly generated visions does not involve any real increase in their scope or dignity. The inexperienced mind remains a thin mind, no matter how much its vapours may be heated and blown about by natural passion. It was a capital error in Fichte and Schopenhauer to assign essential fertility to the will in the creation of ideas. They mistook, as human nature will do, even when at times it professes pessimism, an ideal for a reality: and because they saw how much the will clings to its objects, how it selects and magnifies them, they imagined that it could breed them out of itself. A man who thinks clearly will see that such self-determination of a will is inconceivable, since what has no external relation and no diversity of structure cannot of itself acquire diversity of functions. Such inconceivability, of course, need not seem a great objection to a man of impassioned inspiration; he may even claim a certain consistency in positing, on the strength of his preference, the inconceivable to be a truth.

The alleged fertility of the will is, however, disproved by experience, from which metaphysics must in the end draw its analogies and plausibility. The passions discover, they do not create, their occasions; a fact which is patent when we observe how they seize upon what objects they find, and how reversible, contingent, and transferable the emotions are in respect to their objects. A doll will be loved instead of a child, a child instead of a lover, God instead of everything. The differentiation of the passions, as far as consciousness is concerned, depends on the variety of the objects of experience,—that is, on the differentiation of the senses and of the environment which stimulates them.

When the "infinite" spirit enters the human body, it is determined to certain limited forms of life by the organs which it wears; and its blank potentiality becomes actual in thought and deed, according to the fortunes and relations of its organism. The ripeness of the passions may thus precede the information of the mind and lead to groping in by-paths without issue; a phenomenon which appears not only in the obscure individual whose abnormalities the world ignores but also in the starved, half-educated genius that pours the whole fire of his soul into trivial arts or grotesque superstitions. The hysterical forms of music and religion are the refuge of an idealism that has lost its way; the waste and failures of life flow largely in those channels. The carnal temptations of youth are incidents of the same maladaptation, when passions assert themselves before the conventional order of society can allow them physical satisfaction, and long before philosophy or religion can hope to transform them into fuel for its own sacrificial flames.

Hence flows the greatest opportunity of fiction. We have, in a sense, an infinite will; but we have a limited experience, an experience sadly inadequate to exercise that will either in its purity or its strength. To give form to our capacities nothing is required but the appropriate occasion; this the poet, studying the world, will construct for us out of the materials of his observations. He will involve us in scenes which lie beyond the narrow lane of our daily ploddings; he will place us in the presence of important events, that we may feel our spirit rise momentarily to the height of his great argument. The possibilities of love or glory, of intrigue and perplexity, will be opened up before us; if he gives us a good plot, we can readily furnish the characters, because each of them will be the realization of some stunted potential self of our own. It is by the plot, then, that the characters will be vivified, because it is by the plot that our own character will be expanded into its latent possibilities.

The description of an alien character can serve this purpose only very imperfectly; but the presentation of the circumstances in which that character manifests itself will make description unnecessary, since our instinct will supply all that is requisite for the impersonation. Thus it seems that Aristotle was justified in making the plot the chief element in fiction: for it is by virtue of the plot that the characters live, or, rather, that we live in them, and by virtue of the plot accordingly that our soul rises to that imaginative activity by which we tend at once to escape from the personal life and to realize its ideal. This idealization is, of course, partial and merely relative to the particular adventure in which we imagine ourselves engaged. But in some single direction our will finds self-expression, and understands itself; runs through the career which it ignorantly coveted, and gathers the fruits and the lesson of that enterprise.

This is the essence of tragedy: the sense of the finished life, of the will fulfilled and enlightened: that purging of the mind so much debated upon, which relieves us of pent-up energies, transfers our feelings to a greater object, and thus justifies and entertains our dumb passions, detaching them at the same time for a moment from their accidental occasions in our earthly life. An episode, however lurid, is not a tragedy in this nobler sense, because it does not work itself out to the end; it pleases without satisfying, or shocks without enlightening. This enlightenment, I need hardly say, is not a matter of theory or of moral maxims; the enlightenment by which tragedy is made sublime is a glimpse into the ultimate destinies of our will. This discovery need not be an ethical gain—Macbeth and Othello attain it as much as Brutus and Hamlet—it may serve to accentuate despair, or cruelty, or indifference, or merely to fill the imagination for a moment without much affecting the permanent tone of the mind. But without such a glimpse of the goal of a passion the passion has not been adequately read, and the fiction has served to amuse us without really enlarging the frontiers of our ideal experience. Memory and emotion have been played upon, but imagination has not brought anything new to the light.

The dramatic situation, however, gives us the environment of a single passion, of life in one of its particular phases; and although a passion, like Romeo's love, may seem to devour the whole soul, and its fortunes may seem to be identical with those of the man, yet much of the man, and the best part of him, goes by the board in such a simplification. If Leonardo da Vinci, for example, had met in his youth with Romeo's fate, his end would have been no more ideally tragic than if he had died at eighteen of a fever; we should be touched rather by the pathos of what he had missed, than by the sublimity of what he had experienced. A passion like Romeo's, compared with the ideal scope of human thought and emotion, is a thin dream, a pathological crisis.

Accordingly Aristophanes, remembering the original religious and political functions of tragedy, blushes to see upon the boards a woman in love. And we should readily agree with him, but for two reasons,—one, that we abstract too much, in our demands upon art, from nobility of mind, and from the thought of totality and proportion; the other, that we have learned to look for a symbolic meaning in detached episodes, and to accept the incidental emotions they cause, because of their violence and our absorption in them, as in some sense sacramental and representative of the whole. Thus the picture of an unmeaning passion, of a crime without an issue, does not appear to our romantic apprehension as the sorry farce it is, but rather as a true tragedy. Some have lost even the capacity to conceive of a true tragedy, because they have no idea of a cosmic order, of general laws of life, or of an impersonal religion. They measure the profundity of feeling by its intensity, not by its justifying relations; and in the radical disintegration of their spirit, the more they are devoured the more they fancy themselves fed. But the majority of us retain some sense of a meaning in our joys and sorrows, and even if we cannot pierce to their ultimate object, we feel that what absorbs us here and now has a merely borrowed or deputed power; that it is a symbol and foretaste of all reality speaking to the whole soul. At the same time our intelligence is too confused to give us any picture of that reality, and our will too feeble to marshal our disorganized loves in a religion consistent with itself and harmonious with the comprehended universe. A rational ideal eludes us, and we are the more inclined to plunge into mysticism.

Nevertheless, the function of poetry, like that of science, can only be fulfilled by the conception of harmonies that become clearer as they grow richer. As the chance note that comes to be supported by a melody becomes in that melody determinate and necessary, and as the melody, when woven into a harmony, is explicated in that harmony and fixed beyond recall; so the single emotion, the fortuitous dream, launched by the poet into the world of recognizable and immortal forms, looks in that world for its ideal supports and affinities. It must find them or else be blown back among the ghosts. The highest ideality is the comprehension of the real. Poetry is not at its best when it depicts a further possible experience, but when it initiates us, by feigning something which as an experience is impossible, into the meaning of the experience which we have actually had.

The highest example of this kind of poetry is religion; and although disfigured and misunderstood by the simplicity of men who believe in it without being capable of that imaginative interpretation of life in which its truth consists, yet this religion is even then often beneficent, because it colours life harmoniously with the ideal. Religion may falsely represent the ideal as a reality, but we must remember that the ideal, if not so represented, would be despised by the majority of men, who cannot understand that the value of things is moral, and who therefore attribute to what is moral a natural existence, thinking thus to vindicate its importance and value. But value lies in meaning, not in substance; in the ideal which things approach, not in the energy which they embody.

The highest poetry, then, is not that of the versifiers, but that of the prophets, or of such poets as interpret verbally the visions which the prophets have rendered in action and sentiment rather than in adequate words. That the intuitions of religion are poetical, and that in such intuitions poetry has its ultimate function, are truths of which both religion and poetry become more conscious the more they advance in refinement and profundity. A crude and superficial theology may confuse God with the thunder, the mountains, the heavenly bodies, or the whole universe; but when we pass from these easy identifications to a religion that has taken root in history and in the hearts of men, and has come to flower, we find its objects and its dogmas purely ideal, transparent expressions of moral experience and perfect counterparts of human needs. The evidence of history or of the senses is left far behind and never thought of; the evidence of the heart, the value of the idea, are alone regarded.

Take, for instance, the doctrine of transubstantiation. A metaphor here is the basis of a dogma, because the dogma rises to the same subtle region as the metaphor, and gathers its sap from the same soil of emotion. Religion has here redis-covered its affinity with poetry, and in insisting on the truth of its mystery it unconsciously vindicates the ideality of its truth. Under the accidents of bread and wine lies, says the dogma, the substance of Christ's body, blood, and divinity. What is that but to treat facts as an appearance, and their ideal im-port as a reality? And to do this is the very essence of poetry, for which everything visible is a sacrament—an outward sign of that inward grace for which the soul is thirsting.

In this same manner, where poetry rises from its elementary and detached expressions in rhythm, euphuism, characteriza-tion, and story-telling, and comes to the consciousness of its highest function, that of portraying the ideals of experience and destiny, then the poet becomes aware that he is essentially a prophet, and either devotes himself, like Homer or Dante, to the loving expression of the religion that exists, or like Lucre-tius or Wordsworth, to the heralding of one which he believes to be possible. Such poets are aware of their highest mission; others, whatever the energy of their genius, have not con-ceived their ultimate function as poets. They have been will-ing to leave their world ugly as a whole, after stuffing it with a sufficient profusion of beauties. Their contemporaries, their fellow-countrymen for many generations, may not perceive this defect, because they are naturally even less able than the poet himself to understand the necessity of so large a harmony. If he is short-sighted, they are blind, and his poetic world may seem to them sublime in its significance, because it may sug-gest some partial lifting of their daily burdens and some par-tial idealization of their incoherent thoughts.

Such insensibility to the highest poetry is no more extra-ordinary than the corresponding indifference to the highest religion; nobility and excellence, however, are not dependent on the suffrage of half-baked men, but on the original disposition of the clay and the potter; I mean on the conditions of the art and the ideal capacities of human nature. Just as a note is better than a noise because, its beats being regular, the ear and brain can react with pleasure on that regularity, so all the stages of harmony are better than the confusion out of which they come, because the soul that perceives that harmony welcomes it as the fulfilment of her natural ends. The Pythagoreans were therefore right when they made number the essence of the knowable world, and Plato was right when he said harmony was the first condition of the highest good. The good man is a poet whose syllables are deeds and make a harmony in Nature. The poet is a rebuilder of the imagination, to make a harmony in that. And he is not a complete poet if his whole imagination is not attuned and his whole experience composed into a single symphony.

For his complete equipment, then, it is necessary, in the first place, that he sing; that his voice be pure and well pitched, and that his numbers flow; then, at a higher stage, his images must fit with one another; he must be euphuistic, colouring his thoughts with many reflected lights of memory and suggestion, so that their harmony may be rich and profound; again, at a higher stage, he must be sensuous and free, that is, he must build up his world with the primary elements of experience, not with the conventions of common sense or intelligence; he must draw the whole soul into his harmonies, even if in doing so he disintegrates the partial systematizations of experience made by abstract science in the categories of prose. But finally, this disintegration must not leave the poet weltering in a chaos of sense and passion; it must be merely the ploughing of the ground before a new harvest, the kneading of the clay before the modelling of a more perfect form. The expression of emotion should be rationalized by derivation from character and by reference to the real objects that arouse it—to Nature, to history, and to the universe of truth; the experience imagined should be conceived as a destiny, governed by principles, and issuing in the discipline and enlightenment of the will. In this way alone can poetry become an interpretation of life and not merely an irrelevant excursion into the realm of fancy, multiplying our images without purpose, and distracting us from our business without spiritual gain.

If we may then define poetry, not in the formal sense of giving the minimum of what may be called by that name, but in the ideal sense of determining the goal which it approaches and the achievement in which all its principles would be fulfilled, we may say that poetry is metrical and euphuistic discourse, expressing thought which is both sensuous and ideal.

Such is poetry as a literary form; but if we drop the limitation to verbal expression, and think of poetry as that subtle fire and inward light which seems at times to shine through the world and to touch the images in our minds with ineffable beauty, then poetry is a momentary harmony in the soul amid stagnation or conflict,—a glimpse of the divine and an incitation to a religious life.

Religion is poetry become the guide of life, poetry substituted for science or supervening upon it as an approach to the highest reality. Poetry is religion allowed to drift, left without points of application in conduct and without an expression in worship and dogma; it is religion without practical efficacy and without metaphysical illusion. The ground of this abstractness of poetry, however, is usually only its narrow scope; a poet who plays with an idea for half an hour, or constructs a character to which he gives no profound moral significance, forgets his own thought, or remembers it only as a fiction of his leisure, because he has not dug his well deep enough to tap the subterraneous springs of his own life. But when the poet enlarges his theatre and puts into his rhapsodies the true visions of his people and of his soul, his poetry is the consecration of his deepest convictions, and contains the whole truth of his religion. What the religion of the vulgar adds to the poet's is simply the inertia of their limited apprehension, which takes literally what he meant ideally, and degrades into a false extension of this world on its own level what in his mind was a true interpretation of it upon a moral plane.

This higher plane is the sphere of significant imagination, of relevant fiction, of idealism become the interpretation of the reality it leaves behind. Poetry raised to its highest power is then identical with religion grasped in its inmost truth; at their point of union both reach their utmost purity and beneficence, for then poetry loses its frivolity and ceases to demoralize, while religion surrenders its illusions and ceases to deceive.

BRANDER MATTHEWS

James Brander Matthews (1852-1929) was born in New Orleans, Louisiana, and grew up in the custom of traveling widely in the United States and in Europe, but for most of his life made New York City his home. Graduated from Columbia College in 1871, he began to write reviews and critical essays for "little" magazines. In 1880 and 1881 he published two volumes of critical commentary on the French theater, and in the next twenty years he established a considerable reputation as playwright, novelist, and author of short stories and of literary criticism. He became a regular contributor to British and American magazines, in which he expounded the idea of the well-made play, and interpreted French literature, particularly the drama, to the reading publics in Great Britain and the United States. He had a wide acquaintance among literary personalities: he was one of the founders of the Authors' Club, of the Players, and of the National Institute of Arts and Letters, and he belonged to numerous literary societies. In 1892 Matthews became professor of literature, and in 1900 of dramatic literature, at Columbia. His latter appointment was the first such chair in an American college. Until the 1890s literature had been taught primarily by professors of rhetoric; Matthews' appointment to the chair in dramatic literature was symptomatic of a change in teaching drama and imaginative writing, for which Matthews himself was largely responsible.

His several collections of lectures, as professor of dramatic literature, comprise a thorough analysis of authorship and of the craft of writing. Curiously, there is no collected edition of his writing, and there is scarcely any critical commentary on his works. This belies the extraordinary influence he had as a journeyman writer, literary critic, teacher and man of letters.

"Apology for Technic" first appeared in the *North American Review,* June 1905, and was then included in *Inquiries and Opinions* (1907), the source of this text. The essay is characteristic of Matthews' principal subject, the process of authorship, of his catholic view of the subject, of the scope of his illustration—including prose fiction, painting, sculpture, and playwriting, and of the explanatory quality of most of his essays, which were first delivered as lectures to academic colleagues and to his students.

AN APOLOGY FOR TECHNIC

IF the chief end of all art is delight, there is small blame to be attached to most of us in that we are glad to take our pleasure carelessly and to give little thought to the means whereby we have been moved. Properly enough, the enjoyment of most of us is unthinking; and in the appreciation of the masterpieces of the several arts few of us are wont to consider curiously the craftsmanship of the men who wrought these marvels, their skill of hand, their familiarity with the mechanics of their art, their consummate knowledge of technic. Our regard is centered rather on the larger aspects of the masterwork, on its meaning and on its veracity, on its intellectual elevation, and on its moral appeal. No doubt this is best, for it is only by its possession of these nobler qualities that a work of art endures. On the other hand, these nobler qualities by themselves will not suffice to confer immortality, unless they are sustained by the devices of the adroit craftsman. As Massinger asserted long ago:

> No fair colors
> Can fortify a building faintly joined.

Technic is most successful when its existence is least suspected, and this is one reason why it is often overlooked and neglected in the very achievements which owe to its aid their vitality. Perhaps this happens the more frequently because it is the affectation of many an artist to hurry his tools out of sight as swiftly as he can, and to sweep up the chips of his workshop as soon as may be, so that the result of his effort shall seem almost as if it were the sudden effect of the inspiration that is believed to visit a genius now and again. He may have toiled at it unceasingly for months, joying in the labor

and finding keen pleasure in every workmanlike artifice he
had used to attain his end; and yet he refrains from confess-
ing his many struggles with his rebellious material, wisely preferring to let what he has done speak for itself, simply and
without commentary. But the artists know that the pathway to
achievement is never along the line of least resistance; and
they smile when they hear Mascarille, in Molière's little comedy, tell the affected young ladies whom he is seeking to impress that all he did "was done without effort." By this the
artists at once perceive the fellow to be a pretender, who had
never accomplished anything and who never would. They
know, as no others can know, that there is no cable-road to the
tops of the twin-peaks of Parnassus, and that he who would
climb to these remote heights must trudge afoot,—even if he is
lucky enough now and again to get a lift on Pegasus.

What the artists do not care to parade, it is the duty of the
commentators to point out; and an understanding of the technic of any art, of its possibilities and of its limitations, is as
necessary for the critics as for the creators. Perhaps it is not
pedantic to suggest that the critic who seeks to be of service
ought to be able to see in every masterpiece the result of the
combined action of three forces, without any one of which
that work of art could not have come into being. First, there
is the temperament of the artist himself, his native endowment
for the practise of that special art, his gift of story-telling or of
play-making, as the case may be. Second, there is the training
of the artist, his preparation for his work, his slowly acquired
mastery of the processes of his craft, his technical accomplishments. And, thirdly, there is the man's own character, his intelligence, and energy, and determination, his moral sense,
his attitude toward life and its insistent problems. Now, of
these three necessary factors—first, his native gift; second, his
technic; and, third his character—only the second is improv-
able by taking thought. The native gift must remain ever what
it is, neither more nor less; and it cannot be enlarged by any
effort of will. So also the character, which is conditioned by

much that is beyond a man's control,—which can be bettered, perhaps, but only as the man himself climbs upward.

Technic, however, can be had for the asking. Any man can acquire it if he will but pay the price,—the needful study and experiment. Any man can make himself a master of his craft, if he will but serve his apprenticeship loyally. The beginner in painting, for example, can go into the studio of an older practitioner to get grounded in the grammar of his art, and to learn slowly how to speak its language, not eloquently at first, but so as to make his meaning clear. In that workshop he soon awakens to the fact that permanent success is never won by any audacity of ignorance, and that the most famous artists are those who acquainted themselves with every artifice of their craft and with every trick of their trade. They went to school to certain of their elders to acquire that tradition of technic, past along from hand to hand, enriched by the devices of one after another of the strong men who had practised the art, following each in the other's footsteps and broadening the trail blazed by those who went first.

Every generation is privileged to stand on the shoulders of its predecessors, and it is taller by what they accomplished. The art of fiction, for example, is a finer art today than it was yesterday; and so is every other art, even tho the artists themselves are no greater now than then, and even tho genius is no more frequent than it was formerly. Ghirlandajo and Marlowe and Cervantes were men of genius; but their technic is seen today to be as primitive as their native talent is indisputable. We can perceive them doubtfully feeling for a formula, fumbling in the dark, for want of the model which they themselves were to aid in establishing and which every novice nowadays has ready to his hand, even tho he may lack the temperament to profit by what is set before him.

It is significant that not a few of the masters, in the days when they were but novices, found so much satisfaction in this mere acquiring of the secrets of the craft, that they chose to linger in the apprentice-stage longer than might seem necessary. In their earlier work they were content modestly to put in practise the technical principles they had just been acquiring; and for a little while they sought scarcely more than mere technical adroitness. Consider the firstlings of Shakspere's art and of Molière's; and observe how they reveal these prentice playwrights at work, each seeking to display his cleverness and each satisfied when he had done this. In "Love's Labor's Lost," Shakspere is trying to amuse by inventive wit and youthful gaiety and ingenuity of device, just as Molière in the "Étourdi" is enjoying his own complicating of comic imbroglios, not yet having anything of importance to say on the stage, but practising against the time when he should want to say something. Neither in the English comedy nor in the French is there any purpose other than the desire to please by the devices of the theater.

There is so little hint of a deeper meaning in either "Love's Labor's Lost" or the "Étourdi," of a moral, so to speak, of a message of ulterior significance, that, if Shakspere and Molière had died after these plays were produced, nobody would ever have suspected that either youthful playwright had it in him to develop into a philosophic observer of the deeper realities of life. Of course, neither of them was long satisfied with this dexterous display of technical adroitness alone; and, as they grew in years, we find their plays getting richer in meaning and dealing more seriously with the larger problems of existence. But technic was never despised; and, if it was not always the chief end of the playwright, it remained the means whereby he was enabled to erect the solid framework of masterpieces like "Othello" and "Tartuffe," in which the craftsmanship is overshadowed by the nobler qualities, no doubt, but in which the stark technical skill is really more abundant than in the earlier and emptier plays.

As Shakspere and Molière matured mentally and morally, so also did they grow in facility of accomplishment, in the ease with which they could handle the ever-present problems of exposition and construction. The student of dramaturgy notes with increasing delight the ingenuity with which the first appearance of Tartuffe is prepared; and he finds an almost equal joy in the bolder beginnings of "Romeo and Juliet" and of "Hamlet," where the difficulty was less, it may be, but where the interest of the craftsman in the excellence of his device is quite as obvious. Shakspere was the greatest of dramatic poets and Molière was the greatest of comic dramatists; and both of them were good workmen, taking an honest pride in the neatness with which they finished a job. In his later years, Shakspere seems to have relaxed a little his interest in technic, and the value of his work is at once seen to suffer. Altho his mind is as powerful as ever up to the last years of his stay in London, "Cymbeline" and "A Winter's Tale" are far inferior to "Hamlet" and to "Macbeth"; and the cause is apparently little more than a carelessness of technic, an unwillingness to take the trouble needful to master his material and to present it in due proportion.

If Shakspere and Molière ever meet in that other world which was so much in the mind of the one and so little in the thought of the other, and if they chance to fall into chat—Shakspere spoke French, pretty certainly, even if Molière knew no English—we may rest assured that they will not surprise each other by idle questions about the meaning of this play or that, its moral purpose or its symbolic significance. We may be confident that their talk would turn promptly to technic; and, perhaps, Shakspere would congratulate Molière on his advantages in coming later, when the half-open, semi-medieval playhouse, with which the English dramatist had perforce to be contented, had been superseded by a more modern theater, roofed and lighted and set with scenery. And, in his turn, Molière might be curious to inquire how the English playwright was able to produce upon the spectators the effect of a change of scene when, in fact, there was no actual scenery to change.

To suggest that these two masters of the dramatic art would probably confine their conversation to matters of mere technic is not so vain or adventurous as it may seem, since technic is the one theme the dramatists from Lope de Vega to Legouvé

have always chosen to discuss, whenever they have been em-
boldened to talk about their art in public. Lope's "New Art
of Writing Plays" is in verse, and it has taken for its remote
model Horace's "Art of Poetry," but none the less does it contain the practical counsels of a practical playwright, advising
his fellow-craftsmen how best to succeed on the stage; and it is
just as technical in its precepts as Mr. Pinero's acute lecture on
the probable success of Robert Louis Stevenson as a dramatist,
if only the Scots romancer had taken the trouble to learn the
rules of the game, as it is played in the theater of today.

In thus centering the interest of their public utterance upon
the necessities of craftsmanship, the dramatists are in accord
with the customs of the practitioners of all the other arts. Consider the criticism of poetry by the poets themselves, for example,—how narrowly it is limited to questions of vocabulary
or of versification, whether the poet-critic is Dryden or Wordsworth or Poe. Consider the criticism of painting by the painters
themselves,—how frankly it is concerned with the processes of
the art, whether the painter-critic is Fromentin or La Farge.
It is La Farge who records that Rembrandt was a "workman
following his trade of painting to live by it," and who reminds
us that "these very great artists"—Rembrandt and his fellows—
"are primarily workmen, without any pose or assumption of
doing more than a daily task." What they did was all in the
day's work. One of the most distinguished of American sculptors was once standing before a photograph of the Panathenaic
frieze, and a critical friend by his side exprest a wonder as to
"what those old Greeks were thinking of when they did work
like that?" The professional artist smiled and responded: "I
guess that, like the rest of us, they were thinking how they
could pull it off!"

The method, the tricks of the trade, the ingenious devices
of one kind or another, these are what artists of all sorts like
to discuss with fellow-practitioners of the art; and it is by this
interchange of experiences that the means of expression are
multiplied. The inner meaning of what they have wrought,
its message, its morality, its subtler spirit, the artists do not

care ever to talk over, even with each other. This is intangible and incommunicable; and it is too personal, too intimate, to be vulgarized in words; it is to be felt rather than phrased. Above all, it must speak for itself, for it is there because it had to be there, and not because the artist put it there deliberately. If he has not builded better than he knew, then is the result of his labor limited and narrow. A story is told of Thorwaldsen in his old age, when a friend found him disconsolate before a finished statue and inquired if he was despondent because he had not been able to realize his ideal. And the sculptor responded that, on the contrary, he had realized his ideal, and therefore he was downcast; for the first time his hand had been able to accomplish all that his mind had planned.

"Neither in life, nor even in literature and in art, can we always do what we intend to do," M. Brunetière once asserted, adding that, "in compensation, we have not always intended to do all that we have actually accomplished." Often no one is more astonished than the artist himself—be he poet or painter —at what the critics sometimes find in his work; and he is frankly unaware of any intention on his part to do all the fine things which he is told that he has done. But the critics may be justified, despite the disclaimer of the artist; and the fine things are, of a truth, to be discovered even tho they get into the work by accident, as it were, and even tho they may be the result of an intention which was either unconscious on the artist's part, or subconscious.

We cannot help feeling the sublimity so obvious in the frescos of the Sistine Chapel; and yet it is equally obvious—if we care to look for the evidence—that while he was at this work the mind of Michelangelo was absorbed by the conquest of a host of technical difficulties. Of course, it would be going too far to assert that the great artist did not actually intend the sublimity that we admire and wonder at; but we may be sure that this sublimity is not something deliberately planned and achieved by him. It is there because the theme evoked it, and because Michelangelo was himself a man of the noblest character and of the loftiest imagination. It was inherent and latent in him, and it had to come out, inevitably and mightily, when he was engaged on a piece of work that tasked all his powers.

An ideal, a significance, a moral, that has to be inserted into a work of art and that might have been omitted, is not likely to be firmly joined; and it is liable to fall apart sooner or later. Morality, for example, is not something to be put in or left out, at the caprice of the creator; it is, as Mr. Henry James once called it, "a part of the essential richness of inspiration." Therefore the artist need not give thought to it. If his own soul is as clean as may be, and if his vision is clear, the moral of his work may be left to take care of itself. Nearly always when an artist has been over-anxious to charge his work with a moral message, written so plain that all who run may read, he has failed to attain either of his ends, the ethical or the esthetic. There is a purpose plainly exprest in Miss Edgeworth's "Moral Tales" and in her "Parent's Assistant"; and the result is that healthy girls and wholesome boys are revolted. There was no moral intent in her ever-delightful "Castle Rackrent"; and yet it has an ethical significance which few of its readers can have failed to feel.

Perhaps "Castle Rackrent" is the finest of Miss Edgeworth's stories, because it is the only one in which she had set herself a technical problem of exceeding difficulty. She chose to use the faithful old retainer to tell the tale of the family's downfall in consequence of its weakness, its violence, and its vice. Thady has never a word of blame for any son of the house he has served generation after generation. Indeed, he is forever praising his succession of masters; but so artfully does the author utilize the device of transparency that the reader is put in possession of the damning facts, one by one, and is soon able to see the truth of the matter which Thady himself has no thought of revealing,—which, indeed, he would probably deny indignantly if it was suggested by anyone else.

The chief reason why the novel is still held to be inferior to the drama is to be found in its looseness of form. The novel is not strictly limited, as the play must be by the practical neces-

sities of the theater; and the practitioners of the art of fiction
permit themselves a license of structure which cannot but be
enfeebling to the artists themselves. Few of the novelists have
ever gone about a whole winter with a knot in their foreheads,
such as Hawthorne carried there while he was thinking out
the "Scarlet Letter." And only by strenuous grappling with
his obstacles was he able to attain the masterly simplicity of
that Puritan tragedy. A resolute wrestling with difficulty is
good not only for the muscles but also for the soul; and it may
be because they know this, that artists are inclined to go afield
in search of difficulties to be overthrown, that they set themselves problems, that they accept limitations. Herein we may
see a cause for the long popularity of the sonnet, with its re-
stricted scheme of rimes. Herein, again, we may see a reason
for the desire of the novelist to try his fate as a dramatist. "To
work successfully beneath a few grave, rigid laws," so Mr.
James once declared, "is always a strong man's highest ideal of
success." The novelist often fails as a dramatist, because he
has the gift of the story-teller only, and not that of the play-
maker, but more often still because the writing of fiction has
provided him with no experience in working beneath any law
other than his own caprice.

The modern sculptor, by the mere fact that he may now
order marble of any shape and of any size, finds his work far
easier and, therefore, far less invigorating than it was long ago,
when the artist needed to have an alerter imagination to perceive in a given piece of marble the beautiful figure he had to
cut out of that particular block and no other. Professor Ma-
haffy has suggested that the decay of genius may be traced to
the enfeebling facilities of our complex civilization. "In art,"
he maintained, "it is often the conventional shackles,—the
necessities of rime and meter, the triangle of a gable, the cir-
cular top of a barrel—which has led the poet, the sculptor, or
the painter, to strike out the most original and perfect products of their art. Obstacles, if they are extrinsic and not intrinsic, only help to feed the flame." Professor Butcher has declared that genius "wins its most signal triumphs from the

very limitations within which it works." And this is what Gautier meant when he declared that the greater the difficulty the more beautiful the work; or, as Mr. Austin Dobson has paraphrased it:

> Yes; when the ways oppose—
> When the hard means rebel,
> Fairer the work outgrows,—
> More potent far the spell.

Not only has a useful addition to the accepted devices of the craft been the guerdon of a victorious grapple with a difficulty, but the successful effort to solve a purely technical problem has often led to an ennobling enlargement of the original suggestion, with which the artist might have rested content if he had not been forced to the struggle. From the history of sculpture and of architecture here in the United States during the last years of the nineteenth century, it is easy to select two instances of this enrichment of the fundamental idea, as the direct consequence of an unexpected obstacle which the artist refused to consider a stumbling-block, preferring to make it a stepping-stone to a loftier achievement.

When the city of New York was making ready to welcome the men of the navy on their return from Manila and Santiago, the Architectural League offered to design a triumphal arch. The site assigned, in front of Madison Square, just where Broadway slants across Fifth Avenue, forced the architect to face a difficulty seemingly unsurmountable. The line of march was to be along Fifth Avenue, and, therefore, the stately monument was set astride that street. But the line of approach, for most of the multitude certain to come to gaze on the temporary addition to civic beauty, was along Broadway; and the arch built squarely across the avenue would seem askew to all who first caught sight of it from the other street. To avoid this unfortunate effect the designer devised a colonnade, extending north and south, up and down the avenue. Thus he corrected the apparent slant by emphasizing the fact that it was the avenue in which the arch was placed and not the more popular highway that chanced to cut across it. But this colonnade, invented solely to solve a difficulty, lent itself readily to rich adornment. It became at once an integral element of the architectural scheme, to which it gave breadth as well as variety. It was accepted instantly as a welcome modification of the tradition,—as an amplification not to be wantonly disregarded by any architect hereafter called upon to design a triumphal arch.

To this illustration from architecture may be added another from sculpture, as suggestive and as useful in showing how a conquest of technical difficulty is likely ever to increase the resources of the art. The sculptor of the statue of Lincoln which ennobles a park of Chicago was instructed that the work of his hands was to stand upon a knoll, visible from all sides, stark against the sky, unprotected by any background of entablature or canopy. The gaunt figure of Lincoln is not a thing of beauty to be gazed at from all the points of the compass; and the stern veracity of the artist would not permit him to disguise the ill-fitting coat and trousers by any arbitrary draperies, mendaciously cloaking the clothes which were intensely characteristic of the man to be modeled. To shield the awkwardness of the effigy when seen from the rear, a chair was placed behind it; and so the sculptor was led to present Lincoln as the Chief Magistrate of the Republic, arisen from the chair of state, to address the people from whom he had received his authority. And thus, at that late day, at the end of the nineteenth century, Mr. Saint-Gaudens did a new thing; altho there had been standing statues and seated statues, no sculptor had ever before designed a figure just rising from his seat.

It is by victories like these over technical difficulties that the arts advance; and it is in combats like these that the true artist finds his pleasure. The delight of battle is his, as he returns to the attack, again and again, until at last he wins the day and comes home laden with the spoil. The true artist hungers after technic for its own sake, well knowing the nourishment it affords. He even needlessly puts on fetters now and again, that he may find sharper zest in his effort. This ravenous appetite for technic leads many an artist to go outside his own art in search of unforeseen but fascinating difficulties. The painter is tempted to stretch his muscles by a tussle with the unknown obstacles of the sculptor; and the sculptor in his turn contends with the limitations of the painter. Michelangelo called himself a sculptor and pretended to be no more; but in time he took up the craft of the architect, of the painter and of the poet. And this interchange of field in search of new worlds to conquer seems to be characteristic of the great periods of artistic activity and achievement. In all such periods, the more accomplished craftsmen have never wearied of technical experiment to the constant enrichment of the processes of their art.

It is the uncreative critics, it is never the creative craftsmen, who dwell on the danger of taking too much interest in technic. The critics may think that the more attention the artist pays to his manner, the less he has for his matter, and that he is in peril of sacrificing content to form. But the craftsmen themselves know better; they know that no one may surely separate manner and matter, form and content, Siamese twins often, coming into being at a single birth. Furthermore, the artist knows that technic is the one quality he can control, every man for himself, every man improving himself as best he can. His native gift, his temperament,—this is what it is; and what it is it must be; and no man can better it by any effort. His character, also, the personality of the artist, that which gives a large meaning to his work,—how little can any man control this result of heredity and environment?

If an artist has anything to say it will out, sooner or later, however absorbed he may be in finding the best way of saying it. If he has nothing to say, if he has no message for the heart of man, he may at least give some pleasure to his contemporaries by the sheer dexterity of his craftsmanship. There would have been no more meaning in Poe's verse, if there had been less melody, if the poet had less devotedly studied the "book of iambs and pentameters." There would have been no larger significance in the painted epigrams of Gérôme, if that master of line had cared less for draftsmanship. There would have been no more solid value in the often amusing plays of Sardou, if he had not delighted in the ingenuity of his dramaturgical devices. At bottom, Sardou, Gérôme, and Poe, had little or nothing to say; that is their misfortune, no doubt; but it is not their fault, for, apparently, each one of them made the best of his native gift.

In his time Milton was the most careful and conscientious of artists in verse-making, and so, in his turn, was Pope, whose ideals were different, but whose skill was no less in its kind. So, again, was Tennyson untiring in seeking to attain ultimate perfection of phrase, consciously employing every artifice of alliteration, assonance and rime. But, if Milton's verse seems to us now noble and lofty, while Pope's appears to us as rather petty and merely clever, surely this is because Milton himself was noble and his native endowment lofty, and because Pope himself was petty and his gift only cleverness; surely it is not because they were both of them as much interested in the mechanics of their art as was Tennyson after them.

One of the wittiest critics of our modern civilization, the late Clarence King, remarked, some ten years ago, that the trouble with American fiction just then lay in the fact that it had the most elaborate machinery,—and no boiler. But the fault of our fiction at that time was to be sought in the absence of steam,—and not in the machinery itself which stood ready to do its work, to the best advantage and with the utmost economy of effort, just so soon as the power might be applied.

T. S. ELIOT

Thomas Stearns Eliot (1888-   ) was born in St. Louis, Missouri. His parents were of New England stock, and Eliot went to college at Harvard, where he earned an A.B. degree (1909) and an A.M. degree (1910), and where Irving Babbitt and George Santayana were among his teachers. He studied philosophy for a year at the University of Paris and then at the Graduate School at Harvard (1911-14). While at Harvard, he was an assistant in philosophy, as well as a student of Sanskrit and of Pali, but, granted a traveling fellowship, Eliot left before completing the requirements for a doctorate. After a summer in Germany, he married and settled in England; he spent a year studying at Oxford, two years teaching school, and eight years in the service of Lloyd's Bank. He joined the staff of the publishing house of Faber & Gwyer (now Faber & Faber) in 1925, and two years later, at the age of thirty-nine, he became a British subject and a member of the Church of England.

Eliot's first volume of poems was *Prufrock and Other Observations* (1917), and his first published critical study was *Ezra Pound: His Metric and Poetry* (1917). The second, revised edition (1934) of *Selected Essays* (1932), *The Use of Poetry and the Use of Criticism* (1933), and *Essays, Ancient and Modern* (1936) collect most of his critical writings; and *The Complete Poems and Plays, 1900-1950* (1952) is, to date, the definitive collection of his poetry.

Acknowledging both the merits and the limitations of his own literary criticism, Eliot calls it "workshop criticism": a prolongation of the thinking that has gone into the formation of his own verse. His criticism, he says, has the obvious limitation of being primarily relevant to the critic's own poetry. Nevertheless, it is faithful to what Eliot believes to be the function of criticism, which is to promote the understanding and enjoyment of literature. To understand a poem, he explains, it is necessary to "endeavor to grasp what the poem is aiming to be." Eliot acknowledges two preoccupations which, since the writings of Coleridge, have extended the frontiers of literary criticism: the preoccupation with the origins of the poem, and the preoccupation with an intense analysis of its text. His cautious response is to warn us of the misuse of these enthusiasms, and to point out that speculations about a poem's origin or about the intent of its author are likely to put off an understanding of the poem in its own terms.

First published in two parts, in *Egoist*, September-October, November-December, 1919, "Tradition and the Individual Talent" was reprinted in Eliot's *The Sacred Wood* (1920), and again in his *Selected Essays, 1917-1932* (1932), the source of this text.

TRADITION AND THE INDIVIDUAL TALENT

I

IN English writing we seldom speak of tradition, though we occasionally apply its name in deploring its absence. We cannot refer to "the tradition" or to "a tradition"; at most, we employ the adjective in saying that the poetry of So-and-so is "traditional" or even "too traditional." Seldom, perhaps, does the word appear except in a phrase of censure. If otherwise, it is vaguely approbative, with the implication, as to the work approved, of some pleasing archaeological reconstruction. You can hardly make the word agreeable to English ears without this comfortable reference to the reassuring science of archaeology.

Certainly the word is not likely to appear in our appreciations of living or dead writers. Every nation, every race, has not only its own creative, but its own critical turn of mind; and is even more oblivious of the shortcomings and limitations of its critical habits than of those of its creative genius. We know, or think we know, from the enormous mass of critical writing that has appeared in the French language the critical method or habit of the French; we only conclude (we are such unconscious people) that the French are "more critical" than we, and sometimes even plume ourselves a little with the fact, as if the French were the less spontaneous. Perhaps they are; but we might remind ourselves that criticism is as inevitable as breathing, and that we should be none the worse for articulating what passes in our minds when we read a book and feel an emotion about it, for criticizing our own minds in their work of criticism. One of the facts that might come to light in this process is our tendency to insist, when we praise a poet, upon those aspects of his work in which he least resembles anyone else. In these aspects or parts of his work we pretend to find what is individual, what is the peculiar essence of the man. We dwell with satisfaction upon the poet's difference from his predecessors, especially his immediate predecessors; we endeavour to find something that can be isolated in order to be enjoyed. Whereas if we approach a poet without his prejudice we shall often find that not only the best, but the most individual parts of his work may be those in which the dead poets, his ancestors, assert their immorality most vigorously. And I do not mean the impressionable period of adolescence, but the period of full maturity.

Yet if the only form of tradition, of handing down, consisted in following the ways of the immediate generation before us in a blind or timid adherence to its successes, "tradition" should positively be discouraged. We have seen many such simple currents soon lost in the sand; and novelty is better than repetition. Tradition is a matter of much wider significance. It cannot be inherited, and if you want it you must obtain it by great labour. It involves, in the first place, the historical sense, which we may call nearly indispensable to anyone who would continue to be a poet beyond his twenty-fifth year; and the historical sense involves a perception, not only of the pastness of the past, but of its presence; the historical sense compels a man to write not merely with his own generation in his bones, but with a feeling that the whole of the literature of Europe from Homer and within it the whole of the literature of his own country has a simultaneous existence and composes a simultaneous order. This historical sense, which is a sense of the timeless as well as of the temporal and

of the timeless and of the temporal together, is what makes a
writer traditional. And it is at the same time what makes a
writer most acutely conscious of his place in time, of his con-
temporaneity.

No poet, no artist of any art, has his complete meaning
alone. His significance, his appreciation is the appreciation of
his relation to the dead poets and artists. You cannot value
him alone; you must set him, for contrast and comparison,
among the dead. I mean this as a principle of aesthetic, not
merely historical, criticism. The necessity that he shall conform, that he shall cohere, is not one-sided; what happens
when a new work of art is created is something that happens
simultaneously to all the works of art which preceded it. The
existing monuments form an ideal order among themselves,
which is modified by the introduction of the new (the really
new) work of art among them. The existing order is complete
before the new work arrives; for order to persist after the su-
pervention of novelty, the *whole* existing order must be, if
ever so slightly, altered; and so the relations, proportions,
values of each work of art toward the whole are readjusted;
and this is conformity between the old and the new. Whoever
has approved this idea of order, of the form of European, of
English literature, will not find it preposterous that the past
should be altered by the present as much as the present is
directed by the past. And the poet who is aware of this will be
aware of great difficulties and responsibilities.

In a peculiar sense he will be aware also that he must inevitably be judged by the standards of the past. I say judged, not
amputated, by them; not judged to be as good as, or worse or
better than, the dead; and certainly not judged by the canons
of dead critics. It is a judgment, a comparison, in which two
things are measured by each other. To conform merely would
be for the new work not really to conform at all; it would not
be new, and would therefore not be a work of art. And we do
not quite say that the new is more valuable because it fits in;
but its fitting in is a test of its value—a test, it is true, which
can only be slowly and cautiously applied, for we are none

of us infallible judges of conformity. We say: it appears to conform, and is perhaps individual, or it appears individual, and
may conform; but we are hardly likely to find that it is one
and not the other.

To proceed to a more intelligible exposition of the relation
of the poet to the past: he can neither take the past as a lump,
an indiscriminate bolus, nor can he form himself wholly on
one or two private admirations, nor can he form himself
wholly upon one preferred period. The first course is inadmissible, the second is an important experience of youth, and the
third is a pleasant and highly desirable supplement. The poet
must be very conscious of the main current, which does not at
all flow invariably through the most distinguished reputations.
He must be quite aware of the obvious fact that art never im-
proves, but that the material of art is never quite the same.
He must be aware that the mind of Europe—the mind of his
own country—a mind which he learns in time to be much
more important than his own private mind—is a mind which
changes, and that this change is a development which aban-
dons nothing *en route,* which does not superannuate either
Shakespeare, or Homer, or the rock drawing of the Magda-
lenian draughtsmen. That this development, refinement perhaps, complication, certainly, is not, from the point of view of
the artist, any improvement. Perhaps not even an improvement from the point of view of the psychologist or not to the
extent which we imagine; perhaps only in the end based upon
a complication in economics and machinery. But the difference between the present and the past is that the conscious
present is an awareness of the past in a way and to an extent
which the past's awareness of itself cannot show.

Some one said: "The dead writers are remote from us because we *know* so much more than they did." Precisely, and
they are that which we know.

I am alive to a usual objection to what is clearly part of my
programme for the *métier* of poetry. The objection is that the
doctrine requires a ridiculous amount of erudition (pedantry),
a claim which can be rejected by appeal to the lives of poets

in any pantheon. It will even be affirmed that much learning
deadens or perverts poetic sensibility. While, however, we persist in believing that a poet ought to know as much as will not
encroach upon his necessary receptivity and necessary laziness,
it is not desirable to confine knowledge to whatever can be put
into a useful shape for examinations, drawing-rooms, or the
still more pretentious modes of publicity. Some can absorb
knowledge, the more tardy must sweat for it. Shakespeare acquired more essential history from Plutarch than most men
could from the whole British Museum. What is to be insisted
upon is that the poet must develop or procure the consciousness of the past and that he should continue to develop this
consciousness throughout his career.

What happens is a continual surrender of himself as he is at
the moment to something which is more valuable. The progress of an artist is a continual self-sacrifice, a continual extinc-
tion of personality.

There remains to define this process of depersonalization
and its relation to the sense of tradition. It is in this depersonalization that art may be said to approach the condition of
science. I shall, therefore, invite you to consider, as a suggestive analogy, the action which takes place when a bit of finely
filiated platinum is introduced into a chamber containing oxy-
gen and sulphur dioxide.

II

Honest criticism and sensitive appreciation is directed not
upon the poet but upon the poetry. If we attend to the confused cries of the newspaper critics and the susurrus of popular repetition that follows, we shall hear the names of poets in
great numbers; if we seek not Blue-book knowledge but the
enjoyment of poetry, and ask for a poem, we shall seldom find
it. In the last article I tried to point out the importance of the
relation of the poem to other poems by other authors, and
suggested the conception of poetry as a living whole of all the
poetry that has ever been written. The other aspect of this Im-

personal theory of poetry is the relation of the poem to its author. And I hinted, by an analogy, that the mind of the mature poet differs from that of the immature one not precisely in any valuation of "personality," not being necessarily more interesting, or having "more to say," but rather by being a more finely perfected medium in which special, or very varied, feelings are at liberty to enter into new combinations.

The analogy was that of the catalyst. When the two gases previously mentioned are mixed in the presence of a filament of platinum, they form sulphurous acid. This combination takes place only if the platinum is present; nevertheless, the newly formed acid contains no trace of platinum, and the platinum itself is apparently unaffected; has remained inert, neutral, and unchanged. The mind of the poet is the shred of platinum. It may partly or exclusively operate upon the experience of the man himself; but, the more perfect the artist, the more completely separate in him will be the man who suffers and the mind which creates; the more perfectly will the mind digest and transmute the passions which are its material.

The experience, you will notice, the elements which enter the presence of the transforming catalyst, are of two kinds: emotions and feelings. The effect of a work of art upon the person who enjoys it is an experience different in kind from any experience not of art. It may be formed out of one emotion, or may be a combination of several; and various feelings, inhering for the writer in particular words or phrases or images, may be added to compose the final result. Or great poetry may be made without the direct use of any emotion whatever: composed out of feelings solely. Canto XV of the *Inferno* (Brunetto Latini) is a working up of the emotion evident in the situation; but the effect, though single as that of any work of art, is obtained by considerable complexity of detail. The last quatrain gives an image, a feeling attaching to an image, which "came," which did not develop simply out of what precedes, but which was probably in suspension in the poet's mind until the proper combination arrived for it to add itself to. The poet's mind is in fact a receptacle for seizing and storing up numberless feelings, phrases, images, which remain there until all the particles which can unite to form a new compound are present together.

If you compare several representative passages of the greatest poetry you see how great is the variety of types of combination, and also how completely any semi-ethical criterion of "sublimity" misses the mark. For it is not the "greatness," the intensity, of the emotions, the components, but the intensity of the artistic process, the pressure, so to speak, under which the fusion takes place, that counts. The episode of Paolo and Francesca employs a definite emotion, but the intensity of the poetry is something quite different from whatever intensity in the supposed experience it may give the impression of. It is no more intense, furthermore, than Canto XXVI, the voyage of Ulysses, which has not the direct dependence upon an emotion. Great variety is possible in the process of transmutation of emotion: the murder of Agamemnon, or the agony of Othello, gives an artistic effect apparently closer to a possible original than the scenes from Dante. In the *Agamemnon*, the artistic emotion approximates to the emotion of an actual spectator; in *Othello* to the emotion of the protagonist himself. But the difference between art and the event is always absolute; the combination which is the murder of Agamemnon is probably as complex as that which is the voyage of Ulysses. In either case there has been a fusion of elements. The ode of Keats contains a number of feelings which have nothing particular to do with the nightingale, but which the nightingale, partly, perhaps, because of its attractive name, and partly because of its reputation, served to bring together.

The point of view which I am struggling to attack is perhaps related to the metaphysical theory of the substantial unity of the soul: for my meaning is, that the poet has, not a "personality" to express, but a particular medium, which is only a medium and not a personality, in which impressions and experiences combine in peculiar and unexpected ways. Impressions and experiences which are important for the man may take no place in the poetry, and those which become important in the poetry may play quite a negligible part in the man, the personality.

I will quote a passage which is unfamiliar enough to be regarded with fresh attention in the light—or darkness of these observations:

> And now methinks I could e'en chide myself
> For doating on her beauty, though her death
> Shall be revenged after no common action.
> Does the silkworm expend her yellow labours
> For thee? For thee does she undo herself?
> Are lordships sold to maintain ladyships
> For the poor benefit of a bewildering minute?
> Why does yon fellow falsify highways,
> And put his life between the judge's lips,
> To refine such a thing—keep horse and men
> To beat their valours for her? . . .

In this passage (as is evident if it is taken in its context) there is a combination of positive and negative emotions: an intensely strong attraction toward beauty and an equally intense fascination by the ugliness which is contrasted with it and which destroys it. This balance of contrasted emotion is in the dramatic situation to which the speech is pertinent, but that situation alone is inadequate to it. This is, so to speak, the structural emotion, provided by the drama. But the whole effect, the dominant tone, is due to the fact that a number of floating feelings, having an affinity to this emotion by no means superficially evident, have combined with it to give us a new art emotion.

It is not in his personal emotions, the emotions provoked by particular events in his life, that the poet is in any way remarkable or interesting. His particular emotions may be simple, or crude, or flat. The emotion in his poetry will be a very complex thing, but not with the complexity of the emotions of people who have very complex or unusual emotions in life. One error, in fact, of eccentricity in poetry is to seek for new human emotions to express; and in this search for novelty in the wrong place it discovers the perverse. The business of the poet is not to find new emotions, but to use the ordinary ones and, in working them up into poetry, to express feelings which are not in actual emotions at all. And emotions which he has never experienced will serve his turn as well as those familiar to him. Consequently, we must believe that "emotion recollected in tranquillity" is an inexact formula. For it is neither emotion, nor recollection, nor, without distortion of meaning, tranquillity. It is a concentration, and a new thing resulting from the concentration, of a very great number of experiences which to the practical and active person would not seem to be experiences at all; it is a concentration which does not happen consciously or of deliberation. These experiences are not "recollected," and they finally unite in an atmosphere which is "tranquil" only in that it is a passive attending upon the event. Of course this is not quite the whole story. There is a great deal, in the writing of poetry, which must be conscious and deliberate. In fact, the bad poet is usually unconscious where he ought to be conscious, and conscious where he ought to be unconscious. Both errors tend to make him "personal." Poetry is not a turning loose of emotion, but an escape from emotion; it is not the expression of personality, but an escape from personality. But, of course, only those who have personality and emotions know what it means to want to escape from these things.

III

This essay proposes to halt at the frontier of metaphysics or mysticism, and confine itself to such practical conclusions as can be applied by the responsible person interested in poetry. To divert interest from the poet to the poetry is a laudable aim: for it would conduce to a juster estimation of actual poetry, good and bad. There are many people who appreciate the expression of sincere emotion in verse, and there is a smaller number of people who can appreciate technical excellence. But very few know when there is expression of *significant* emotion, emotion which has its life in the poem and not in the history of the poet. The emotion of art is impersonal.

And the poet cannot reach this impersonality without surrendering himself wholly to the work to be done. And he is not likely to know what is to be done unless he lives in what is not merely the present, but the present moment of the past, unless he is conscious, not of what is dead, but of what is already living.

H. L. MENCKEN

Henry Louis Mencken (1880-1956) was born in Baltimore, Maryland. After training as an engineer and working in his father's tobacco business, he turned to newspaper reporting (1899), and became successively city editor (1903-05) and editor (1905-06) on the Baltimore *Morning Herald,* and, for the next twenty-five years, foreign correspondent, editor and editorial writer, and columnist on the staff of the Baltimore *Evening Sun.* With George Jean Nathan, Mencken was co-editor (1914-23) of *Smart Set,* in which capacity he was both a vigorous satirist of the American mind and manners and an enthusiastic sponsor of young British, Irish, and American writers. With Nathan he founded the *American Mercury* (1924) and he continued, as its editor (until 1933), "to attempt a realistic presentation of the whole, gaudy, gorgeous American scene." From his several editorial chairs, particularly during the 1920s, Mencken provoked a continuing reappraisal of literary opinion in America.

Mencken's published writing, from his only volume of verse (1903) to the anthology of his essays, *A Mencken Chrestomathy* (1949), is both large and various. This canon is distinguished primarily by Mencken's study of the development of the English language in the United States, *The American Language* (1919), which he continued to enlarge and revise through its fifth edition (1948). He was the editor of numerous translations, anthologies, and selections of contemporary writing; he was the author of three autobiographical volumes, of two plays (one with a collaborator), and of volumes and pamphlets of editorial pronouncements on almost every subject that came to his mind. But the bulk of his writing is composed primarily of critical essays, variously literary, philosophical, and social. Among these, *A Book of Prefaces* (1917) and six collections of essays (1919-27), called *Prejudices,* comprise most of his literary criticism. In this criticism, Mencken's response to social Darwinism and his abhorrence of the genteel conventions of Victorian thought shaped his enthusiasm for literary naturalism and for a more vigorous, honest, and skeptical national literature; and Mencken's boisterous iconoclasm made these literary convictions even more controversial. There have been numerous selections (but no collected edition) of his writing, which have kept alive Mencken's notoriety.

This essay was originally published as "The Motive of the Critic," in the *New Republic*, October 26, 1921, and reprinted as "Footnote on Criticism" in *Prejudices, Third Series* (1922). The essay was revised by Mencken and included, under the present title, in *A Mencken Chrestomathy* (1949), the source of this text.

THE CRITICAL PROCESS

NEARLY all the discussions of criticism that I am acquainted with start off with a false assumption, to wit, that the primary motive of the critic, the impulse which makes a critic of him instead of, say, a politician or a stockbroker, is pedagogical—that he writes because he is possessed by a passion to advance the enlightenment, to put down error and wrong, to disseminate some specific doctrine: psychological, epistemological, historical, or esthetic. But this is true, it seems to me, only of bad critics, and its degree of truth increases in direct ratio to their badness. The motive of the critic who is really worth reading—the only critic of whom, indeed, it may be said truthfully that it is at all possible to read him, save as an act of mental penitence—is something quite different. That motive is not the motive of the pedagogue, but the motive of the artist. It is no more and no less than the simple desire to function freely and beautifully, to give outward and objective form to ideas that bubble inwardly and have a fascinating lure in them, to get rid of them dramatically and make an articulate noise in the world.

When, years ago, I devoted myself diligently to critical pieces upon the writings of Theodore Dreiser, I found that practically everyone who took any notice of my proceedings at all fell into either one of two assumptions about my underlying purpose: (a) that I had a fanatical devotion to Mr. Dreiser's ideas and desired to propagate them, or (b) that I was an ardent patriot, and yearned to lift up American literature. Both assumptions were false. I had, in fact, very little interest in many of Mr. Dreiser's main ideas; when we met we usually quarreled about them. And I was and am wholly devoid of public spirit, and haven't the least lust to improve American literature; if it ever came to what I regard as perfection my job would be gone. What, then, was my motive in writing about Mr. Dreiser so copiously? My motive, well known to Mr. Dreiser himself and to everyone else who knew me as intimately as he did, was simply and solely to sort out and give coherence to the ideas of Mr. Mencken, and to put them into suave and ingratiating terms, and to discharge them with a flourish, and maybe with a phrase of pretty song into the dense fog that blanketed the Republic.

The critic's choice of criticism rather than of what is called creative writing is chiefly a matter of temperament, with accidents of education and environment to help. The feelings that happen to be dominant in him at the moment the scribbling frenzy seizes him are feelings inspired, not directly by life itself, but by books, pictures, music, sculpture, architecture, religion, philosophy—in brief, by some other man's feelings about life. They are thus, in a sense, second-hand, and it is no wonder that creative artists so easily fall into the theory that they are also second-rate. Perhaps they usually are. If, indeed, the critic continues on this plane—if he lacks the intellectual agility and enterprise needed to make the leap from the work of art to the vast and mysterious complex of phenomena behind it—then they *always* are, and he remains no more than a fugleman or policeman to his betters. But if anything resembling a genuine artist is concealed within him—if his feelings are in any sense profound and original, and his capacity for self-expression above the average of educated men—then he moves inevitably from the work of art to life itself, and begins to take on a dignity that he formerly lacked.

It is impossible to think of a man of any actual force and originality, universally recognized as having those qualities, who spent his whole life appraising and describing the work of other men. Did Goethe, or Carlyle, or Matthew Arnold, or Sainte-Beuve, or Macaulay, or even, to come down a few pegs, Lewes, or Lowell, or Hazlitt? Certainly not. The thing that becomes most obvious about the writings of all such men, once they are examined carefully, is that the critic is always being swallowed up by the creative artist—that what starts out as the review of a book, or a play, or other work of art, usually develops very quickly into an independent essay upon the theme of that work of art, or upon some theme that it suggests —in a word, that it becomes a fresh work of art, and only indirectly related to the one that suggested it. This fact, indeed, is so plain that it scarcely needs statement. What the pedagogues always object to in, for example, the *Quarterly* reviewers is that they forgot the books they were supposed to review, and wrote long papers—often, in fact, small books—expounding ideas suggested (or not suggested) by the books under review. But every critic who is worth reading falls inevitably into the same habit. He cannot stick to his ostensible task: what is before him is always infinitely less interesting to him than what is within him. If he is genuinely first-rate—if what is within him stands the test of type, and wins an audience, and produces the reactions that every artist craves—then he usually ends by abandoning the criticism of specific works of art altogether, and setting up shop as a merchant in general ideas, i.e., as an artist working in the materials of life itself.

Mere reviewing, however conscientiously and competently it is done, is plainly a much inferior business. Like writing poetry, it is chiefly a function of intellectual immaturity. The young literatus just out of the university, having as yet no capacity for grappling with the fundamental mysteries of existence, is put to writing reviews of books, or plays, or music, or painting. Very often he does it pretty well; it is, in fact, not hard to do well, for even decayed pedagogues often do it. But if he continues to do it, whether well or ill, it is a sign to all the world that his growth ceased when they made him *artium baccalaureus*. Gradually he becomes, whether in or out of the academic grove, a professor, which is to say, a man devoted to diluting and retailing the ideas of his superiors—not an artist, not even a bad artist, but almost the antithesis of an artist. He is learned, he is sober, he is painstaking and accurate—but he is as hollow as a jug. Nothing is in him save the ghostly echoes of other men's thoughts and feelings. If he were a genuine artist he would have thoughts and feelings of his own, and the impulse to give them objective form would be irresistible. An artist can no more withstand that impulse than a politician can withstand the temptations of a job. There are no mute, inglorious Miltons, save in the hallucinations of poets. The one sound test of a Milton is that he functions as a Milton. His difference from other men lies precisely in the superior vigor of his impulse to self-expression, not in the superior beauty and loftiness of his ideas. Other men, in point of fact, often have the same ideas, or perhaps even loftier ones, but they are able to suppress them, usually on grounds of decorum, and so they escape being artists, and are respected by right-thinking persons, and die with money in the bank, and are forgotten in two weeks.

Obviously, the critic whose performance we are commonly called upon to investigate is a man standing somewhere along the path leading from the beginning that I have described to the goal. He has got beyond being a mere cataloguer and valuer of other men's ideas, but he has not yet become an autonomous artist—he is not yet ready to challenge attention with his own ideas alone. But it is plain that his motion, in so far as he is moving at all, must be in the direction of that autonomy, that is, unless one imagines him sliding backward into senile infantilism—a spectacle not unknown to literary pathology, but too pathetic to be discussed here. Bear this motion in mind, and the true nature of his aims and purposes becomes clear; more, the incurable falsity of the aims and purposes usually credited to him becomes equally clear. He is not actually trying to perform an impossible act of arctic justice upon the artist whose work gives him a text. He is not trying with mathematical passion to find out exactly what was in that artist's mind at the moment of creation, and to display it precisely and in an ecstasy of appreciation. He is not trying to bring the work discussed into accord with some transient theory of esthetics, or ethics, or truth, or to determine its degree of departure from that theory. He is not trying to lift up the fine arts, or to defend democracy against sense, or to promote happiness at the domestic hearth, or to convert sophomores into right-thinkers, or to serve God. He is not trying to fit a group of novel phenomena into the orderly process of history. He is not even trying to discharge the catalytic office that I myself, in a romantic moment, once sought to force upon him. He is, first and last, simply trying to express himself. He is trying to arrest and challenge a sufficient body of readers, to make them pay attention to him, to impress them with the charm and novelty of his ideas, to provoke them into an agreeable (or shocked) awareness of him, and he is trying to achieve thereby for his own inner ego the grateful feeling of a function performed, a tension relieved, a *katharsis* attained which Wagner achieved when he wrote "Die Walküre," and a hen achieves every time she lays an egg.

Joseph Conrad was moved by that necessity to write romances; Mozart was moved to write music; poets are moved to write poetry; critics are moved to write criticism. The form is nothing; the only important thing is the motive power, and it is the same in all cases. It is the pressing yearning of nearly every man who has actual ideas in him to empty them upon the world, to hammer them into plausible and ingratiating shapes, to compel the attention and respect of his equals, to lord it over his inferiors. So seen, the critic becomes a far more transparent and agreeable fellow than ever he was in the discourses of the psychologists who sought to make him a mere appraiser in an intellectual customs house, a gauger in a distillery of the spirit, a just and infallible judge upon the cosmic bench. Such offices, in point of fact, never fit him. He always bulges over their confines. When he is thus labeled and estimated, it inevitably turns out that the critic under examination is a very bad one, or no critic at all.

But when he is thought of, not as pedagogue, but as artist, then he begins to take on reality, and, what is more, dignity. Carlyle was surely no just and infallible judge; on the contrary, he was full of prejudices, biles, naïvetés, humors. Yet he is read, consulted, attended to. Macaulay was unfair, inaccurate, fanciful, lyrical—yet his essays live. Arnold had his faults too, and so did Sainte-Beuve, and so did Goethe, and so did many another of that line—and yet they are remembered today, and all the learned and conscientious critics of their time, laboriously concerned with the precise intent of the artists under review, and passionately determined to set it forth with god-like care and to relate it exactly to this or that great stream of ideas—all these pedants are forgotten. What saved Carlyle, Macaulay and company is as plain as day. They were first-rate artists. They could make the thing charming, and that is always a million times more important than making it true.

Truth, indeed, is something that is believed in completely only by persons who have never tried personally to pursue it to its fastnesses and grab it by the tail. It is the adoration of second-rate men—men who always receive it as second-hand. Pedagogues believe in immutable truths and spend their lives trying to determine them and propagate them; the intellectual progress of man consists largely of a concerted effort to block and destroy their enterprise. Nine times out of ten, in the arts as in life, there is actually no truth to be discovered; there is only error to be exposed. In whole departments of human inquiry it seems to me quite unlikely that the truth ever *will* be discovered. Nevertheless, the rubber-stamp thinking of the world always makes the assumption that the exposure of an error is identical with the discovery of the truth —that error and truth are simply opposites. They are nothing of the sort. What the world turns to, when it has been cured of one error, is usually simply another error, and maybe one worse than the first one. This is the whole history of the intellect in brief. The average man of today does not believe in precisely the same imbecilities that the Greek of the Fourth Century before Christ believed in, but the things that he *does* believe in are often quite as idiotic.

Perhaps this statement is a bit too sweeping. There is, year by year, a gradual accumulation of what may be called, provisionally, truths—there is a slow accretion of ideas that somehow manage to meet all practicable human tests, and so survive. But even so, it is risky to call them absolute truths. All that one may safely say of them is that no one, as yet, has demonstrated that they are errors. Soon or late, if experience teaches us anything, they are likely to succumb too. The profoundest truths of the Middle Ages are now laughed at by schoolboys. The profoundest truths of democracy will be laughed at, a few centuries hence, even by school-teachers.

In the department of esthetics, wherein critics mainly disport themselves, it is almost impossible to think of a so-called truth that shows any sign of being permanently true. The most profound of principles begins to fade and quiver almost as soon as it is stated. But the work of art, as opposed to the theory behind it, has a longer life, particularly if that theory be obscure and questionable, and so cannot be determined accurately. "Hamlet," the Mona Lisa, "Dixie," "Parsifal," "Mother Goose," "Annabel Lee," "Huckleberry Finn"—these things, so baffling to pedagogy, so contumacious to the categories, so mysterious in purpose and utility—these things live. And why? Because there is in them the flavor of salient, novel and attractive personality, because the quality that shines from them is not that of correct demeanor but that of creative passion, because they pulse and breathe and speak, because they are genuine works of art.

So with criticism. Let us forget all the heavy effort to make a science of it; it is a fine art, or nothing. If the critic, retiring to his cell to concoct his treatise upon a book or play or whatnot, produces a piece of writing that shows sound structure, and brilliant color, and the flash of new and persuasive ideas, and civilized manners, and the charm of an uncommon personality in free function, then he has given something to the

world that is worth having, and sufficiently justified his existence. Is Carlyle's "Frederick" true? Who cares? As well ask if
the Parthenon is true, or the C Minor Symphony, or "Wiener
Blut." Let the critic who is an artist leave such necropsies to
professors of esthetics, who can no more determine the truth
than he can, and will infallibly make it unpleasant and a bore.

It is, of course, not easy to practise this abstention. Two
forces, one within and one without, tend to bring even a Hazlitt under the campus pump. One is the almost universal human susceptibility to messianic delusions—the irresistible tendency to practically every man, once he finds a crowd in front
of him, to strut and roll his eyes. The other is the public
demand, born of such long familiarity with conventional criticism that no other kind is readily conceivable, that the critic
teach something as well as say something—in the Rotarian
phrase, that he be constructive. Both operate powerfully
against his free functioning, and especially the former. He
finds it hard to resist the flattery of his customers, however
little he may actually esteem it. If he knows anything at all,
he knows that his following, like that of every other artist in
ideas, is chiefly made up of the congenitally subaltern type of
man and woman—natural converts, lodge joiners, me-toos,
stragglers after parades. It is precious seldom that he ever gets
a positive idea out of them; what he usually gets is mere unintelligent ratification. But this troop, despite its obvious fail-
ings, corrupts him in various ways. For one thing, it enormously re-enforces his belief in his own ideas, and so tends to
make him stiff and dogmatic—in brief, precisely everything
that he ought not to be. And for another thing, it tends to
make him (by a curious contradiction) a bit pliant and poli-
tic: he begins to estimate new ideas, not in proportion as they
are amusing or beautiful, but in proportion as they are likely
to please. So beset, front and rear, he sometimes sinks supinely
to the level of a professor and his subsequent proceedings are
interesting no more.

The true aim of a critic is certainly not to make converts.
He must know that very few of the persons who are susceptible

to conversion are worth converting. Their minds are intrinsically flabby and parasitical, and it is certainly not sound sport to agitate minds of that sort. Moreover, the critic must always harbor a grave doubt about most of the ideas that they lap up so greedily—it must occur to him not infrequently, in the silent watches of the night, that much that he writes is sheer buncombe. As I have said, I can't imagine any idea—that is, in the domain of esthetics—that is palpably and incontrovertibly sound. All that I am familiar with, and in particular all that I announce most vociferously, seem to me to contain a core of quite obvious nonsense. I thus try to avoid cherishing them too lovingly, and it always gives me a shiver to see anyone else gobble them at one gulp. Criticism, at bottom, is indistinguishable from skepticism. Both launch themselves, the one by esthetic presentations and the other by logical presentations, at the common human tendency to accept whatever is approved, to take in ideas ready-made, to be responsive to mere rhetoric and gesticulation. A critic who believes in anything absolutely is bound to that something quite as helplessly as a Christian is bound to the Freudian garbage in the Book of Revelation. To that extent, at all events, he is unfree and unintelligent, and hence a bad critic.

The demand for "constructive" criticism is based upon the ancient assumption that immutable truths exist in the arts, and that the artist will be improved by being made aware of them. This notion, whatever the form it takes, is always absurd—as much so, indeed, as its brother delusion that the critic, to be competent, must be a practitioner of the specific art he ventures to deal with, i.e., that a doctor, to cure a belly-ache, must have a belly-ache. As practically encountered, it is disingenuous as well as absurd, for it comes chiefly from bad artists who tire of serving as performing monkeys, and crave the greater ease and safety of sophomores in class. They demand to be taught in order to avoid being knocked about. In their demand is the theory that instruction, if they could get it, would profit them—that they are capable of doing better work than they do. As a practical matter, I doubt that this is ever true. Bad poets never actually grow any better; they invariably grow worse and worse. In all history there has never been, to my knowledge, a single practitioner of any art who, as a result of "constructive" criticism, improved his work. The curse of all the arts, indeed, is the fact that they are constantly invaded by persons who are not artists at all—persons whose yearning to express their ideas and feelings is unaccompanied by the slightest capacity for charming expression—in brief, persons with absolutely nothing to say.

This is particularly true of the art of letters, which interposes very few technical obstacles to the vanity and garrulity of such invaders. Any effort to teach them to write better is an effort wasted, as every editor discovers for himself; they are as incapable of it as they are of jumping over the moon. The only sort of criticism that can deal with them to any profit is the sort that employs them frankly as laboratory animals. It cannot cure them, but it can at least make an amusing and perhaps edifying show of them. It is idle to argue that the good in them is thus destroyed with the bad. The simple answer is that there *is* no good in them. Suppose Poe had wasted his time trying to dredge good work out of Rufus Dawes, author of "Geraldine." He would have failed miserably—and spoiled a capital essay, still diverting after a century. Suppose Beethoven, dealing with Gottfried Weber, had tried laboriously to make an intelligent music critic of him. How much more apt, useful and durable the simple note: "Arch-ass! Double-barreled ass!" Here was absolutely sound criticism. Here was a judgment wholly beyond challenge. Moreover, here was a small but perfect work of art.

Upon the low practical value of "constructive" criticism I can offer testimony out of my own experience. My books have been commonly reviewed at length, and many critics have devoted themselves to pointing out what they conceive to be my errors, both of fact and of taste. Well, I cannot recall a case in which any suggestion offered by a "constructive" critic has helped me in the slightest, or even actively interested me. Every such wet-nurse of letters has sought fatuously to make

me write in a way differing from that in which the Lord God
Almighty, in His infinite wisdom, impels me to write—that is,
to make me write stuff which, coming from me, would be as
false as an appearance of decency in a Congressman. All the
benefits I have ever got from the critics of my work have come
from the destructive variety. A hearty slating always does me
good, particularly if it be well written. It begins by enlisting
my professional respect; it ends by making me examine my
ideas coldly in the privacy of my chamber. Not, of course, that
I usually revise them, but I at least examine them. If I decide
to hold fast to them, they are all the dearer to me thereafter,
and I expound them with a new passion and plausibility. If,
on the contrary, I discern holes in them, I shelve them in a
pianissimo manner, and set about hatching new ones to take
their place. But "constructive" criticism irritates me. I do not
object to being denounced, but I can't abide being schoolmas-
tered, especially by men I regard as imbeciles.

I find, as a practising critic, that very few men who write
books are even as tolerant as I am—that most of them, soon or
late, show signs of extreme discomfort under criticism, however polite its terms. Perhaps this is why enduring friendships
between authors and critics are so rare. All artists, of course,
dislike one another more or less, but that dislike seldom rises
to implacable enmity, save between opera singer and opera
singer, and creative author and critic. Even when the latter
two keep up an outward show of good-will, there is always
bitter antagonism under the surface. Part of it, I daresay,
arises out of the impossible demands of the critic, particularly
if he be tinged with the constructive madness. Having favored
an author with his good opinion, he expects the poor fellow
to live up to that good opinion without the slightest compromise or faltering, and this is commonly beyond human power.
He feels that any letdown compromises *him*—that his hero is
stabbing him in the back, and making him ridiculous—and
this feeling rasps his vanity. The most bitter of all literary
quarrels are those between critics and creative artists, and
most of them arise in just this way. As for the creative artist,

he on his part naturally resents the critic's air of pedagogical superiority and he resents it especially when he has an uneasy feeling that he has fallen short of his best work, and that the discontent of the critic is thus justified. Injustice is relatively easy to bear; what stings is justice.

Under it all, of course, lurks the fact that I began with: the fact that the critic is himself an artist, and that his creative impulse, soon or late, is bound to make him neglect the punctilio. When he sits down to compose his criticism, his artist ceases to be a friend and becomes mere raw material for his work of art. It is my experience that artists invariably resent this cavalier use of them. They are pleased so long as the critic confines himself to the modest business of interpreting them—preferably in terms of their own estimate of themselves—but the moment he proceeds to adorn their theme with variations of his own, the moment he brings new ideas to the enterprise and begins contrasting them with their ideas, that moment they grow restive. It is precisely at this point, of course, that criticism becomes genuine criticism; before that it was mere reviewing. When a critic passes it he loses his friends. By becoming an artist, he becomes the foe of all other artists.

But the transformation, I believe, has good effects upon him: it makes him a better critic. Too much *Gemütlichkeit* is as fatal to criticism as it would be to surgery or politics. When it rages unimpeded it leads inevitably either to a dull professorial sticking on of meaningless labels or to log-rolling, and often it leads to both. One of the most hopeful signs in the Republic is the revival of acrimony in criticism—the renaissance of the doctrine that esthetic matters are important, and that it is worth the while of a healthy male to take them seriously, as he takes business, sport and amour. In the days when American literature was showing its first vigorous growth, the native criticism was extraordinarily violent and even vicious; in the days when American literature swooned upon the tomb of the Puritan *Kultur* it became flaccid and childish. The typical critic of the first era was Poe, as the typical critic of the second was Howells. Poe carried on his criti-

cal jehads with such ferocity that he sometimes got into law-
suits, and now and again ran no little risk of having his head
cracked. He regarded literary questions as exigent and momen-
tous. The lofty aloofness of the don was simply not in him.
When he encountered a book that seemed to him to be bad,
he attacked it almost as sharply as an archbishop would attack
Jesus. His opponents replied in the same Berserker manner.
Much of Poe's surviving ill-fame, as a drunkard and dead-beat,
is due to their inordinate denunciations of him. They were
not content to refute him; they constantly tried to dispose of
him altogether. The very ferocity of that ancient row shows
that the native literature, in those days, was in a healthy state.
Books of genuine value were produced.

Literature always thrives best, in fact, in an atmosphere of
hearty strife. Poe, surrounded by admiring professors, never
challenged, never aroused to the emotions of revolt, would
probably have written poetry indistinguishable from the hollow stuff of, say, George E. Woodberry. It took the persistent
(and often grossly unfair and dishonorable) opposition of Gris-
wold *et al.* to stimulate him to his highest endeavors. He
needed friends, true enough, but he also needed enemies.

IRVING BABBITT

Irving Babbitt (1865-1933) was born in Dayton, Ohio, and was educated at Harvard and at the Sorbonne. He was a professor of Romance languages at Williams (1893-94) before joining the faculty at Harvard, where, from 1912 until his death, he was a professor of French literature. His early publications included editions of certain writings of Taine, Renan, Voltaire, and Racine; but his scholarly and critical achievements are primarily represented in six volumes of essays which he published from 1908 to 1932. These essays define his philosophy of humanism, and measure both literature and education by its principles.

Babbitt believed that the uniqueness of human experience lay in its compassing both natural and supernatural phenomena; that the knowledge of this experience was moral knowledge; and that the function of literature was to convey moral knowledge. The validity of any writing, he insisted, lay largely in its sense of proportion. An emphasis on the merely natural or on the merely supernatural could produce only an eccentric individualism. These convictions resulted, for instance, in Babbitt's indictment of romanticism, of the faith in scientific knowledge, and of humanitarianism. Babbitt was impressed by the responsibility of any imaginative writing. Only that literature, he argued, which embodied both a moral and a historical awareness could convey the sense of permanence which makes experience meaningful. In all these essays, Babbitt was insistently partisan; yet, curiously, the singular quality of his polemical writing is the clarity with which it presents the subject at issue and defines both poles of an argument—Babbitt's own and his opponents'.

Many of Babbitt's lectures and essays remain uncollected. A seventh volume of essays, *Spanish Character and Other Essays,* posthumously published (1940), contains an "Index to the Collected Works of Irving Babbitt."

Babbitt's indictment of Mencken, in "The Critic and American Life," he published in his volume, *On Being Creative, and Other Essays* (1932), from which this text is taken.

The essay first appeared in *Forum,* February 1928; and symptoms of the controversies in which the New Humanism was continually involved are found in a response to Babbitt's article: H. M. Jones, "Professor Babbitt Cross-Examined," *New Republic,* March 21, 1928; and in a response to Jones: A. R. Thompson, "In Defense of Professor Babbitt," *New Republic,* June 27, 1928.

THE CRITIC AND AMERICAN LIFE

A FREQUENT remark of the French about Americans is: "They're children"; which, interpreted, means that from the French point of view Americans are childishly uncritical. The remark is relevant only in so far as it refers to general critical intelligence. In dealing with the special problems of a commercial and industrial society, Americans have shown that they can be abundantly critical. Certain Americans, for example, have developed a critical keenness in estimating the value of stocks and bonds that is nothing short of uncanny. The very persons, however, who are thus keen in some particular field, are, when confronted with questions that call for general critical intelligence, often puerile. Yet in an age like the present, which is being subjected to a constant stream of propaganda in everything from the choice of its religion to its cigarettes, general critical intelligence would seem desirable.

As a matter of fact, most persons nowadays aspire to be not critical but creative. We have not merely creative poets and novelists, but creative readers and listeners and dancers. Lately a form of creativeness has appeared that may in time swallow up all the others—creative salesmanship. The critic himself has caught the contagion and also aspires to be creative. He is supposed to become so when he receives from the creation of another, conceived as pure temperamental overflow, so vivid an impression that, when passed through his temperament, it issues forth as a fresh creation. What is eliminated in both critic and creator is any standard that is set above temperament and that therefore might interfere with their eagerness to get themselves expressed.

This notion of criticism as self-expression is important for our present subject, for it has been adopted by the writer who is, according to the *Encyclopedia Britannica* "the greatest critical force in America"—Mr. H. L. Mencken. Creative self-expression, as practiced by himself and others, has, according to Mr. Mencken, led to a salutary stirring up of the stagnant pool of American letters: "Today for the first time in years there is strife in American criticism. . . . Heretics lay on boldly and the professors are forced to make some defence. Often going further they attempt counter-attacks. Ears are bitten off, noses are bloodied. There are wallops both above and below the belt."

But it may be that criticism is something more than Mr. Mencken would have us believe, more in short than a squabble between Bohemians, each eager to capture the attention of the public for his brand of self-expression. To reduce criticism indeed to the satisfaction of a temperamental urge, to the uttering of one's gustos and disgustos (in Mr. Mencken's case chiefly the latter) is to run counter to the very etymology of the word which implies discrimination and judgment. The best one would anticipate from a writer like Mr. Mencken, possessing an unusual verbal virtuosity and at the same time temperamentally irresponsible, is superior intellectual vaudeville. One must grant him, however, certain genuine critical virtues—for example, a power of shrewd observation within rather narrow limits. Yet the total effect of his writing is nearer to intellectual vaudeville than to serious criticism.

The serious critic is more concerned with achieving a correct scale of values and so seeing things proportionately than with self-expression. His essential virtue is poise. The specific benefit he confers is to act as a moderating influence on the opposite insanities between which mankind in the lump is constantly tending to oscillate—oscillations that Luther compares to the reelings of a drunken peasant on horseback. The critic's survey of any particular situation may very well seem satirical.

The complaint that Mr. Mencken is too uniformly disgruntled in his survey of the American situation rather misses the point. Behind the pleas for more constructiveness it is usually easy to detect the voice of the booster. A critic who did not get beyond a correct diagnosis of existing evils might be very helpful. If Mr. Mencken has fallen short of being such a diagnostician, the failure is due not to his excess of severity but to his lack of discrimination.

The standards with reference to which men have discriminated in the past have been largely traditional. The outstanding fact of the present period, on the other hand, has been the weakening of traditional standards. An emergency has arisen not unlike that with which Socrates sought to cope in ancient Athens. Anyone who is untraditional and seeks at the same time to be discriminating must almost necessarily own Socrates as his master. As is well known, Socrates sought above all to be discriminating in his use of general terms. Before allowing one's imagination and finally one's conduct to be controlled by a general term, it would seem wise to submit it to a Socratic scrutiny.

It is, therefore, unfortunate that at a time like the present, which plainly calls for a Socrates, we should instead have got a Mencken. One may take as an example of Mr. Mencken's failure to discriminate adequately, his attitude towards the term that for several generations past has been governing the imagination of multitudes—democracy. His view of democracy is simply that of Rousseau turned upside down, and nothing, as has been remarked, resembles a hollow so much as a swelling. A distinction of which he has failed to recognize the importance is that between a direct or unlimited and a constitutional democracy. In the latter we probably have the best thing in the world. The former, on the other hand, as all thinkers of any penetration from Plato and Aristotle down have perceived, leads to the loss of liberty and finally to the rise of some form of despotism. The two conceptions of democracy involve not merely incompatible views of government but ultimately of human nature. The desire of the constitutional democrat for institutions that act as checks on the immediate will of the people implies a similar dualism in the individual —a higher self that acts restrictively on his ordinary and impulsive self. The partisan of unlimited democracy on the other hand is an idealist in the sense the term assumed in connection with the so-called romantic movement. His faith in the people is closely related to the doctrine of natural goodness proclaimed by the sentimentalists of the eighteenth century and itself marking an extreme recoil from the dogma of total depravity. The doctrine of natural goodness favors the free temperamental expansion that I have already noticed in speaking of the creative critic.

It is of the utmost importance, however, if one is to understand Mr. Mencken, to discriminate between two types of temperamentalist—the soft and sentimental type, who cherishes various "ideals," and the hard, or Nietzschean type, who piques himself on being realistic. As a matter of fact, if one sees in the escape from traditional controls merely an opportunity to live temperamentally, it would seem advantageous to pass promptly from the idealistic to the Nietzschean phase, sparing oneself as many as possible of the intermediary disillusions. It is at all events undeniable that the rise of Menckenism has been marked by a certain collapse of romantic idealism in the political field and elsewhere. The numerous disillusions that have supervened upon the War have provided a favoring atmosphere.

The symptoms of Menckenism are familiar: a certain hardness and smartness and disposition to rail at everything that, rightly or wrongly, is established and respected; a tendency to identify the real with what Mr. Mencken terms "the cold and clammy facts" and to assume that the only alternative to facing these facts is to fade away into sheer romantic unreality. These and similar traits are becoming so widely diffused that, whatever one's opinion of Mr. Mencken as a writer and thinker, one must grant him representativeness. He is a chief prophet at present of those who deem themselves emancipated but who are, according to Mr. Brownell, merely unbuttoned.

The crucial point in any case is one's attitude towards the principle of control. Those who stand for this principle in any form or degree are dismissed by the emancipated as reactionaries or, still graver reproach, as Puritans. Mr. Mencken would have us believe that the historical Puritan was not even sincere in his moral rigorism, but was given to "lamentable transactions with loose women and fiery jugs." This may serve as a sample of the assertions, picturesquely indiscriminate, by which a writer wins immediate notoriety at the expense of his permanent reputation. The facts about the Puritan happen to be complex and need to be dealt with very Socratically. It has been affirmed that the point of view of the Puritan was stoical rather than truly Christian, and the affirmation is not wholly false. The present discussion of the relationship between Puritanism and the rise of capitalism with its glorification of the acquisitive life also has its justification. It is likewise a fact that the Puritan was from the outset unduly concerned with reforming others as well as himself, and this trait relates him to the humanitarian meddler or "wowser" of the present day, who is Mr. Mencken's pet aversion.

Yet it remains true that awe and reverence and humility are Christian virtues and that there was some survival of these virtues in the Puritan. For a representative Puritan like Jonathan Edwards they were inseparable from the illumination of grace, from what he terms "a divine and supernatural light." In the passage from the love and fear of God of an Edwards to the love and service of man professed by the humanitarian, something has plainly dropped out, something that is very near the center. What has tended to disappear is the inner life with the special type of control it imposes. With the decline of this inner control there has been an increasing resort to outer control. Instead of the genuine Puritan we then have the humanitarian legalist who passes innumerable laws for the control of people who refuse to control themselves. The activity of our uplifters is scarcely suggestive of any "divine and supernatural light." Here is a discrimination of the first importance that has been obscured by the muddy thinking of our half-baked intelligentsia. One is thus kept from perceiving the real problem, which is to retain the inner life, even though one refuse to accept the theological nightmare with which the Puritan associated it. More is involved in the failure to solve this problem than the Puritan tradition. It is the failure of our contemporary life in general. Yet, unless some solution is reached by a full and free exercise of the critical spirit, one remains a mere modernist and not a thoroughgoing and complete modern; for the modern spirit and the critical spirit are in their essence one.

What happens, when one sets out to deal with questions of this order without sufficient depth of reflection and critical maturity, may be seen in Mr. Sinclair Lewis's *Elmer Gantry*. He has been lured from art into the writing of a wild diatribe which, considered even as such, is largely beside the mark. If the Protestant Church is at present threatened with bankruptcy, it is not because it has produced an occasional Elmer Gantry. The true reproach it has incurred is that, in its drift toward modernism, it has lost its grip not merely on certain dogmas but, simultaneously, on the facts of human nature. It has failed above all to carry over in some modern and critical form the truth of a dogma that unfortunately receives much support from these facts—the dogma of original sin. At first sight Mr. Mencken would appear to have a conviction of evil—when, for example, he reduces democracy in its essential aspect to a "combat between jackals and jackasses"—that establishes at least one bond between him and the austere Christian.

The appearance, however, is deceptive. The Christian is conscious above all of the "old Adam" in himself: hence his humility. The effect of Mr. Mencken's writing, on the other hand, is to produce pride rather than humility, a pride ultimately based on flattery. The reader, especially the young and callow reader, identifies himself imaginatively with Mr. Mencken and conceives of himself as a sort of morose and sardonic divinity surveying from some superior altitude an immeasurable expanse of "boobs." This attitude will not seem especially novel to anyone who has traced the modern movement. One is reminded in particular of Flaubert, who showed a diligence in collecting bourgeois imbecilities comparable to that displayed by Mr. Mencken in his *Americana*. Flaubert's discovery that one does not add to one's happiness in this way would no doubt be dismissed by Mr. Mencken as irrelevant, for he has told us that he does not believe in happiness. Another discovery of Flaubert's may seem to him more worthy of consideration. "By dint of railing at idiots," Flaubert reports, "one runs the risk of becoming idiotic oneself."

It may be that the only way to escape from the unduly complacent cynicism of Mr. Mencken and his school is to reaffirm once more the truths of the inner life. In that case it would seem desirable to disengage, so far as possible, the principle of control on which the inner life finally depends from mere creeds and traditions and assert it as a psychological fact; a fact, moreover, that is neither "cold" nor "clammy." The coldness and clamminess of much so-called realism arises from its failure to give this fact due recognition. A chief task, indeed, of the Socratic critic would be to rescue the noble term "realist" from its present degradation. A view of reality that overlooks the element in man that moves in an opposite direction from mere temperament, the specifically human factor in short, may prove to be singularly one-sided. Is the Puritan, John Milton, when he declares that "he who reigns within himself and rules passions, desires, and fears is more than a king," less real than Mr. Theodore Dreiser when he discourses in his peculiar dialect of "those rearranging chemisms upon which all the morality or immorality of the world is based"?

As a matter of fact, according to the degree and nature of the exercise of the principle of control, one may distinguish two main types of realism which may be denominated respectively religious and humanistic: as the principle of control falls into abeyance, a third type tends to emerge, which may be termed naturalistic realism. That the decline of the traditional controls has been followed by a lapse to the naturalistic level is indubitable. The characteristic evils of the present age arise from unrestraint and violation of the law of measure and not, as our modernists would have us believe, from the tyranny of taboos and traditional inhibitions. The facts cry to heaven. The delicate adjustment that is required between the craving for emancipation and the need of control has been pointed out once for all by Goethe, speaking not as a Puritan but as a clear-eyed man of the world. Everything, he says, that liberates the spirit without a corresponding growth in self-mastery is pernicious. This one sentence would seem to cover the case of our "flaming youth" rather completely.

The movement in the midst of which we are still living was from its inception unsound in its dealing with the principle of control. It is vain to expect from the dregs of this movement what its "first sprightly running failed to give." Mr. Carl Sandburg speaks of the "marvelous rebellion of man at all signs reading 'Keep off.' " An objection to this purely insurrectional attitude is that, as a result of its endless iteration during the past century and more, it has come to savor too strongly of what has been called "the humdrum of revolt." A more serious objection to the attitude is that it encourages an unrestricted and merely temperamental liberty which, paradoxically enough at first sight, affords the modern man no avenue of escape from the web that is being woven about him by the scientific determinist.

Realists of the current type are in point of fact intimately allied with the psychologist—glandular, behavioristic, and psycho-analytical—who, whatever their divergencies among themselves, unite in their deterministic trend and therefore clash fundamentally with both religious and humanistic realists. The proper method of procedure in defending the freedom of the will would seem to be to insist upon it as a fact of experience, a fact so primary that the position of the determinist involves an evasion of one of the immediate data of consciousness in favor of a metaphysical dream. What is genuinely experimental in naturalistic psychology should of course be received with respect; but the facts of which it takes account in its experiments are unimportant compared with the facts it either neglects or denies. Practically it is running into grotesque extremes of pseudo-science that make of it a shining mark for the Socratic critic.

Here at all events is the issue on which all other issues finally hinge; for until the question of moral freedom—the question whether man is a responsible agent or only the plaything of his impulses and impressions—is decided, nothing is decided; and to decide the question under existing circumstances calls for the keenest critical discrimination. Creation that is not sufficiently supported by such discrimination is likely to prove premature.

One may illustrate from Mr. Dreiser's *American Tragedy,* hailed in certain quarters as the "Mount Everest" of recent fiction. He has succeeded in producing in this work something genuinely harrowing; but one is harrowed to no purpose. One has in more than full measure the tragic qualm but without the final relief and enlargement of spirit that true tragedy succeeds somehow in giving, and that without resort to explicit moralizing. It is hardly worth while to struggle through eight hundred and more very pedestrian pages to be left at the end with a feeling of sheer oppression. The explanation of this oppression is that Mr. Dreiser does not rise sufficiently above the level of "rearranging chemisms," in other words, of animal behavior. Tragedy may admit fate—Greek tragedy admits it—but not of the naturalistic variety. Confusion on this point may compromise in the long run the reputation of writers more eminent than Mr. Dreiser—for example, of Thomas Hardy. Fatalism of the naturalistic type is responsible in large measure for the atmosphere of futility and frustration that hangs heavily over so much contemporary writing. One finally comes to feel with a recent poet that "dust" is the common source from which

stream
The cricket's cry and Dante's dream.

Anyone who admits reality only in what derives from the dust, whether in a cricket or a Dante, must, from the point of view of the religious or the humanistic realist, be prepared to make substantial sacrifices. In the first place, he must sacrifice the depth and subtlety that arise from the recognition in some form of the duality of man's nature. For the interest that may arise from the portrayal of the conflict between a law of the spirit and a law of the members, the inordinate interest in sex for its own sake promoted by most of the so-called realists is a rather shabby substitute. A merely naturalistic realism also involves the sacrifice of beauty in almost any sense of that elusive term. Closely related to this sacrifice is the sacrifice of delicacy, elevation, and distinction. The very word realism has come to connote the opposite of these qualities. When we learn, for example, that someone has written a realistic study of a great man, we are sure in advance that he has devoted his main effort to proving that "Plutarch lied." The more the great man is reduced to the level of commonplace or worse, the more we feel he has been "humanized."

Mr. Sherwood Anderson has argued ingeniously that, inasmuch as we ourselves are crude, our literature, if it is not to be unreal and factitious, should be crude likewise. But the writer who hopes to achieve work of importance cannot afford to be too deeply immersed in the atmosphere of the special place and passing moment. Still less can he afford to make us feel, as writers like Mr. Anderson and Mr. Dreiser and Mr. Sinclair Lewis do, that, if there were any lack of vulgarity in what they are depicting, they would be capable of supplying the defect from their own abundance. More is involved here than mere loss of distinction. We have come, indeed, to the supreme sacrifice that every writer must make who does not transcend a naturalistic realism. He must forego the hope of the enduring appeal—the hope that every writer worthy of his salt cherishes in some degree. In the absence of humanistic or religious standards, he is prone to confound the real with the welter of the actual, and so to miss the "grandeur of generality."

Certain books in the current mode are so taken up with the evanescent surfaces of life that they will survive, if at all, not as literature but as sociological documents. The very language in which they are written will, in a generation or two, require a glossary. So far from imposing an orderly pattern on the raw material of experience, they rather emphasize the lack of pattern. The resulting effect, to borrow a phrase from the late Stephen Crane, who has had a marked influence on the recent movement, is that of a "cluttered incoherency." As an extreme example of the tendency one may cite *Manhattan Transfer* by John Dos Passos. In the name of reality, Mr. Dos Passos has perpetrated a literary nightmare. Such a work would seem to have slight value even as a sociological document; unless, indeed, one is prepared to admit that contemporary Manhattan is inhabited chiefly by epileptic Bohemians.

"It is as much a trade," says La Bruyère, "to make a book as it is to make a clock"; in short, literature is largely a matter of technique. The technique of *Manhattan Transfer* is as dubious as its underlying philosophy. Neither can be justified save on the assumption that the aim of art is to exaggerate the clutter and incoherency of the mundane spectacle instead of eliciting its deeper meaning. Technique counts for even more in poetry than in prose. It would be possible to base on technical grounds alone a valid protest against the present preposterous overestimate of Walt Whitman. Fundamental questions need, in these very untraditional days, to be critically elucidated with a view to right definition if the poet is not to lack technique or still worse, if he is not, like certain recent practitioners of free verse, to be hagridden by a false technique. It evidently concerns both the form and substance of poetry, whether one define it with Aristotle as the portrayal of representative human action, or whether one define it with Mr. Carl Sandburg as a "mystic, sensuous mathematics of fire, smokestacks, waffles, pansies, people, and purple sunsets."

There is no doubt much in the America of today that suggests a jazzy impressionism. Still our naturalistic deliquescence has probably not gone so far as one might infer from poetry like that of Mr. Sandburg or fiction like that of Mr. Dos Passos. The public response to some of the realistic novels has been considerable: allowance must be made however for the *succès de scandale,* also for the skill attained by the modern publisher

in the art of merchandizing. The reputation of certain books
one might mention may be regarded as a triumph of "creative" advertising. What has been created is a mirage of masterpieces where no masterpieces are. It is well also to remember
in regard to some of the works that have been most discussed
that, so far from being an authentic reflection of the American scene, they are rather a belated echo of certain European
movements. For it is as certain that in our literary and artistic
modes we follow Europe—usually at an interval of from five to
forty years—as it is that we lead Europe in our bathtubs and
sanitary plumbing. Anyone who resided in Paris in the nine-
ties and later in America, will, as I can testify from personal
experience, have the sense of having lived through the same
literary fads twice. Mr. Dreiser reminds one of Zola and his
school. The technique of Mr. Dos Passos recalls that of the
Goncourts. Our experimenters in free verse have followed in
the wake not merely of Walt Whitman but of the French sym-
bolists, and so on.

We shall presently begin to hear of certain new developments in French literature and critical thought that point,
though indecisively as yet, to a radical departure from what
has been the main current since the eighteenth century and
in some respects since the Renaissance. It is well that we
should become familiar with the writers who reveal in different ways this latest trend—notably with Maritain, Maurras,
Lasserre, Seillière, and Benda; for they give evidence of a quality of cerebration that is rare in our own literati. At the same
time we should not adopt with our usual docility the total out-
look of any of these writers: for no one of them has worked
out a point of view exactly adapted to our requirements. In
general, it is not fitting that a great nation at the very height
of its power should go on indefinitely trailing after Europe.
It is time for us to initiate something of our own. This does
not mean that we should proceed forthwith to inbreed our
own "originality." It means almost the exact opposite. The
most original thing one could do nowadays would be to question the whole theory of originality as mere temperamental

overflow and self-expression that has prevailed from the "geniuses" of the eighteenth century down to one of our youthful
and very minor bards who aspires to "spill his bright illimita-
ble soul."

A genuinely critical survey would make manifest that the
unsatisfactoriness of our creative effort is due to a lack of the
standards that culture alone can supply. Our cultural crudity
and insignificance can be traced in turn to the inadequacy of
our education, especially our higher education. Mr. Mencken's
attack on the "professors" is therefore largely justified; for if
the professors were performing their function properly Mr.
Mencken himself would not be possible. One must add in
common justice that the professors themselves, or at least some
of them, are becoming aware that all is not well with existing
conditions. One could not ask anything more perspicacious
than the following paragraph from a recent report of Com-
mittee G to the American Association of University Professors:

> American education has suffered from the domination,
> conscious or unconscious, direct or indirect, of political and
> sentimental, as well as educational, theories that are demon-
> strably false. If the views of some men are to prevail the in-
> tellectual life of the country is doomed; everybody except
> the sheer idiot is to go to college and pursue chiefly sociol-
> ogy, nature study, child study, and community service—and
> we shall have a society unique only in its mediocrity, ignor-
> ance and vulgarity. It will not do to dismiss lightly even so
> extreme a view as this; it is too indicative. Such influences
> are very strong, their pressure is constant; and if education
> has largely failed in America it has been due primarily to
> them.

In short, as a result of the encroachments of an equalitarian
democracy, the standards of our higher education have suffered in two distinct particulars: first, as regards the quality of
students; second, as regards the quality of the studies these students pursue. The first of these evils is generally recognized.
There is even some prospect of remedial measures. Certain institutions, Harvard, for example, without being as yet severely
selective, are becoming more critical of the incompetent stu-

dent. On the other hand, there seems to be less hope than ever of any righting of the second and more serious evil—the failure to distinguish qualitatively between studies. The main drift is still towards what one may term the blanket degree. (Dartmouth for example, has just merged its bachelor of arts and bachelor of science.) Yet rather than blur certain distinctions it would have been better, one might suppose, to use up all the letters of the alphabet devising new degrees to meet the real or supposed educational needs of the modern man. To bestow the A.B. degree indiscriminately on a student for whom education has meant primarily a specialization in chemistry and on one for whom it has meant primarily an assimilation of the masterpieces of Greek literature is to empty it of any effective meaning. At the present rate, indeed, the time may come when the A.B. will not throw much more light on the cultural quality of its recipient than it would, if, as has been suggested, it were bestowed on every American child at birth.

It goes without saying that those who have been lowering and confusing educational standards have been profuse in their professions of "service." A critical examination, not merely of American education but of American life at the present time will almost necessarily hinge on this term. The attitude of the Socratic critic towards it is not to be confounded with that of Mr. Mencken and the "hard-boiled" contingent. "When a gang of real estate agents," says Mr. Mencken, "bond salesmen, and automobile dealers gets together to sob for Service, it takes no Freudian to surmise that someone is about to be swindled." But if one entertain doubts about this current American gospel, why waste one's ammunition on any such small fry? Other and more exalted personages than the members of the Rotary Club at Zenith have, in Mr. Sinclair Lewis's elegant phrase, been "yipping for Service." If one is to deal with this idea of service Socratically, one needs to consider it in its relation to the two figures who have rightly been taken to be the most representative in our cultural background—Benjamin Franklin and Jonathan Edwards. Franklin's idea of service is already humanitarian. Edwards' idea is still traditionally Christian—service not of man but of God. What Franklin stood for is flourishing prodigiously at the present moment, so much so that he may perhaps be defined in his chief line of influence as the great superrotarian. What Edwards stood for is, on the other hand, largely obsolete or survives only in the form of habits, which, lacking doctrinal support, are steadily declining along with the whole Puritan culture.

Intermediary types are possible. One may in one's character reflect the Puritan background and at the same time in one's idea of service derive rather from Franklin. Precisely that combination is found in the most influential of our recent educational leaders—the late President Eliot. A legitimate admiration for his personal qualities should not interfere with the keenest critical scrutiny of his views about education, for the two things stand in no necessary connection. Practically this means to scrutinize the humanitarian idealism that he probably did more than any other man of his generation to promote. In this respect most of the heads of our institutions of learning have been and still are understudies of President Eliot.

In an address on the occasion of his ninetieth birthday President Eliot warned his hearers against introspection, lest it divert them from a wholehearted devotion to service. Between this attitude and a religious or humanistic attitude there is a clash of first principles. Both humanism and religion require introspection as a prerequisite of the inner life and its appropriate activity. With the disappearance of this activity what is left is the outer activity of the utilitarian, and this leads straight to the one-sided cult of material efficiency and finally to the standardization that is, according to nearly all foreign critics and many of our own, a chief American danger. We cannot return to the introspection of the Puritan. We shudder at the theology an Edwards would impose as the condition of his "divine and supernatural light." Yet it does not follow, as I have already suggested, that we should reject the inner life itself along with this theology. One may recognize innumer-

able incidental advantages in the gospel of service and yet
harbor an uneasy suspicion withal that in the passage from
the older religion to the modern humanitarian dispensation
something vital has disappeared, something for which neither
the outer working of the utilitarian nor again the expansive
sympathy of the sentimentalist can offer an equivalent.

The problem of the inner life is very much bound up with
two other problems that are now pressing for solution in our
higher education, and have as yet found none: the problem of
the specialist and the problem of leisure. The man of leisure is
engaged in an inner and specifically human form of activity, a
form that is, according to Aristotle, needful if he is to compass the end of ends—his own happiness. The question is
whether one should consent like the specialist to forego this
activity and to live partially and as a mere instrument for the
attainment of some outer end—even though this end be the
progress of humanity. We are beginning to hear a great deal
nowadays about the "menace" of leisure. It has been estimated
that with the perfecting of mechanical devices the man of the
future will be able to satisfy his material wants by working
not more than four hours a day. It is vain to anticipate that
the rank and file will use this release from outer activity intel-
ligently unless the leaders, notably those in high academic station, show the way. The notion of true leisure is the ultimate
source of the standards of any education that deserves to be
called liberal. When even a few of our college and university
presidents show that they are thinking to some purpose on the
nature of leisure it will be time enough to talk of "America's
coming of age."

As it is, our institutions of learning seem to be becoming
more and more hotbeds of "idealism." Their failure, on the
whole, to achieve standards as something quite distinct from
ideals, on the one hand, and standardization, on the other,
may prove a fact of sinister import for the future of American
civilization. The warfare that is being waged at the present
time by Mr. Sinclair Lewis and others against a standardized
Philistinism continues in the main the protest that has been

made for several generations past by the temperamentalists, hard or soft, against the mechanizing of life by the utilitarian. This protest has been, and is likely to continue to be, ineffectual. The fruitful opposite of the standardized Philistine is not the Bohemian, nor again the hard temperamentalist or superman, as Mr. Mencken conceives him, but the man of leisure. Leisure involves an inner effort with reference to standards that is opposed to the sheer expansion of temperament, as it is to every other form of sheer expansion.

Perhaps a reason why the standards of the humanist are less popular in this country than the ideals of the humanitarian is that these standards set bounds to the acquisitive life; whereas it seems possible to combine a perfect idealism with an orgy of unrestricted commercialism. It is well for us to try to realize how we appear to others in this matter. Our growing unpopularity abroad is due no doubt in part to envy of our material success, but it also arises from the proneness of the rest of the world to judge us, not by the way we feel about ourselves, but by our actual performance. If we are in our own eyes a nation of idealists, we are, according to a recent French critic, M. André Siegfried, a "nation of Pharisees." The European, M. Siegfried would have us believe, still has a concern for the higher values of civilization, whereas the American is prepared to sacrifice these values ruthlessly to mass production and material efficiency.

It is easy to detect under this assumption the latest form of a "certain condescension in foreigners." The breakdown of cultural standards is European as well as American. It is not clear that M. Siegfried himself has an adequate notion of the form of effort that can alone serve as a counterpoise to the one-sided activity of the utilitarian. At the same time his anatomy of our favorite ideal of service is not without interest. This ideal opposes no effective barrier to our expansiveness. An unchecked expansiveness on the national scale is always imperialistic. Among the ingredients of a possible American imperialism M. Siegfried enumerates the American's "great self-satisfaction, his rather brutal sense of his own interests, and *the consciousness, still more dangerous, of his 'duties'* toward humanity." M. Sieg-fried admits however that our imperialism is likely to be of a new and subtle essence, not concerned primarily with terri-torial aggrandizement.

A proper discussion of Mr. Siegfried's position as well as of other issues I have been raising would transcend the limits of an essay. My end has been accomplished if I have justified in some measure the statement with which I started as to the im-portance of cultivating a general critical intelligence. James Russell Lowell's dictum that before having an American lit-erature we must have an American criticism was never truer than it is today. The obvious reply to those who call for more creation and less criticism is that one needs to be critical above all in examining what now passes for creation. A scrutiny of this kind would, I have tried to show, extend beyond the bounds of literature to various aspects of our national life and would converge finally on our higher education.

We cannot afford to accept as a substitute for this true criti-cism the self-expression of Mr. Mencken and his school, unless indeed we are to merit the comment that is, I am told, made on us by South Americans: "They are not a very serious people!" To be sure, the reader may reflect that I am myself a critic, or would-be critic. I can only express the hope that, in my magnifying of the critical function, I do not offer too close a parallel to the dancing-master in Molière who averred, it will be remembered, that "all the mistakes of men, the fatal reverses that fill the world's annals, the shortcomings of states-men, and the blunders of great captains arise from not know-ing how to dance."

JOHN CROWE RANSOM

John Crowe Ransom (1888-   ) was born in Pulaski, Tennessee. Graduated from Vanderbilt University in 1909, he was a Rhodes Scholar at Oxford (1910-13), where he studied classics and mathematics. For two years, during World War I, he served in the United States army. He joined the faculty of Vanderbilt in 1914 and from 1927 to 1937 was a professor of English. Since 1937 he has been Carnegie Professor of Poetry at Kenyon College.

Ransom is one of a group of southern writers who have made their contemporaries aware of regionalism. He was a founder and editor of the *Fugitive* (1922-25), a magazine of verse; he founded (1938), and has since edited, the *Kenyon Review;* and he has published both poetry and literary criticism. He has been a Guggenheim Fellow and is a member of the American Academy of Arts and Letters.

Ransom's theory of literary criticism grows from the assumption that literature is beyond moral judgment; and on this score his quarrel with traditional criticism has attracted the most attention. Nevertheless, he contends that the poem is a whole experience in itself and, therefore, that it compasses *both* moral and aesthetic awareness. On the one hand, as he battles the critics who would measure a poem by moral standards, so, on the other hand, Ransom indicts that poetry which is merely intellectual, theoretical, or objective. Among the poets without laurels, for Ransom, are those moderns who have assumed that aesthetic effect exists by itself, and whose verse, consequently, is partial and fragmentary. Ransom's philosophical defense of poetry is based upon his notion of the wholeness of experience.

"Poets Without Laurels" first appeared in the *Yale Review,* Spring 1935; it was then published in a collection of Ransom's essays, *The World's Body* (1938), from which this text is taken.

POETS WITHOUT LAURELS

THE poets I refer to in the title are the "moderns"; those whom a small company of adept readers enjoys, perhaps enormously, but the general public detests; those in whose hands poetry as a living art has lost its public support.

Consequently I do not refer to such poets as Edna St. Vincent Millay and Robert Frost, who are evidently influenced by modernism without caring to "go modern" in the sense of joining the revolution; which is very much as if they had stopped at a mild or parlor variety of socialism, when all about them the brave, or at least the doctrinaire, were marching under the red banner. Probably they are wise in their time; they have laurels deservedly and wear them gracefully. But they do not define the issue which I wish to discuss. And still less do I refer to poets like E. A. Robinson, Sturge Moore, and John Masefield, who are even less modern; though I have no intention of questioning their laurels either. I refer to poets with no laurels.

I do not wish to seem to hold the public responsible for their condition, as if it had suddenly become phlegmatic, cruel, and philistine. The poets have certainly for their part conducted themselves peculiarly. They could not have estranged the public more completely if they had tried; and smart fellows as they are, they know very well what they have been doing, and what they are still stubborn in doing, and what the consequences are.

For they have failed more and more flagrantly, more and more deliberately, to identify themselves with the public interests, as if expressly to renounce the kind of affections which poets had courted for centuries. Accordingly, they do not only encounter public indifference, they sometimes encounter active hostility. A Pulitzer committeeman, I hear, says about some modernist poet whose book is up for judgment: "He will never get the award except over my dead body." The violence of the remark seems to exceed the occasion, but it is not exceptional.

Poets used to be bards and patriots, priests and prophets, keepers of the public conscience, and, naturally, men of public importance. Society crowned them with wreaths of laurel, according to the tradition which comes to us from the Greeks and is perpetuated by official custom in England—and in Oklahoma. Generally the favor must have been gratefully received. But modern poets are of another breed. It is as if all at once they had lost their prudence as well as their piety, and formed a compact to unclasp the chaplet from their brows, inflicting upon themselves the humility of delaureation, and retiring from public responsibility and honors. It is this phenomenon which has thrown critical theory into confusion.

Sir Philip Sidney made the orthodox defense of poetry on the ground of the poet's service to patriotism and virtue:

> He doth not only show the way, but giveth so
> sweet a prospect into the way, as will
> entice any man to enter it.

And what was the technique of enticement?

> With a tale forsooth he cometh unto you, with a
> tale which holdeth children from play,
> and old men from the chimney corner.

The poets, therefore, told entrancing tales, which had morals. But the fact was, also, that the poets were not always content to win virtue by indirection, or enticement, but were prepared to preach with almost no disguise, and to become sententious and repetitious, and the literature which they created is crowded with precise maxims for the moralists. There it stands on the shelves now. Sometimes the so-called poet has been only a moralist with a poetic manner. And all the poets famous in our tradition, or very nearly all, have been poets of a powerful moral cast.

So I shall try a preliminary definition of the poet's traditional function on behalf of society: he proposed to make virtue delicious. He compounded a moral effect with an aesthetic effect. The total effect was not a pure one, but it was rich, and relished highly. The name of the moral effect was goodness; the name of the aesthetic effect was beauty. Perhaps these did not have to coexist, but the planners of society saw to it that they should; they called upon the artists to reinforce morality with charm. The artists obliged.

When they had done so, the public did not think of attempting to distinguish in its experience as reader the glow which was aesthetic from the glow which was moral. Most persons probably could not have done this; many persons cannot do it today. There is yet no general recognition of the possibility that an aesthetic effect may exist by itself, independent of morality or any other useful set of ideas. But the modern poet is intensely concerned with this possibility, and he has disclaimed social responsibility in order to secure this pure aesthetic effect. He cares nothing, professionally, about morals, or God, or native land. He has performed a work of dissociation and purified his art.

There are distinct styles of "modernity," but I think their net results, psychologically, are about the same. I have in mind what might be called the "pure" style and what might be called the "obscure" style.

A good "pure" poem is Wallace Stevens' "Sea Surface Full of Clouds"—famous perhaps, but certainly not well known. I shall have to deal with it summarily. Time and place, "In that November off Tehuantepec." The poem has five uniform stanzas, presenting as many surface effects beheld at breakfast time "after the slopping of the sea by night grew still." The first surface made one think of rosy chocolate and gilt umbrellas; the second, of chophouse chocolate and sham umbrellas; the third, of porcelain chocolate and pied umbrellas; the fourth, of musky chocolate and frail umbrellas; the fifth, of Chinese chocolate and large umbrellas. Nothing could be more discriminating than these details, which induct us respectively into the five fields of observation. The poem has a calculated complexity, and its technical competence is so high that to study it, if you do that sort of thing, is to be happy. That it has not been studied by a multitude of persons is due to a simple consideration which strikes us at once: the poem has no moral, political, religious, or sociological values. It is not about "res publica," the public thing. The subject matter is trifling.

Poetry of this sort, as it was practised by some French poets of the nineteenth century, and as it is practised by many British and American poets now, has been called pure poetry, and the name is accurate. It is nothing but poetry; it is poetry for poetry's sake, and you cannot get a moral out of it. But it was to be expected that it would never win the public at large. The impulse which led readers to the old poetry was at least as much moral as it was aesthetic, while the new poetry cannot count on any customers except those specializing in strict aesthetic effects. But the modern poets intend to rate only as poets, and would probably think it meretricious to solicit patronage by making moral overtures.

As an example of "obscure" poetry, though not the most extreme one, I cite Allen Tate's "Death of Little Boys." Here are some of its verses:

> Then you will touch at the bedside, torn in two,
> Gold curls now deftly intricate with gray
> As the windowpane extends a fear to you
> From one peeled aster drenched with the wind all
>   day . . . .
> Till all the guests, come in to look, turn down
> Their palms; and delirium assails the cliff
> Of Norway where you ponder, and your little town
> Reels like a sailor drunk in his rotten skiff.

There is evidently a wide difference between Stevens and Tate, as poets. Tate has an important subject, and his poem is a human document, with a contagious fury about it: Stevens, pursuing purity, does not care to risk such a subject. But Tate, as if conscious that he is close to moralizing and sententiousness, builds up deliberately, I imagine, an effect of obscurity; for example, he does not care to explain the private meaning of his windowpane and his Norwegian cliff; or else, by some feat, he permits these bright features to belong to his total image without permitting them to reveal any precise meaning, either for himself or for his reader. Stevens, however, is objective from beginning to end; he completes all his meanings, knowing these will have little or no moral importance.

Pure or obscure, the modern poet manages not to slip into the old-fashioned moral-beautiful compound. If pure, he will not consider a subject which lends itself to moralization; that is, a subject of practical interest. It is his chief problem to find then a subject which has any interest at all. If, however, he prefers the other road, he may take the subject nearest his own humanity, a subject perhaps of terrifying import; but in treating it will stop short of all moral or theoretical conclusions, and confuse his detail to the point where it leaves no positive implications.

To be more technical; it is as if the pure poet presented a subject and declined to make any predication about it or even to start predication; and as if the obscure poet presented a subject in order to play with a great deal of important predication without ever completing any.

Personally, I prefer the rich obscure poetry to the thin pure poetry. The deaths of little boys are more exciting than the sea surfaces. It may be that the public preference, however, is otherwise. The public is inclined simply to ignore the pure poetry, because it lacks practical usefulness; but to hate the obscure poetry, because it looks important enough to attend to, and yet never yields up any specific fruit. Society, through its spokesmen the dozens of social-minded critics, who talk about the necessity of "communication," is now raging with indignation, or it may be with scorn, against the obscure poetry which this particular generation of poets has deposited. Nevertheless, both types of poetry, obscure as well as pure, aim at poetic autonomy; that is, speaking roughly, at purity.

Modern poetry in this respect is like modern painting. European painting used to be nearly as social a thing as poetry. It illustrated the sacred themes prescribed by the priests, whether popularly (Raphael) or esoterically and symbolically (Michelangelo); did the portraits of kings and cardinals, and the scenes of battles and great occasions; worked up allegorical and sentimental subjects. But more or less suddenly it asserted its independence. So we find Impressionists, doing the most innocent tricks with landscapes and mere objects; and we find Cézanne, painting so many times and so lovingly his foolish little bowl of fruits. The procedure was a strange one for the moral laity, who could detect nothing of importance there; and indeed nothing of public importance was there, only matters of technical interest to painters, and to persons who found painting sufficient. Later, and today, we find painters taking up the most heroic human material again in the most promising manner, yet arriving at no explicit meaning and, on the whole, simply playing with its powerful symbols. (Not all painters, of course.)

Apostate, illaureate, and doomed to outlawry the modern poets may be. I have the feeling that modernism is an unfortunate road for them to have taken. But it was an inevitable one. It is not hard to defend them from imputations against their honor and their logic. It is probably a question of whether we really know them, and understand their unusual purpose, and the powerful inhibitions they impose upon themselves.

But let us approach the matter from a slightly different angle. Poets have had to become modern because the age is modern. Its modernism envelops them like a sea, or an air. Nothing in their thought can escape it.

Modern poetry is pure poetry. The motive behind it cannot be substantially different from the motive behind the other modern activities, which is certainly the driving force of all our modernism. What is its name? "Purism" would be exact, except that it does not have the zealous and contriving sound we want. "Platonism" would do, provided there were time to come to an agreement about the essential meaning of Plato's act. I think the name "Puritanism" will describe this motive, if I may extend a little a term whose application in history has been mostly religious and moral.

Our period differs outwardly from other periods because it first differs inwardly. Its spiritual temper is puritanical; that is, it craves to perfect the parts of experience separately or in their purity, and is a series of isolated perfections. These have often been brilliant. But perhaps the modern program, on the whole, is not the one under which men maintain their best health and spirits. A little fear to that effect is beginning to cloud the consciousness of the brilliant moderns.

And here I conclude my defense of the modern poet. He is a good workman, and his purpose is really quite orthodox in its modernism. But it is no better.

The development of modern civilization has been a grand progression in which Puritanism has invaded first one field and then another.

The first field perhaps was religion. The religious impulse used to join itself and dominate and hold together nearly all the fields of human experience; politics, science, art, and even industry, and by all means moral conduct. But Puritanism came in the form of the Protestant Reformation and separated religion from all its partners. Perhaps the most important of these separations was that which lopped off from religion the aesthetic properties which simple-hearted devotees and loving artists had given it. The aesthetic properties constituted the myth, which to the temperamental Protestants became superstition, and the ceremonial, which became idolatry. Under the progressive zeal of the Reformation the being of God has become rarefied in the degree that it has been purified, until we find difficulty in grasping it, and there are people who tell me, just as there are people who tell the reader, that religion as a living force here in the Western world is spent. Theology is purer or more abstract than ever before, but it would seem to belong exclusively to theologians, and it cannot by itself assemble together all those who once delighted in the moral precepts, the music and the pomp, the social communion, and the concrete Godhead, of the synthetic institution which was called religion.

Next, or perhaps at the same time, Puritanism applied itself to morality. Broad as the reach of morality may be, it is distinct enough as an experience to be capable of purification. We may say that its destiny was to become what we know as sociology, a body of positivistic science. It had to be emancipated from its religious overlords, whose authority, after all, was not a moral one. Then it had to be emancipated from the dictates of taste, or aesthetic, and this latter emancipation was the harder, and perhaps the more needless. The Greeks, though they were incipient Puritans, scarcely attempted it. They had a compound phrase meaning "beautiful-good," which even their philosophers used habitually as the name of something elemental and indissoluble. Suspicion was aroused in Greeks by a goodness which could not produce beauty, just as to a man like Spenser the idea of virtue was incomplete until it flowered into poetic form, and just as to the sympathetic French artist our new American liberty was not quite won until identifiable with an able-bodied demi-goddess lifting a torch. The splitting up of the moral-beautiful compound for the sake of the pure moral article is visibly at work in the New Testament, and in the bourgeois cult of plainness in seventeenth-century England, and in the finicky private life of a Puritan moralist like Kant, and today in moral or sociological treatises (and authors) which neither exhibit nor discuss charm. Now, it is true that we moralize with "maximum efficiency" when we do it technically, or abstractly, but when that comes to be the rule we no longer approach a moral discussion with anything but a moral interest. To be moral is no longer to be "decent," and it looks as if moral appeal had become something less wide and less instant than it was.

Then Puritanism worked upon politics. I am not prepared to go deeply into this, but it is evident that purification consisted in taking the state away from the church, from the monarch, from the feudal aristocracy, from any other concrete attachments, in order that it might propel itself by the force of pure statecraft. Progress in this direction meant constitutionalism, parliamentarianism, republicanism. A modern state like ours is transparent in the perfection of its logic. But that does not make it the more realistic. It is obliged to count upon a universal and continuous will on the part of the citizens to accept an abstract formula of political action. But such a will may not be there. The population, not being composed exclusively of politicians, is inclined to delegate statecraft to those who profess it. The old mixed states had a greater variety of loyalties to appeal to.

Puritanism is an ideal which not all persons are strong enough to realize, but only those with great power of concentration. Its best chance of success lies in individual projects. Accordingly, Puritanism fairly came into its own in the vast multitude of private enterprises which go together to make modern science. Galileo and Kepler found science captive to religious dogma. America, the paradise of Puritanism, was not yet in being, but England was; and there presently, while other Puritanisms were going on, Lord Bacon was able to anticipate the complete emancipation of science by virtue of its adoption of the pure experimental method. Now, there have been other incubi besides religion resting upon science at one time or another; and chiefly the tendency of poetry to haunt its deliberations. Poetry is a figurative way of expression, science is a technical or abstract way; but since science employs language, the figurative associations are hard to keep out. In earlier days poetry kept close to science, and it did not seem so strange if Lucretius wanted to set forth the body of accepted science in verse. But poetry now cannot attend science into its technical labyrinth. The result is greater success for scientists, but not necessarily their greater happiness as men; and the general understanding on our part that we will follow science if we are scientists, but otherwise will leave it to the scientists.

It was but one step that Puritanism had to go from there into the world of business, where the material sciences are systematically applied. The rise of the modern business world is a development attendant upon the freedom which it has enjoyed; upon business for business' sake, or pure business, or "laissez faire," with such unconditioned principles as efficiency, technological improvement, and maximum productivity. If I wished to attack the record of business, I should by now have been long anticipated. It is common opinion that business as a self-contained profession has created business men who are defective in their humanity; that the conduct of business has made us callous to personal relations and to social justice; and that many of the occupations which business has devised are, in the absence of aesthetic standards, servile.

All these exclusions and specializations, and many more, have been making modern life what it is. It is significant that every specialization on the list has had to resist the insidious charms of aesthetic experience before its own perfection could arise. (Evidently the aesthetic interest is remarkably catholic among our faculties in its affinities; ready to attach itself easily to almost any sort of moment; a ubiquitous element in experience, it might be thought, which it would be unhealthy to cast out.) But the energy of so deep an impulse as Puritanism had to flow through all the channels, and to come to its last outlet in a pure art, a pure poetry. Those who have not observed the necessity may choose to hold its predestined agents the poets in contempt, or in amazement. The poets are in the spirit of their time. On the one hand, they have been pushed out of their old attachments, whereby they used to make themselves useful to public causes, by the specialists who did not want the respective causes to be branded with amateurism. On the other hand, they are moved by a universal tendency into their own appropriate kind of specialization, which can be, as they have been at pains to show, as formidable as any other.

Considerations of this kind, I feel sure, have been more or less precisely within the intuition of all modern poets, and have motivated their performance. Technically, they are quite capable of writing the old compound poetry, but they cannot bring themselves to do it; or rather, when they have composed it in unguarded moments, as modern poets still sometimes do, they are under the necessity of destroying it immediately. There is no baffling degree of virtuosity in the old lines,

Roll on, thou deep and dark blue Ocean, roll!
Ten thousand fleets sweep over thee in vain:
Man marks the earth with ruin, his control
Stops with the shore.

The modern poet can accomplish just as elegant a rumination as this; but thinks it would commit him to an anachronism, for this is the style of an older period. In that period, though it was a comparatively late one, and though this poet thought he was in advance of it, the prophets of society were still numbering and tuning their valuable reflections before they saw fit to release them; and morality, philosophy, religion, science, and art could still meet comfortably in one joint expression, though perhaps not with the same distinction they might have gained if they had had their pure and several expressions. A passage of Byron's, if sprung upon an unsuspecting modern would be felt immediately as "dating"; it would be felt as something that did very well for those dark ages before the modern mind achieved its own disintegration and perfected its faculties serially.

Even as readers, we must testify readily to the force of this time-principle. We sometimes pore over an old piece of poetry for so long that we fall under its spell and forget that its spirit is not our spirit. But we began to read it in a peculiar manner; by saying to ourselves, This is early Greek epic, This is seventeenth-century English drama. By means of one of the ripest and subtlest powers in us, that is, the historical sense, we made an adaptation of our minds to its mind, and were able to suspend those centuries which had intervened. Those centuries had made our minds much more knowing and at the same time, it is to be feared, much less suggestible. Yet it is not exactly with our own minds that we are reading the old poetry; otherwise we could not read it. For when we come back to our own world there begins to function in us a different style of consciousness altogether. And if we had begun to read a poetry of this old sort by saying, This was written last night by the poet around the corner, we could not have put up with it. If we throw away impatiently a contemporaneous poetry which displays archaisms of diction, what will we do with that which displays archaisms of temper? It looks spurious; for we require our art, and the living artists require it too, to be as contemporaneous as our banking or our locomotion.

What, then, is the matter with a pure poetry? The question is really more theoretical than practical. A school, an age, is involved by such a question, not merely some small poem or poet. And there is nothing the matter with this particular branch of purity which is not the matter with our modern activities. All are affected by Puritanism, just as the vegetation is affected, generally and indifferently, by the climate.

It is impossible to answer the question categorically because the items are intangible. But we find ourselves reasoning about it as well as we can, which is as follows.

You may dissociate the elements of experience and exploit them separately. But then at the best you go on a schedule of small experiences, taking them in turn, and trusting that when the rotation is complete you will have missed nothing. And at the worst you will become so absorbed in some one small experience that you will forget to go on and complete the schedule; in that case you will have missed something. The theory that excellence lies in the perfection of the single functions, and that society should demand that its members be hard specialists, assumes that there is no particular harm in missing something. But I do not see why. A maniac with a fixed idea is a variety of specialist, and an absorbing specialty is a small mania.

As for poetry, it seems to me a pity that its beauty should have to be cloistered and conventual, if it is "pure," or teasing and evasive, if it is "obscure." The union of beauty with goodness and truth has been common enough to be regarded as natural. It is the dissociation which is unnatural and painful.

But when we talk about simple and compound experiences, we are evidently employing a chemical mode of speech to represent something we cannot quite make out. Units of con-

sciousness are hard to handle scientifically; it takes more science than we have. Max Eastman thinks the future of literary
criticism is bound up with the future of psychology, and very
likely it is; but it is difficult to share his sanguine expectations
of that science. It cannot become as effective a science as chemistry.

Nevertheless, I shall make a tentative argument from the
analogy of chemistry. Lemonade is only a mechanical mixture,
not very interesting to chemists. Aside from the water, a drop
of lemonade contains lemon and sugar in no standard proportions. If it tastes too sour, add sugar, and if it tastes too sweet,
add lemon. (And do not forget to stir the mixture.) No matter
what the final proportions, you can still detect in the lemonade the sweet taste and the sour; though this is too abstract a
matter to bother about if the lemonade is satisfactory, for in
that case you simply drink it.

Table salt, however, is a true chemical compound; a molecule of it is NaCl. Understanding this, you do not claim to
know the taste either of sodium or of chlorine when you say
you are acquainted with the taste of salt. Whatever the Na
was and however it tasted by itself, it gave up that identity
when it compounded with Cl; and vice versa.

NaCl is found in the state of nature, where it is much com-
moner than either of its constituents. But suppose the chemists
decided to have nothing to do with NaCl because of its com-
poundness, and undertook to extract from it the pure Na and
Cl to serve on the table. Suppose they made war on all the
natural compounds, broke them down into the hundred or so
atomic elements, and asked us to live on these alone. The bene-
ficiaries would regard this service as well-meaning but mistaken.

But we provide the necessities for our minds and affections
with more harshness than we dare use on our stomachs and
bodies—so inferior in precision is our knowledge of minds
to our knowledge of bodies. Poets are now under the influence
of a perfectly arbitrary theory which I have called Puritanism.
They pursue A, an aesthetic element thought always to have

the same taste and to be the one thing desirable for poets. They will not permit the presence near it of M, the moral element, because that will produce the lemonade MA, and they do not approve of lemonade. In lemonade the A gets itself weakened and neutralized by the M.

But it is possible that MA is not a drop of lemonade after all, but a true molecule, into which the separate M and the separate A have disappeared and out of which an entirely new taste is born. The effects which we attribute to a poet like Virgil, or Milton, are on the following order: pious, philosophical, imaginative, sonorous, and the like. But perhaps the effect which we actually receive from the poetry is not that of an aggregate or series or mechanical mixture of distinct properties but only the single effect of a compound. In that event the properties will exist separate only in our minds, by a later act of qualitative analysis, and they will not really be in the poetry in their own identities.

Is the old-fashioned full poetry a mechanical mixture like lemonade or a chemical compound like table salt? That is probably the most important question which the modern critics have opened up to speculation. There are many corollary questions along with it, like these: When does the display of doctrine in poetry incur the charge of didacticism? And must the poet also bear arms—that is, like the economist and the social reformer, view his performance in the light of a utility rather than an end?

Now some poetry, so called, is not even lemonade, for the ingredients have not been mixed, much less compounded. Lumps of morality and image lie side by side, and are tasted in succession. T. S. Eliot thinks that this has been the character of a great deal of English poetry since the age of Dryden. Such poetry occupies some of the best room in the library, and takes up some of the best time of the earnest student of literature. It is decidedly one of the causes of that revulsion of feeling on the part of the modern poet which drives him away from the poetic tradition.

When our critical theory is complete, perhaps we shall be

able to distinguish various combinations of elements passing for poetry; thus, poetry by assemblage, poetry by mixture, and poetry by composition. The last of these sounds the best.

I suggest that critics and philosophers fix their most loving attention upon certain natural compounds in human experience. But I say so diffidently, and not too hopefully. It will take a long time to change the philosophical set which has come over the practice of the poets. The intellectual climate in which they live will have to be altered first.

ROBERT FROST

Robert Lee Frost (1875-   ) was born in San Francisco, California, and, at the age of ten, after the death of his father, moved with his mother to her home in Lawrence, Massachusetts. He attended college at Dartmouth for a few months, and at Harvard for two years, between which experiences of formal education he married and held jobs as a mill worker, schoolteacher, newspaper reporter, and shoemaker. After leaving college—his high marks did not compensate for the irksome discipline of classes—he lived for twelve years on a farm in New Hampshire, where he wrote and taught school. Frost sold his property and moved to England (1912-15), where he established a literary reputation by publishing two volumes of poems: *A Boy's Will* (1913) and *North of Boston* (1914). Returning to New England, he became a professor of English at Amherst, and during his tenure there (1916-38) published seven volumes of poems. Then, while continuing to write (several volumes of new poems, two verse plays, and editions of both selected and collected poems), he became a peripatetic teacher, poet-in-residence, or lecturer in dozens of colleges. During the past thirty years he has received wide acclaim—academic degrees, three Pulitzer Prizes, the gold medal of the National Institute of Arts and Letters, honorary lectureships, and other tokens of homage.

Although the first *Collected Poems of Robert Frost* appeared in 1930, this preface was not added until the edition of 1939. It has since appeared in all editions of this title. Frost has written two other prefatory essays (he is cautious, he says, about getting the sound of prose in his head): "The Constant Symbol," in *The Poems of Robert Frost* (1946); and "The Prerequisites," in *Aforesaid* (1954), a limited edition of selected poems.

THE FIGURE A POEM MAKES

ABSTRACTION is an old story with the philosophers, but it has been like a new toy in the hands of the artists of our day. Why can't we have any one quality of poetry we choose by itself? We can have in thought. Then it will go hard if we can't in practice. Our lives for it.

Granted no one but a humanist much cares how sound a poem is if it is only *a* sound. The sound is the gold in the ore. Then we will have the sound out alone and dispense with the inessential. We do till we make the discovery that the object in writing poetry is to make all poems sound as different as possible from each other, and the resources for that of vowels, consonants, punctuation, syntax, words, sentences, meter are not enough. We need the help of context—meaning—subject matter. That is the greatest help towards variety. All that can be done with words is soon told. So also with meters—particularly in our language where there are virtually but two, strict iambic and loose iambic. The ancients with many were still poor if they depended on meters for all tune. It is painful to watch our sprung-rhythmists straining at the point of omitting one short from a foot for relief from monotony. The possibilities for tune from the dramatic tones of meaning struck across the rigidity of a limited meter are endless. And we are back in poetry as merely one more art of having something to say, sound or unsound. Probably better if sound, because deeper and from wider experience.

Then there is this wildness whereof it is spoken. Granted again that it has an equal claim with sound to being a poem's better half. If it is a wild tune, it is a poem. Our problem then is, as modern abstractionists, to have the wildness pure; to be wild with nothing to be wild about. We bring up as aberrationists, giving way to undirected associations and kicking ourselves from one chance suggestion to another in all directions as of a hot afternoon in the life of a grasshopper.

Theme alone can steady us down. Just as the first mystery was how a poem could have a tune in such a straightness as meter, so the second mystery is how a poem can have wildness and at the same time a subject that shall be fulfilled.

It should be of the pleasure of a poem itself to tell how it can. The figure a poem makes. It begins in delight and ends in wisdom. The figure is the same as for love. No one can really hold that the ecstasy should be static and stand still in one place. It begins in delight, it inclines to the impulse, it assumes direction with the first line laid down, it runs a course of lucky events, and ends in a clarification of life—not necessarily a great clarification, such as sects and cults are founded on, but in a momentary stay against confusion. It has denouement. It has an outcome that though unforeseen was predestined from the first image of the original mood—and indeed from the very mood. It is but a trick poem and no poem at all if the best of it was thought of first and saved for the last. It finds its own name as it goes and discovers the best waiting for it in some final phrase at once wise and sad—the happy-sad blend of the drinking song.

No tears in the writer, no tears in the reader. No surprise for the writer, no surprise for the reader. For me the initial delight is in the surprise of remembering something I didn't know I knew. I am in a place, in a situation, as if I had materialized from cloud or risen out of the ground. There is a glad recognition of the long lost and the rest follows. Step by step the wonder of unexpected supply keeps growing. The impressions most useful to my purpose seem always those I was unaware of and so made no note of at the time when taken, and the conclusion is come to that like giants we are always hurling experience ahead of us to pave the future with against the day when we may want to strike a line of purpose across it for somewhere. The line will have the more charm for not being mechanically straight. We enjoy the straight crookedness of a good walking stick. Modern instruments of precision are being used to make things crooked as if by eye and hand in the old days.

I tell how there may be a better wildness of logic than of inconsequence. But the logic is backward, in retrospect, after the act. It must be more felt than seen ahead like prophecy. It must be a revelation, or a series of revelations, as much for the poet as for the reader. For it to be that there must have been the greatest freedom of the material to move about in it and to establish relations in it regardless of time and space, previous relation, and everything but affinity. We prate of freedom. We call our schools free because we are not free to stay away from them till we are sixteen years of age. I have given up my democratic prejudices and now willingly set the lower classes free to be completely taken care of by the upper classes. Political freedom is nothing to me. I bestow it right and left. All I would keep for myself is the freedom of my material—the condition of body and mind now and then to summons aptly from the vast chaos of all I have lived through.

Scholars and artists thrown together are often annoyed at the puzzle of where they differ. Both work from knowledge; but I suspect they differ most importantly in the way their knowledge is come by. Scholars get theirs with conscientious thoroughness along projected lines of logic; poets theirs cavalierly and as it happens in and out of books. They stick to nothing deliberately, but let what will stick to them like burrs where they walk in the fields. No acquirement is on assignment, or even self-assignment. Knowledge of the second kind is much more available in the wild free ways of wit and art. A schoolboy may be defined as one who can tell you what he knows in the order in which he learned it. The artist must value himself as he snatches a thing from some previous order in time and space into a new order with not so much as a ligature clinging to it of the old place where it was organic.

More than once I should have lost my soul to radicalism if it had been the originality it was mistaken for by its young converts. Originality and initiative are what I ask for my country. For myself the originality need be no more than the freshness of a poem run in the way I have described: from delight to wisdom. The figure is the same as for love. Like a piece of ice on a hot stove the poem must ride on its own melting. A poem may be worked over once it is in being, but may not be worried into being. Its most precious quality will remain its having run itself and carried away the poet with it. Read it a hundred times: it will forever keep its freshness as a metal keeps its fragrance. It can never lose its sense of a meaning that once unfolded by surprise as it went.

EDMUND WILSON

Edmund Wilson (1895-   ) was born in Red Bank, New Jersey. He was graduated from Princeton (1916), became a reporter for the New York *Evening Sun,* and then served in France for two years during World War I. Upon his return, he joined the staff of *Vanity Fair,* and became its managing editor (1921-22). He was an associate editor of the *New Republic* (1926-31). Author and critic, as well as editor, he has twice held Guggenheim fellowships; he has published poetry, fiction, plays and dialogues, and essays in literary and social criticism; and he was book reviewer for *The New Yorker* (1944-48).

Wilson's criticism is confined to no particular literary movement. On the contrary, he has usually been preoccupied, in appraising imaginative writing, with the relationships between aesthetic and social awareness. He has attacked that dogma of poetic tradition which distinguishes between verse and prose, arguing that technical distinctions are far less important than the common denominator of all literature, which is ideology. But he has also attacked the ideological extremes of contemporary literary criticism—notably Marxist criticism and the New Humanism—for their narrow views and the impossibly severe demands they make upon literature. In his own criticism Wilson has developed a singular historical method, recreating a context of continuing social values for the literary text even as he proceeds with a resourceful technical analysis of the work.

"Philoctetes: The Wound and the Bow" is characteristic of both Wilson's method and the success of his perceptions. First printed in the *New Republic,* April 21, 1941, this became the concluding essay in *The Wound and the Bow* (1941), which deals primarily with Victorian and contemporary novelists. This text is taken from the 1947 edition of the book.

PHILOCTETES: THE WOUND AND THE BOW

THE *Philoctetes* of Sophocles is far from being his most popular play. The myth itself has not been one of those which have excited the modern imagination. The idea of Philoctetes' long illness and his banishment to the bleak island is dreary or distasteful to the young, who like to identify themselves with men of action—with Heracles or Perseus or Achilles; and for adults the story told by Sophocles fails to set off such emotional charges as are liberated by the crimes of the Atreidai and the tragedies of the siege of Troy. Whatever may have been dashing in the legend has been lost with the other plays and poems that dealt with it. Philoctetes is hardly mentioned in Homer; and we have only an incomplete account of the plays of Aeschylus and Euripides, which hinged on a critical moment of the campaign of the Greeks at Troy and which seem to have exploited the emotions of Greek patriotism. We have only a few scattered lines and phrases from that other play by Sophocles on the subject, the *Philoctetes at Troy,* in which the humiliated hero was presumably to be cured of his ulcer and to proceed to his victory over Paris.

There survives only this one curious drama which presents Philoctetes in exile—a drama which does not supply us at all with what we ordinarily expect of Greek tragedy, since it culminates in no catastrophe, and which indeed resembles rather our modern idea of a comedy (though the records of the lost plays of Sophocles show that there must have been others like it). Its interest depends almost as much on the latent interplay of character, on a gradual psychological conflict, as that of *Le Misanthrope.* And it assigns itself, also, to a category even more special and less generally appealing through the fact (though this, again, was a feature not uncommon with Sophocles) that the conflict is not even allowed to take place between a man and a woman. Nor does it even put before us the spectacle—which may be made exceedingly thrilling—of the individual in conflict with his social group, which we get in such plays devoid of feminine interest as *Coriolanus* and *An Enemy of the People*. Nor is the conflict even a dual one, as most dramatic conflicts are—so that our emotions seesaw up and down between two opposed persons or groups: though Philoctetes and Odysseus struggle for the loyalty of Neoptolemus, he himself emerges more and more distinctly as representing an independent point of view, so that the contrast becomes a triple affair which makes more complicated demands on our sympathies.

A French dramatist of the seventeenth century, Chateaubrun, found the subject so inconceivable that, in trying to concoct an adaptation which would be acceptable to the taste of his time, he provided Philoctetes with a daughter named Sophie with whom Neoptolemus was to fall in love and thus bring the drama back to the reliable and eternal formula of Romeo and Juliet and the organizer who loves the factory-owner's daughter. And if we look for the imprint of the play on literature since the Renaissance, we shall find a very meager record: a chapter of Fenelon's *Télémaque,* a discussion in Lessing's *Laocoön,* a sonnet of Wordsworth's, a little play by André Gide, an adaptation by John Jay Chapman—this is all, so far as I know, that has any claim to interest.

And yet the play itself *is* most interesting, as some of these writers have felt; and it is certainly one of Sophocles' masterpieces. If we come upon it in the course of reading him, without having heard it praised, we are surprised to be so charmed, so moved—to find ourselves in the presence of something that is so much less crude in its subtlety than either a three-cornered modern comedy like *Candida* or *La Parisienne* or an underplayed affair of male loyalty in a story by Ernest Hemingway, to both of which it has some similarity. It is as if having the three men on the lonely island has enabled the highly sophisticated Sophocles to get further away from the framework of the old myths on which he has to depend and whose barbarities, anomalies and absurdities, tactfully and realistically though he handles them, seem sometimes almost as much out of place as they would in a dialogue by Plato. The people of the *Philoctetes* seem to us more familiar than they do in most of the other Greek tragedies; and they take on for us a more intimate meaning. Philoctetes remains in our mind, and his incurable wound and his invincible bow recur to us with a special insistence. But what is it they mean? How is it possible for Sophocles to make us accept them so naturally? Why do we enter with scarcely a stumble into the situation of people who are preoccupied with a snakebite that lasts forever and a weapon that cannot fail?

Let us first take account of the peculiar twist which Sophocles seems to have given the legend, as it had come to him from the old epics and the dramatists who had used it before him.

The main outline of the story ran as follows: The demigod Heracles had been given by Apollo a bow that never missed its mark. When, poisoned by Deianeira's robe, he had himself burned on Mount Oeta, he had persuaded Philoctetes to light the pyre and had rewarded him by bequeathing to him this weapon. Philoctetes had thus been formidably equipped when he had later set forth against Troy with Agamemnon and Menelaus. But on the way they had to stop off at the tiny island of Chrysè to sacrifice to the local deity. Philoctetes approached the shrine first, and he was bitten in the foot by a snake. The infection became peculiarly virulent; and the groans of Philoctetes made it impossible to perform the sacrifice, which would be spoiled by ill-omened sounds; the bite began to suppurate with so horrible a smell that his companions could not bear to have him near them. They removed him to Lemnos, a neighboring island which was much larger than Chrysè and uninhabited, and sailed away to Troy without him.

Philoctetes remained there ten years. The mysterious wound never healed. In the meantime, the Greeks, hard put to it at Troy after the deaths of Achilles and Ajax and baffled by the confession of their soothsayer that he was unable to advise them further, had kidnaped the soothsayer of the Trojans and had forced him to reveal to them that they could never win till they had sent for Neoptolemus, the son of Achilles, and given him his father's armor, and till they had brought Philoctetes and his bow.

Both these things were done. Philoctetes was healed at Troy by the son of the physician Asclepius; and he fought Paris in single combat and killed him. Philoctetes and Neoptolemus became the heroes of the taking of Troy.

Both Aeschylus and Euripides wrote plays on this subject long before Sophocles did; and we know something about them from a comparison of the treatments by the three different dramatists which was written by Dion Chrysostom, a rhetorician of the first century A.D. Both these versions would seem to have been mainly concerned with the relation of Philoctetes to the success of the Greek campaign. All three of the plays dealt with the same episode: the visit of Odysseus to Lemnos for the purpose of getting the bow; and all represented Odysseus as particularly hateful to Philoctetes (because he had been one of those responsible for abandoning him on the island), and obliged to resort to cunning. But the emphasis of Sophocles' treatment appears fundamentally to have differed from that of the other two. In the drama of Aeschylus, we are told, Odysseus was not recognized by Philoctetes, and he seems simply to have stolen the bow. In Euripides, he was disguised by Athena in the likeness of another person, and he pretended that he had been wronged by the Greeks as Philoctetes had been. He had to compete with a delegation of Trojans, who had been sent to get the bow for their side and who arrived at the same time as he; and we do not know precisely what happened. But Dion Chrysostom regarded the play as "a masterpiece of declamation" and "a model of ingenious debate," and Jebb thinks it probable that Odysseus won the contest by an appeal to Philoctetes' patriotism. Since Odysseus was pretending to have been wronged by the Greeks, he could point to his own behavior in suppressing his personal resentments in the interests of saving Greek honor. The moral theme thus established by Aeschylus and Euripides both would have been

simply, like the theme of the wrath of Achilles, the conflict between the passions of an individual—in this case, an individual
suffering from a genuine wrong—and the demands of duty to a
common cause.

This conflict appears also in Sophocles; but it takes on a
peculiar aspect. Sophocles, in the plays of his we have, shows
himself particularly successful with people whose natures have
been poisoned by narrow fanatical hatreds. Even allowing for
the tendency of Greek heroes, in legend and history both, to
fly into rather childish rages, we still feel on Sophocles' part
some sort of special point of view, some sort of special sympathy, for these cases. Such people—Electra and the embittered
old Oedipus—suffer as much as they hate: it is because they
suffer they hate. They horrify, but they waken pity. Philoctetes is such another: a man obsessed by a grievance, which in
his case he is to be kept from forgetting by an agonizing physical ailment; and for Sophocles his pain and hatred have a
dignity and an interest. Just as it is by no means plain to
Sophocles that in the affair of Antigone *versus* Cleon it is the
official point of view of Cleon, repesenting the interests of his
victorious faction, which should have the last word against Antigone, infuriated by a personal wrong; so it is by no means
plain to him that the morality of Odysseus, who is lying and
stealing for the fatherland, necessarily deserves to prevail over
the animus of the stricken Philoctetes.

The contribution of Sophocles to the story is a third person
who will sympathize with Philoctetes. This new character is
Neoptolemus, the young son of Achilles, who, along with
Philoctetes, is indispensable to the victory of the Greeks and
who has just been summoned to Troy. Odysseus is made to
bring him to Lemnos for the purpose of deceiving Philoctetes
and shanghai-ing him aboard the ship.

The play opens with a scene between Odysseus and the boy,
in which the former explains the purpose of their trip. Odysseus will remain in hiding in order not to be recognized by
Philoctetes, and Neoptolemus will go up to the cave in which
Philoctetes lives and win his confidence by pretending that

the Greeks have robbed him of his father's armor, so that he, too, has a grievance against them. The youth in his innocence and candor objects when he is told what his rôle is to be, but Odysseus persuades him by reminding him that they can only take Troy through his obedience and that once they have taken Troy, he will be glorified for his bravery and wisdom. "As soon as we have won," Odysseus assures him, "we shall conduct ourselves with perfect honesty. But for one short day of dishonesty, allow me to direct you what to do—and then forever after you will be known as the most righteous of men." The line of argument adopted by Odysseus is one with which the politics of our time have made us very familiar. "Isn't it base, then, to tell falsehoods?" Neoptolemus asks. "Not," Odysseus replies, "when a falsehood will bring our salvation."

Neoptolemus goes to talk to Philoctetes. He finds him in the wretched cave—described by Sophocles with characteristic realism: the bed of leaves, the crude wooden bowl, the filthy bandages drying in the sun—where he has been living in rags for ten years, limping out from time to time to shoot wild birds or to get himself wood and water. The boy hears the harrowing story of Philoctetes' desertion by the Greeks and listens to his indignation. The ruined captain begs Neoptolemus to take him back to his native land, and the young man pretends to consent. (Here and elsewhere I am telescoping the scenes and simplifying a more complex development.) But just as they are leaving for the ship, the ulcer on Philoctetes' foot sets up an ominous throbbing in preparation for one of its periodical burstings: "She returns from time to time," says the invalid, "as if she were sated with her wanderings." In a moment he is stretched on the ground, writhing in abject anguish and begging the young man to cut off his foot. He gives Neoptolemus the bow, telling him to take care of it till the seizure is over. A second spasm, worse than the first, reduces him to imploring the boy to throw him into the crater of the Lemnian volcano: so he himself, he says, had lit the fire which consumed the tormented Heracles and had got in return these arms, which he is now handing on to Neoptolemus. The pain abates a little; "It comes and goes," says Philoctetes; and he entreats the young man not to leave him. "Don't worry about that. We'll stay." "I shan't even make you swear it, my son." "It would not be right to leave you" (it would not be right, of course, even from the Greeks' point of view). They shake hands on it. A third paroxysm twists the cripple; now he asks Neoptolemus to carry him to the cave, but shrinks from his grasp and struggles. At last the abscess bursts, the dark blood begins to flow. Philoctetes, faint and sweating, falls asleep.

The sailors who have come with Neoptolemus urge him to make off with the bow. "No," the young man replies. "He cannot hear us; but I am sure that it will not be enough for us to recapture the bow without him. It is he who is to have the glory—it was he the god told us to bring."

While they are arguing, Philoctetes awakes and thanks the young man with emotion: "Agamemnon and Menelaus were not so patient and loyal." But now they must get him to the ship, and the boy will have to see him undeceived and endure his bitter reproaches. "The men will carry you down," says Neoptolemus. "Don't trouble them: just help me up," Philoctetes replies. "It would be too disagreeable for them to take me all the way to the ship." The smell of the suppuration has been sickening. The young man begins to hesitate. The other sees that he is in doubt about something: "You're not so overcome with disgust at my disease that you don't think you can have me on the ship with you?"—

> οὐ δή σε δυσχέρεια τοῦ νοσήματος
> ἔπεισεν ὥστε μή μ'ἄγειν ναύτην ἔτι;

The answer is one of the most effective of those swift and brief speeches of Sophocles which for the first time make a situation explicit (my attempts to render this dialogue colloquially do no justice to the feeling and point of the verse):

> ἅπαντα δυσχέρεια, τὴν αὑτοῦ φύσιν
> ὅταν λιπών τις δρᾷ τὰ μὴ προσεικότα.

"Everything becomes disgusting when you are false to your own nature and behave in an unbecoming way."

He confesses his real intentions; and a painful scene occurs. Philoctetes denounces the boy in terms that would be appropriate for Odysseus; he sees himself robbed of his bow and left to starve on the island. The young man is deeply worried: "Why did I ever leave Scyros?" he asks himself. "Comrades, what shall I do?"

At this moment, Odysseus, who has been listening, pops out from his hiding place. With a lash of abuse at Neoptolemus, he orders him to hand over the arms. The young man's spirit flares up: when Odysseus invokes the will of Zeus, he tells him that he is degrading the gods by lending them his own lies. Philoctetes turns on Odysseus with an invective which cannot fail to impress the generous Neoptolemus: Why have they come for him now? he demands. Is he not still just as ill-omened and loathsome as he had been when they made him an outcast? They have only come back to get him because the gods have told them they must.

The young man now defies his mentor and takes his stand with Philoctetes. Odysseus threatens him: if he persists, he will have the whole Greek army against him, and they will see to it that he is punished for his treason. Neoptolemus declares his intention of taking Philoctetes home; he gives him back his bow. Odysseus tries to intervene; but Philoctetes has got the bow and aims an arrow at him. Neoptolemus seizes his hand and restrains him. Odysseus, always prudent, beats a quiet retreat.

Now the boy tries to persuade the angry man that he should, nevertheless, rescue the Greeks. "I have proved my good faith," says Neoptolemus; "you know that I am not going to coerce you. Why be so wrongheaded? When the gods afflict us, we are obliged to bear our misfortunes; but must people pity a man who suffers through his own choice? The snake that bit you was an agent of the gods, it was the guardian of the goddess's shrine, and I swear to you by Zeus that the son of Asclepius will cure you if you let us take you to Troy." Philoctetes is incredulous, refuses. "Since you gave me your word," he says, "take me home again." "The Greeks will attack me and ruin me." "I'll defend you." "How can you?" "With my bow." Neoptolemus is forced to consent.

But now Heracles suddenly appears from the skies and declares to Philoctetes that what the young man says is true, and that it is right for him to go to Troy. He and the son of Achilles shall stand together like lions and shall gloriously carry the day.—The *deus ex machina* here may of course figure a change of heart which has taken place in Philoctetes as the result of his having found a man who recognizes the wrong that has been done him and who is willing to champion his cause in defiance of all the Greek forces. His patron, the chivalrous Heracles, who had himself performed so many generous exploits, asserts his influence over his heir. The long hatred is finally exorcised.

In a fine lyric utterance which ends the play, Philoctetes says farewell to the cavern, where he has lain through so many nights listening to the deep-voiced waves as they crashed against the headland, and wetted by the rain and the spray blown in by the winter gales. A favorable wind has sprung up; and he sails away to Troy.

It is possible to guess at several motivations behind the writing of the *Philoctetes*. The play was produced in 409, when—if the tradition of his longevity be true—Sophocles would have been eighty-seven; and it is supposed to have been followed by the *Oedipus Coloneus,* which is assigned to 405 or 406. The latter deals directly with old age; but it would appear that the *Philoctetes* anticipates this theme in another form. Philoctetes, like the outlawed Oedipus, is impoverished, humbled, abandoned by his people, exacerbated by hardship and chagrin. He is accursed: Philoctetes' ulcer is an equivalent for the abhorrent sins of Oedipus, parricide and incest together, which have made of the ruler a pariah. And yet somehow both are sacred persons who have acquired superhuman powers, and who are destined to be purged of their guilt. One passage from the earlier play is even strikingly repeated in the later. The conception of the wave-beaten promontory and the sick man lying in his cave assailed by the wind and rain turns up in the *Oedipus Coloneus* (Coloneus was Sophocles' native deme) with a figurative moral value. So the ills of old age assail Oedipus. Here are the lines, in A. E. Housman's translation:

> This man, as me, even so,
> Have the evil days overtaken;
> And like as a cape sea-shaken
> With tempest at earth's last verges
> And shock of all winds that blow,
> His head the seas of woe,
> The thunders of awful surges
> Ruining overflow.
> Blown from the fall of even,
>   Blown from the dayspring forth,
> Blown from the noon in heaven,
>   Blown from night and the North.

But Oedipus has endured as Philoctetes has endured in the teeth of all the cold and the darkness, the screaming winds and the bellowing breakers: the blind old man is here in his own person the headland that stands against the storm.

We may remember a widely current story about the creator of these two figures. It is said that one of Sophocles' sons brought him into court in his advanced old age on the complaint that he was no longer competent to manage his property. The old poet is supposed to have recited a passage from the play which he had been writing: the chorus in praise of Coloneus, with its clear song of nightingales, its wine-dark ivy, its crocus glowing golden and its narcissus moist with dew, where the stainless stream of the Cephisus wanders through the broad-swelling plain and where the gray-leaved olive grows of itself beneath the gaze of the gray-eyed Athena—shining Coloneus, breeder of horses and of oarsmen whom the Nereids lead. The scene had been represented on the stage and Sophocles had been made to declare: "If I am Sophocles, I am not mentally incapable; if I am mentally incapable, I am not Sophocles." In any case, the story was that the tribunal, composed of his fellow clansmen, applauded and acquitted the poet and censored the litigating son. The ruined and humiliated heroes of Sophocles' later plays are still persons of mysterious virtue, whom their fellows are forced to respect.

There is also a possibility, even a strong probability, that Sophocles intended Philoctetes to be identified with Alcibiades. This brilliant and unique individual, one of the great military leaders of the Athenians, had been accused by political opponents of damaging the sacred statues of Hermes and burlesquing the Eleusinian mysteries, and had been summoned to stand trial at Athens while he was away on his campaign against Sicily. He had at once gone over to the Spartans, commencing that insolent career of shifting allegiances which ended with his returning to the Athenian side. At a moment of extreme danger, he had taken over a part of the Athenian fleet and had defeated the Spartans in two sensational battles in 411 and 410, thus sweeping them out of the Eastern Aegean and enabling the Athenians to dominate the Hellespont. The *Philoctetes* was produced in 409, when the Athenians already wanted him back and were ready to cancel the charges against him and to restore him to citizenship. Alcibiades was a startling example of a bad character who was indispensable. Plutarch says that Aristophanes well describes the Athenian feeling about Alcibiades when he writes: "They miss him and hate him and long to have him back." And the malady of Philoctetes may have figured his moral defects: the unruly and unscrupulous nature which, even though he seems to have been innocent of the charges brought against him, had given them a certain plausibility. It must have looked to the Athenians, too, after the victories of Abydos and Cyzicus, as if he possessed an invincible bow. Plutarch says that the men who had served under him at the taking of Cyzicus did actually come to regard themselves as undefeatable and refused to share quarters with other soldiers who had fought in less successful engagements.

Yet behind both the picture of old age and the line in regard to Alcibiades, one feels in the *Philoctetes* a more general and fundamental idea: the conception of superior strength as inseparable from disability.

For the superiority of Philoctetes does not reside merely in the enchanted bow. When Lessing replied to Winckelmann, who had referred to Sophocles' cripple as if he were an example of the conventional idea of impassive classical fortitude, he pointed out that, far from exemplifying impassivity, Philoctetes becomes completely demoralized every time he has one of his seizures, and yet that this only heightens our admiration for the pride which prevents him from escaping at the expense of helping those who have deserted him. "We despise," say the objectors, "any man from whom bodily pain extorts a shriek. Ay, but not always; not for the first time, nor if we see that the sufferer strains every nerve to stifle the expression of his pain; not if we know him otherwise to be a man of firmness; still less if we witness evidences of his firmness in the very midst of his sufferings, and observe that, although pain may have extorted a shriek, it has extorted nothing else from him, but that on the contrary he submits to the prolongation of his pain rather than renounce one iota of his resolutions, even where such a concession would promise him the termination of his misery."

For André Gide, in his *Philoctète,* the obstinacy of the invalid hermit takes on a character almost mystical. By persisting in his bleak and lonely life, the Philoctetes of Gide wins the love of a more childlike Neoptolemus and even compels the respect of a less hard-boiled Odysseus. He is practicing a kind of virtue superior not only to the virtue of the latter, with his code of obedience to the demands of the group, but also to that of the former, who forgets his patriotic obligations for those of a personal attachment. There is something above the gods, says the Philoctetes of Gide; and it is virtue to devote oneself to this. But what is it? says Neoptolemus. I do not know, he answers; oneself! The misfortune of his exile on the island has enabled him to perfect himself: "I have learned to express myself better," he tells them, "now that I am no longer with men. Between hunting and sleeping, I occupy myself with thinking. My ideas, since I have been alone so that nothing, not even suffering, disturbs them, have taken a subtle course which sometimes I can hardly follow. I have come to know more of the secrets of life than my masters had ever revealed to me. And I took to telling the story of my sufferings, and if the phrase was very beautiful, I was by so much consoled; I even sometimes forgot my sadness by uttering it. I came to understand that words inevitably become more beautiful from the moment they are no longer put together in response to the demands of others . . . ." The Philoctetes of Gide is, in fact, a literary man: at once a moralist and an artist, whose genius becomes purer and deeper in ratio to his isolation and outlawry. In the end, he lets the intruders steal the bow after satisfying himself that Neoptolemus can handle it, and subsides into a blissful tranquillity, much relieved that there is no longer any reason for people to seek him out.

With Gide we come close to a further implication, which even Gide does not fully develop but which must occur to the modern reader: the idea that genius and disease, like strength and mutilation, may be inextricably bound up together. It is significant that the only two writers of our time who have especially interested themselves in Philoctetes—André Gide and John Jay Chapman—should both be persons who have not only, like the hero of the play, stood at an angle to the morality of society and defended their position with stubbornness, but who have suffered from psychological disorders which have made them, in Gide's case, ill-regarded by his fellows; in Chapman's case excessively difficult. Nor is it perhaps accidental that Charles Lamb, with his experience of his sister's insanity, should in his essay on The Convalescent choose the figure of Philoctetes as a symbol for his own "nervous fever."

And we must even, I believe, grant Sophocles some special insight into morbid psychology. The tragic themes of all three of the great dramatists—the madnesses, the murders and the incests—may seem to us sufficiently morbid. The hero with an incurable wound was even a stock subject of myth not confined to the Philoctetes legend: there was also the story of Telephus, also wounded and also indispensable, about which both Sophocles and Euripides wrote plays. But there is a dif-

ference between the treatment that Sophocles gives to these
conventional epic subjects and the treatments of the other
writers. Aeschylus is more religious and philosophical; Euripides more romantic and sentimental. Sophocles by comparison is clinical. Arthur Platt, who had a special interest in the
scientific aspect of the classics, says that Sophocles was scrupu-
lously up-to-date in the physical science of his time. He was
himself closely associated by tradition with the cult of the
healer Asclepius, whose son is to cure Philoctetes: Lucian had
read a poem which he had dedicated to the doctor-god; and
Plutarch reports that Asclepius was supposed to have visited
his hearth. He is said also to have been actually a priest of another of the medical cults. Platt speaks particularly of his medical knowledge—which is illustrated by the naturalism and precision of his description of Philoctetes' infected bite.

But there is also in Sophocles a cool observation of the behavior of psychological derangements. The madness of Ajax is
a genuine madness, from which he recovers to be horrified at
the realization of what he has done. And it was not without
good reason that Freud laid Sophocles under contribution for
the naming of the Oedipus complex—since Sophocles had not
only dramatized the myth that dwelt with the violation of the
incest taboo, but had exhibited the suppressed impulse behind
it in the speech in which he makes Jocasta attempt to reassure
Oedipus by reminding him that it was not uncommon for men
to dream about sleeping with their mothers—"and he who
thinks nothing of this gets through his life most easily." Those
who do not get though life so easily are presented by Sophocles
with a very firm grasp on the springs of their abnormal conduct. Electra is what we should call nowadays schizophrenic:
the woman who weeps over the urn which is supposed to contain her brother's ashes is not "integrated," as we say, with
the fury who prepares her mother's murder. And certainly
the fanaticism of Antigone—"fixated," like Electra, on her
brother—is intended to be abnormal, too. The banishment by
Jebb from Sophocles' text of the passage in which Antigone
explains the unique importance of a brother and his juggling

of the dialogue in the scene in which she betrays her indifference to the feelings of the man she is supposed to marry are certainly among the curiosities of Victorian scholarship—though he was taking his cue from the complaint of Goethe that Antigone had been shown by Sophocles as acting from trivial motives and Goethe's hope that her speech about her brother might some day be shown to be spurious. Aristotle had cited this speech of Antigone's as an outstanding example of the principle that if anything peculiar occurs in a play the cause must be shown by the dramatist. It was admitted by Jebb that his rewriting of these passages had no real textual justification; and in one case he violates glaringly the convention of the one-line dialogue. To accept his emendation would involve the assumption that Aristotle did not know what the original text had been and was incapable of criticizing the corrupted version. No: Antigone forgets her fiancé and kills herself for her brother. Her timid sister (like Electra's timid sister) represents the normal feminine point of view. Antigone's point of view is peculiar, as Aristotle says. (The real motivation of the Antigone has been retraced with unmistakable accuracy by Professor Walter R. Agard in *Classical Philology*, of July, 1937.)

These insane or obsessed people of Sophocles all display a perverse kind of nobility. I have spoken of the authority of expiation which emanates from the blasted Oedipus. Even the virulence of Electra's revenge conditions the intensity of her tenderness for Orestes. And so the maniacal fury which makes Ajax run amok, the frenzy of Heracles in the Nessus robe, terribly though they transform their victims, can never destroy their virtue of heroes. The poor disgraced Ajax will receive his due of honor after his suicide and will come to stand higher in our sympathies than Menelaus and Agamemnon, those obtuse and brutal captains, who here as in the *Philoctetes* are obviously no favorites of Sophocles'. Heracles in his final moments bids his spirit curb his lips with steel to keep him from crying out, and carry him through his self-destructive duty as a thing that is to be desired.

Some of these maladies are physical in origin, others are psychological; but they link themselves with one another. The case of Ajax connects psychological disorder as we get it in Electra, for example, with the access of pain and rage that causes Heracles to kill the herald Lichas; the case of Heracles connects a poisoning that produces a murderous fury with an infection that, though it distorts the personality, does not actually render the victim demented: the wound of Philoctetes, whose agony comes in spasms like that of Heracles. All these cases seem intimately related.

It has been the misfortune of Sophocles to figure in academic tradition as the model of those qualities of coolness and restraint which that tradition regards as classical. Those who have never read him—remembering the familiar statue—are likely to conceive something hollow and marmoreal. Actually, as C. M. Bowra says, Sophocles is "passionate and profound." Almost everything that we are told about him by the tradition of the ancient world suggests equanimity and amiability and the enjoyment of unusual good fortune. But there is one important exception: the anecdote in Plato's *Republic* in which Sophocles is represented as saying that the release from amorous desire which had come to him in his old age had been like a liberation from an insane and cruel master. He *has* balance and logic, of course: those qualities that the classicists admire; but these qualities only count because they master so much savagery and madness. Somewhere even in the fortunate Sophocles there had been a sick and raving Philoctetes.

And now let us go back to the *Philoctetes* as a parable of human character. I should interpret the fable as follows. The victim of a malodorous disease which renders him abhorrent to society and periodically degrades him and makes him helpless is also the master of a superhuman art which everybody has to respect and which the normal man finds he needs. A practical man like Odysseus, at the same time coarse-grained and clever, imagines that he can somehow get the bow without having Philoctetes on his hands or that he can kidnap Philoctetes the bowman without regard for Philoctetes the invalid.

But the young son of Achilles knows better. It is at the moment when his sympathy for Philoctetes would naturally inhibit his cheating him—so the supernatural influences in Sophocles are often made with infinite delicacy to shade into subjective motivations—it is at this moment of his natural shrinking that it becomes clear to him that the words of the seer had meant that the bow would be useless without Philoctetes himself. It is in the nature of things—of this world where the divine and the human fuse—that they cannot have the irresistible weapon without its loathsome owner, who upsets the processes of normal life by his curses and his cries, and who in any case refuses to work for men who have exiled him from their fellowship.

It is quite right that Philoctetes should refuse to come to Troy. Yet it is also decreed that he shall be cured when he shall have been able to forget his grievance and to devote his divine gifts to the service of his own people. It is right that he should refuse to submit to the purposes of Odysseus, whose only idea is to exploit him. How then is the gulf to be got over between the ineffective plight of the bowman and his proper use of his bow, between his ignominy and his destined glory? Only by the intervention of one who is guileless enough and human enough to treat him, not as a monster, nor yet as a mere magical property which is wanted for accomplishing some end, but simply as another man, whose sufferings elicit his sympathy and whose courage and pride he admires. When this human relation has been realized, it seems at first that it is to have the consequence of frustrating the purpose of the expedition and ruining the Greek campaign. Instead of winning over the outlaw, Neoptolemus has outlawed himself as well, at a time when both the boy and the cripple are desperately needed by the Greeks. Yet in taking the risk to his cause which is involved in the recognition of his common humanity with the sick man, in refusing to break his word, he dissolves Philoctetes' stubbornness, and thus cures him and sets him free, and saves the campaign as well.

RICHARD P. BLACKMUR

Richard Palmer Blackmur (1904-   ) was born in Spring-
field, Massachusetts, and lives in Princeton, New Jersey. He
was a free-lance poet and critic and a contributor to "little"
magazines before he joined the faculty at Princeton (1940)
where (since 1951) he has been a professor of English. A Guggenheim Fellow, and a member of the Institute of Advanced
Study (1944-45), he has published volumes of poetry and literary criticism.

Blackmur's criticism grows from his extraordinary capacity
for investigating language. He has written no comprehensive
ars criteria, but it is plain, from his appraisal of specific writings, that he believes the substance and the technique of
imaginative writing to be inseparable. For Blackmur, the
success of a poem lies in the degree to which its language
represents its substance. He is likely to assume the nature of
this substance—be it a fact, a condition, or a feeling—and to
press his attentions upon its articulation. He assumes that it
is the critic's reasonable responsibility to acquire and to use
any demands for knowledge that the poet makes; and his
criticisms are characteristically built around careful linguis-
tic research: the precise, and often exhaustive, analysis of
sources and frequency and usages of words, and of the way
they are put together.

One of the Mesures Lectures for 1942 at Princeton, "Language as Gesture" first appeared in *Accent,* Summer 1943; it
was then published as the title essay of a collection of studies
in poetry (1952). The text is taken from the book.

LANGUAGE AS GESTURE

IF there is a puzzle in my title, it is because, like Sweeney
with his ladies in Eliot's *Fragment of an Agon,* "I've gotta
use words when I talk to you." The puzzle is verbal, something we have made ourselves, and may be solved. Language is
made of words, and gesture is made of motion. There is one
half the puzzle. The other half is equally self-evident if only

because it is an equally familiar part of the baggage of our thought. It is the same statement put the other way round. Words are made of motion, made of action or response, at whatever remove; and gesture is made of language—made of the language beneath or beyond or alongside of the language of words. When the language of words fails we resort to the language of gesture. If we stop there, we stop with the puzzle. If we go on, and say that when the language of words most succeeds it *becomes* gesture in its words, we shall have solved the verbal puzzle with which we began by discovering one approach to the central or dead-end mystery of meaningful expression in the language of the arts. We shall have made, too, I take it, an imaginative equivalent for Kenneth Burke's more nearly intellectual thesis, which I share, that the language of poetry may be regarded as symbolic action. The difference between Mr. Burke and myself is that where he is predominantly concerned with setting up methods for analyzing the actions as they are expressed in the symbol, I choose to emphasize the created or dead-end symbol. He explores the puzzle of the language in the process of becoming symbolic. I try to show in a series of varied and progressive examples how the symbol invests the actions in language with poetic actuality. Mr. Burke legislates; I would judge; the executive is between us.

There is a line in *Othello* which I think makes it all plain between us, not just between Mr. Burke and myself, but between all of us. "I understand a fury in your words/But not the words." I do not propose this language as itself a gesture, but it is proposed as a fair example of the situation in which language gains the force of gesture; and indeed it leads to the memory of my own earliest experience of language as gesture. As a small boy of six or seven walking the streets of Cambridge I used often to pass little dead-end streets, each with its signpost which at its top read, say, Trowbridge Place or Irving Terrace, and underneath in letters of a different color and on a separate board, the following mysterious legend: Private Way Dangerous Passing. The legend meant of course merely that the City of Cambridge, since it neither built nor maintained the roadbed of this place or this terrace, would not be responsible for injury to life or property sustained through its use. But to me it meant something else. It meant that there was in passing across its mouth a clear and present danger which might, and especially if it was dusk, suddenly leap out and overcome me. Thus, to say the least of it, I had the regular experience of that heightened, that excited sense of being which we find in poetry, whenever I passed one of those signs. I understood the fury in its words, but not the words. Yet I am not sure at this late and dejected day that in understanding the words I have not become indifferent to a fury of meaning that was actually there. There was a steady over-arching gesture in those words, Dangerous Passing, which because I was included within it and indeed partly created it, meant more and touched me more deeply than any merely communicative words, deprived of their native gesture, can ever do.

For gesture *is* native to language, and if you cut it out you cut roots and get a sapless and gradually a rotting if indeed not a petrifying language. (If I may quote a poem of my own in which there was some effort to make an image for standing dead timber, what in Maine we call dri-kai, "Ghostly, these gestures are beyond repair.") But gesture is not only native to language, it comes before it in a still richer sense, and must be, as it were, carried into it whenever the context is imaginative. Living in Belmont some ten years ago I used to go into Cambridge on an orange-yellow bus which made very good time the first half of the trip. If anyone were ahead of you getting on, you might jump from ten to twenty to forty or fifty miles an hour by the time you had paid your fare and found your seat. So it was for the woman I remember one very high bright noon. She got on with a friend whom I do not remember at all except that she sat directly behind me and no doubt looked over my shoulder seeing just what I saw. But the woman herself I remember very well. She was largish and of a French figure, that is with a noticeable waist and a more noticeable rear, and she had heels too high for her balance in a spurting bus. There she stood holding the chromium rail back of the

driver's seat looking at her friend (and therefore at me) while
the driver made her change. She fair yawed to leeward every
few yards, each time knocking the great floppy hat, which
women of such figure so often wear askew, against the upright
post on which the coin box was set. She had much trouble getting the two fares in the box, and considerably more trouble
getting herself from the box down the aisle, hauling from seat
to seat by their shining handles against the momentum of the
bus, lurching, as she had to, in all directions save the right one.
During the whole business—and this is what I am getting at—
she managed by sniffs and snorts, by smiles, by sticking her
tongue out very sharp, by batting her very blue eyes about,
and generally by cocking her head this way and that, she managed to express fully, and without a single word either uttered
or wanted, the whole mixed, flourishing sense of her discon-
certment, her discomfiture, her uncertainty, together with a
sense of adventure and of gaiety, all of which she wanted to
share with her companion behind me, who took it I was sure,
as I did myself, all smiles. Because I was within the orbit of
her gestures I felt myself, as I felt her, fairly playing in life as
we say that water-lights play in the sun or moon.

That is an example of the gesture that comes before language; but reflecting upon it, it seems also an example of the
gesture which when it goes with language crowns it, and so
animates it as to make it independent of speaker or writer;
reflecting upon it, it seems that the highest use of language
cannot be made without incorporating some such quality of
gesture with it. How without it could the novelist make his
dialogue ring? how could the poet make his cry lyric, his incon-
gruity comic, or his perspective tragic? The great part of our
knowledge of life and of nature—perhaps all our knowledge of
their play and interplay—comes to us as gesture, and we are
masters of the skill of that knowledge before we can ever make
a rhyme or a pun, or even a simple sentence. Nor can we master language purposefully without re-mastering gesture within
it. Gesture, in language, is the outward and dramatic play of
inward and imaged meaning. It is that play of meaningfulness

among words which cannot be defined in the formulas in the dictionary, but which is defined in their use together; gesture is that meaningfulness which is moving, in every sense of that word: what moves the words and what moves us.

Before pursuing the means of access to the mystery of gesture in the art of poetry, let us see quickly how it behaves among the other arts. For if gesture is of such structural importance in poetry as I claim for it, then the other arts should attest for it an equivalent importance; it is in such matters that there must be a substantial unity in all art; there are not two, or three, much less seven, fundamental modes of imagination, but only one. We must use example, not argument, for we wish to remind ourselves not of formulas but of insights, and we wish to get back to poetry with our sense of gesture fortified rather than obstructed.

The clearest and most familiar example of gesture in architecture is the spire on a church, for we have all seen church spires whether we go to church or not. Bad spires weigh a church down and are an affair of carpentry rather than architecture, an example of formula stifling form. A good spire is weightless, springing, an arrow aimed at the Almighty, carrying in its gesture the whole church with it. Though it may have been as much made out of formula as the bad spire, it differs in that the formula has somehow seized enough life to become form again; which is one way of saying what gesture does in art—it is what happens to a form when it becomes identical with its subject. It does this, in the case of a spire, by giving the sense of movement, of aspiration, as a tree or a shrub gives the sense of process of growth, or as a beautiful room gives the effect of extending space rather than enclosing it. This sense of movement in "actually" inert mass and empty space is what we call gesture in architecture. So, too, we feel that pillars are mighty, that a bridge spans or leaps, that a dome covers us, or a crypt appalls us.

In sculpture we have much the same situation as in architecture except that the effects are more specifically human in character; for in sculpture we arrest or fix in physical mass and space those human or animal movements, or those essential shapes of body or object, which, arrested, move within themselves, whether from inward outward or outward inward, so as to make a timeless gesture. Here we get the difference between gesture and act. In bad sculpture, what bores us and annoys us and makes us feel that we are bumping our heads against stones, is the sense that the athlete wants to leap or that the horse is about to canter, or whatever it is; the arrested movement wants to go on and complete itself in action. In good sculpture there is none of this, but rather that in the movement arrested, in the moving stillness, there is a gesture completed at the moment of its greatest significance. Examples in sculpture are easy, as in architecture, but less conspicuous. A good vase shows all the gesture value of roundness; a good nude by Maillol or Lehmbruck or Lachaise gives a deep gesture of the body in some moment of meaningful balance. Let us say that good sculpture has a heaviness or lightness which has nothing to do with stone or wood or the carver's trade, but which has everything to do with the gesture which illumines the medium. It is gesture that makes a stone figure a sphinx, and it is gesture that makes the great Sphinx a smile. By which I mean that there is great momentum in great repose and inexhaustible meaningfulness in any image that makes the gesture, as the sphinx does, of the momentum and the repose in man's brooding upon himself. Sculpture is man breeding shapes out of his brooding.

Painting may combine the effect of the gestures in both sculpture and architecture, since it represents the feeling of physical mass and space, but it does so at a remove. The true play of meaning in painting lies rather in what it does with texture, with light, and especially with what it does with our great, and otherwise ineluctable, visual knowledge of human character. No knowledge is so great or so skilled and no knowledge has been so variously felt as our knowledge of what, literally, we *see* in people. But in our knowledges there is none, too, in which we so fumble when we try to say what we know as in this visual knowledge, except when we use the mode of imaginative painting in the field of the portrait or of figure painting. I think, to reach for things at hand, of Rembrandt's Polish Rider, in the Frick galleries, with all its golden gloom and the light gathering against the rider's face, or, in the same galleries, of Titian's young man in ermine alive in old air—both so full of that maximum human dignity, that rightness and fullness of being, of which no man, seen, can be deprived. Or again there are the portraits of El Greco, brimming, as Marianne Moore's poem says, with inner light—the portrait of the Cardinal in the Metropolitan or that of Brother Felix in the Boston Museum; haunted faces both, haunted with that spiritual life beyond dignity which the flesh cannot ever attain in fact but which is sometimes reached as a gesture of light in eyes and features. How does a painter come by such effects? Look at a society portrait, a prettified portrait, an official portrait—all faithful enough to their sitters; all too faithful, precisely—and is it not plain that their great lack, their yawning vacuity, the almost visible yawn of suppressed inattention, comes about because the painter has rendered them as the average of a long series of unresponsive moments. Nothing is left out but the vital gesture of the single, focal moment, the gesture of some particular state, some long perspective—say the lifelong heaviness of the head upon its little fulcrum—some deep inspiration of the flesh, say the desire *in weariness* for rest, or even, say, just the gaiety and radiance of the features in play with life; nothing is left out but what the great portrait painter puts in: some caught or imagined gesture of awareness that startles the features into a maximum life. The painter puts into his portraits the crossed gesture of knowledge and mystery, of the intolerably familiar and the impossibly alien, which we see in the looking-glass. That is why in great portraits we see ourselves.

In dancing we would seem to have the art that is most directly concerned with gesture, for when the gesture breaks down or does not communicate, the dance does not speak at all. Put the other way around, this means that the gesture in ballet must be built up and infused into what is otherwise "mere" movement. Gesture is what makes dancing buoyant and what makes it possible for it to end. Without gesture there cannot be a beginning or a middle or an end to dance. Gesture is the means through which the movements of the dance complete themselves, and for these movements to become gesture they usually require ritual (as in the Mass), or music (as in the ballet) for both source and background. I think of a rehearsal of one of the ballets based on Mozart where all was dead cluttering movement until Balanchine, by his single example, brought the movements into tune with the music and so made them suddenly into gesture. Again to revert to the Mass, we have the nature of the ritual itself (consecration, sacrifice, communion) determining the scope of the gesture, and on the other hand we reflect that it is the gesture (the posture of prayer, the elevation of the host, the service of the cup and wafer) which transforms the "mere" movements into ritual. Gesture is perhaps the stable *and* moving element in ritual; it is both what is autochthonous—reborn out of the native soil of feeling—and what is autonomous—and independently controls the meaningfulness in ritual. Still again, and not actually far afield, there is Nijinski's remark that it is the costumes of a ballet that determine what the gestures shall be, as the cut of one's cloth determines one's stride; but it is in turn the gestures of the dancers that bring the costumes, or the nakedness, of the bodies to life. Dancing *delivers* gestures otherwise conceived. It is the natural wayward play of the body, controlled.

Control is the key word with regard to gesture in acting, too, and in much the same senses as in dancing; it is the purposive, conventional control of the body's movements that produces meaningful gesture. Or perhaps we should say that it is a kind of reduction, condensation, telescoping, of free instinctive movements that transforms them into residual gestures, almost as closely ordained as the gestures in ritual. Historically, we can remind ourselves, what we call play-acting came out of dumb-show, which was conventionalized mimicry—in short, mummery. Mummery is what the actor calls on apart from his lines when he is making appropriate gestures, and what he calls on in spite of his lines when he is making bad gestures. Of course, as a matter of practice we seldom get familiar enough with a particular version of even a play of Shakespeare to be able to divorce the mummery of it from the lines, but if we could I think we should find that mummery alone is an extraordinarily resourceful and complex art, using the full personality of the actor, rising often through a great span of gesture. Our nearest approach is with a good actor making the best out of bad lines, an affair which, unless we are ourselves mummers, we enjoy apologetically. I recall once having seen Tolstoy's *Living Corpse*, a play which I had not read, produced in German, a language I do not know, with the lead acted by Alessandro Moissi, an actor with whose reputation I was at that time unfamiliar, and in conditions that were hardly propitious: with a straggling handful for audience in the great barn of the Boston Opera House. Yet the experience of the evening proved the case far more than seeing Bernhardt or Duse or Mantell or the Barrymores ever did. For what I saw and heard was nothing but the mummer at his work with movement and posture and voice; the words of the play were transparencies used to time and to bound the acting. What the mere words were, it seemed to me, must have been rubbish; they were so little needed in the face of the fast conventions of voice and movement, conventions that must have been universal to western man since I understood them so well, through which Moissi worked from beauty to lucid beauty of created gesture. The gamut of the actor showed as great as that of any art just because my attention was fastened upon it by being excluded from anything else. Yet I knew at the time that what I felt was good for training short of complete experience; I felt the effect of supreme control without feeling all the controlling force. I missed what the lines of the play called upon Moissi to create; but at least I learned why poor actors ruin the best plays: they have not the knowledge within them which can be called into play. How can a man understand the play of light who has not felt the sun aching in his bones? And how, similarly, can an actor understand the play of words unless they

seem to rise and set within him as his own meaning? Great
acting bodies forth the gestures only of great words: no more.

It is music that of all the arts does more. Like pure acting
its medium may be thought of as entirely in time as time is
filled with sound. It is purer than acting because all its movement is movement of sound. But its greatest purity lies in the
fact that, although other arts may use some of its effects, it
alone of the arts can proceed according to its own purpose
without either anterior or subsequent obligation to any other
art. Roger Sessions, in the essay which he contributed to *The
Intent of the Artist*, says that the purpose of music is to create
gestures of the human spirit, and as my argument is on this
point only a lesser version of his I refer you to it for the completion and confirmation of my own. But I will say this. I do
not know what constitutes the discipline of music from a composer's point of view, except that I am sure it is severe, yet I
feel as a layman that the freedom which that discipline secures
is the freedom of repetition, of development, of variation
within or upon or around a theme to an extent which in any
other major art would be not only ineffectual but boring: the
freedom, in short, to play with the elements of musical meaning until they become gesture. This is no doubt why Pater
said that all the arts tend to the condition of music; the condition is gesture. The rest of music is but the means for the
delivery of gesture, and for the artist who rejoices at all in his
work that is the most blessed circumstance possible to imagine.
It is tantamount to saying that his means—his technique—may
become almost the whole object of attention, both for himself
and for his audience. It is not his theme, once he has it, but
what happens to his theme, that counts; and what happens to
it will be precisely and immitigably what he does within his
means. His form and his substance will be united in process
as well as at the end: united as gesture. No wonder we are
happy when we sing and sing when we are sad. The other arts
take us in parts, and give us roles to play with ourselves looking on; music takes us all round, gesture without remove.

So with gesture in the six arts of which poetry is surely the

natural child, as it shows variously the stigmata of all six and
yet makes a fiery gesture all its own. It is the gesture, I like to
think, of poetic judgment, the judgment of all the gestures, all
the play of meaning, which makes up full being. Poetry is the
meaning of meaning, or at least the prophecy of it. "Behold,
all ye that kindle a fire, that compass yourselves about with
sparks: walk in the light of your fire, and in the sparks that
ye have kindled." In these words of Isaiah there is a motto for
poetry, a judgment of poetry, and a poetic gesture which carries the prophetic meaning of poetry. The words sound with
music, make images which are visual, seem solid like sculpture
and spacious like architecture, repeat themselves like the movements in a dance, call for a kind of mummery in the voice
when read, and turn themselves like nothing but the written
word. Yet is the fury in the words which we understand, and
not the words themselves. Let them serve as text for the rest
of these remarks; for with them to buoy us up we can start on
as low a level as we like.

That is the level of the writer who finds himself inarticulate
because, as he thinks, the words in his pen are not as viable as
the words in his mouth. He says in explanation of why he cannot write—at least one such writer said to me not long ago—
"The trouble is I don't have the benefit of gesture in writing—
or of inflection either." He is wrong; his trouble is that he has
put himself in the position of the stenographer, and what he
wants is what the stenographer cannot take down—on the one
hand rhythm and cadence and interval, the gestures of the
voice that speaks, and on the other hand the look and feel and
movement of the man while speaking, whatever is necessary to
render what we may call the whole gesture of the scene. What
he has to do is to forget the whole theory of stenography or reporting and make the words of his pen do not only what the
words of his mouth did, but also, and most of all, what they
failed to do at those crucial moments when he went off into
physical gesture with face and hands and vocal gesture in shifting inflections. And he must do this by making his written
words sound in the inward ear of his reader, and so play upon

each other by concert and opposition and pattern that they not only drag after them the gestures of life but produce a new gesture of their own. To make words play upon each other both in small units and large is one version of the whole technique of imaginative writing. Since what is being played with is meanings and congeries of meanings, what is wanted cannot be articulated in a formula, but on the other hand it cannot be articulated at all except when delivered within a form. The point is that contrary to the general view there are relatively few formulas and relatively many forms; exactly as many as there are gestures to require them; and for forms there are many rules of thumb. Let us look at a few where the means are small enough to handle.

In a sense any word or congeries of words can be pushed to the condition of gesture either by simple repetition or by a combination of repetition and varied preparation. Macbeth's "Tomorrow and tomorrow and tomorrow," or Lear's "Never never never never," would seem good immediate examples of simple repetition metamorphosing the most familiar words into the most engulfing gesture. To emphasize what has happened in these lines, and to indicate how words sometimes get out of mere verbal meaning when they become gesture, it may be suggested that Macbeth might have said Today and today and today, and Lear said, Always, always always always always, and much the same effect have transpired in either case. It is not at all the meaning the words *had* that counts, but the meaning that repetition, in a given situation, makes them take on. The repetition of the word "will" in the will sonnets, and also all the words that rhyme with will, does much the same thing; the resultant meaning has nothing to do with will, but is an obsessive gesture of Shakespeare the man himself, made out of the single iterated syllable intensified into a half-throttled cry.

A more complex and quite different type of repetition offers itself in Iago's exhortation to Roderigo to leave off thinking of suicide and take up thinking again of Desdemona. I truncate the passage somewhat for the production purposes of these remarks.

"Put money in thy purse; follow thou the wars; defeat thy favour with an usurped beard; I say, put money in thy purse. It cannot be that Desdemona should long continue her love to the Moor—put money in thy purse—nor he his to her: it was a violent commencement, and thou shalt see an unanswerable sequestration; put money in thy purse. These Moors are changeable in their wills:—fill thy purse with money. . . . She must change for youth: when she is sated with his body, she will find the error of her choice: she must have a change, she must: therefore put money in thy purse. If thou wilt needs damn thyself, do it a more delicate way than drowning. Make all the money thou canst: if sanctimony and a frail vow betwixt an erring barbarian and a supersubtle Venetian be not too hard for my wits and all the tribe of Hell, thou shalt enjoy her; therefore make money." . . .

Roderigo questions him. "Wilt thou be fast to my hopes, if I depend on the issue?" and Iago resumes his charge.

"Thou art sure of me: go, make money: I have told thee often, and I re-tell thee again and again, I hate the Moor: my cause is hearted; thine hath no less reason. . . . There are many events in the womb of time, which will be delivered. Traverse; go; provide thy money."

Roderigo as he makes his exit says, "I am changed: I'll go sell all my land," and looking after him Iago begins, "Thus do I ever make my fool my purse."

So we see poor Roderigo bought and sold, bought cheap and sold dear, put on change and quite sold out, half a dozen ways at once, and always in terms of the iterated and focusing phrase, "Put money in thy purse," and the changes rung upon it. Roderigo is indeed a changed man in every sense of the word, and the dark, unclean, unconscious, equivocal nature of that change is made clearer and clearer, brought to a light of its own by Iago's phrase. Unlike the simple syllabic repetitions of Lear and Macbeth, Iago's phrase could not be altered without altering the gesture; it is rather that the material that comes between the different iterations could have been altered to almost anything else providing only that they followed the same general line. As Kenneth Burke remarked, money is a neutral symbol capable of bringing meaningful action into any situation. Money is in this situation the symbol of stored evil, and by rehearsing it Shakespeare has released the gesture of the evil.

In Hamlet's best-known soliloquy there is a passage in which the repetition of two words similarly draws upon the reservoir of chthonic meaning but with a different effect upon the words themselves:

> To die: to sleep;
> No more; and by a sleep to say we end
> The heartache, and the thousand natural shocks
> That flesh is heir to, 'tis a consummation
> Devoutly to be wish'd. To die, to sleep;
> To sleep: perchance to dream; aye, there's the rub;
> For in that sleep of death what dreams may come,
> When we have shuffled off this mortal coil,
> Must give us pause.

Here it is the context that determines the meaningfulness that the words *die* and *sleep* and their variants take on in the process of becoming gesture; but once determined, that meaningfulness, that over-arching gesture, carries on through the rest of the soliloquy and beyond, into Hamlet's answer to Ophelia's query how he is: "I humbly thank you: well, well, well," which as gesture moves us to other than the literal sense. It is all the ill of doubt and trepidation before the unknown prospect which the words "to die: to sleep" release as gesture, which in turn infect the triple, mutilating repetition: "Well, well, well."

But we should put this playing upon the meanings of sleep and death over against another kind of playing, this time from *Macbeth*, on the same words, where all the repetition comes at the beginning and is only implied, in the played-upon sense, through the rest of the passage.

> Methought I heard a voice cry, "Sleep no more
> Macbeth does murder sleep!" the innocent sleep,
> Sleep that knits up the ravell'd sleave of care,

> The death of each day's life, sore labour's bath,
> Balm of hurt minds, great nature's second course.
> Chief nourisher in life's feast.

Where Hamlet's play of gesture was toward condensation, a focusing of the gesture into action, a gesture invading the very plot of the play itself, in the lines from *Macbeth* the context only suggests the gesture and provides it a means to invoke an escape from the context of the action, and sets it, in its little freed world of words, to creating other gestures in the last four phrases, which themselves both play upon each other and all backwards upon sleep. Sore labour plays upon hurt minds, and great nature's second course (meaning a second round or lap in the sense of movement) plays upon the other sense of *course* in connection with life's feast, and life's feast plays directly back upon the death of each day's life: itself sleep, which has already been murdered by Macbeth. What we have here is part prayer and part imprecation, with gesture invoking its substance: the substance of what is lacking and cannot, except in the form of prayer, be had.

What these two passages do in common—and it is their most remarkable deed—is by the power of discovered or invoked gesture to transform the simple name of sleep into a rich and complex symbol. In a large way we are familiar with such metamorphoses in the titles of poems or plays or in the names of great imaginative figures, or sometimes—though very rarely —in the names of particular authors and artists. All the gestures in *Hamlet* combine to make a symbol which has become, with each fresh use, the more inexhaustible and the more complex; so much that we do not need to ask, when we say Hamlet, whether we mean the play as a whole or the figure of a man resolving the agony of doubt in gestures. So with Macbeth and Anna Karenina and Raskolnikov and Don Quixote; and so too with Villon and Dante and Michelangelo and Plato and Baudelaire and Poe. It is the same operation in a small way that we have been watching in the two passages about sleep: the creation of symbols. A symbol, I take it, is what we use to express meaningfulness in a permanent way which cannot be expressed in direct words or formulas of words with any completeness; a symbol is a cumulus of meaning which, once established, attracts further meanings to it until, overloaded, it collapses. The making of symbols is a steady occupation for minds at all aware, and they are especially the objects in which meaning is shared and transmitted by those who have life in common, by lovers, friends, and that version of society which we think of as fellowship. Gestures are the first steps toward the making of symbols, and those symbols which endure are the residuary legatees of the meanings earned through gesture. Returning to our passages about sleep it is only the accident that they are a little too long to be said all at once that has kept them as gestures only, just as, on the same argument, it is their brevity more than their residual possibilities that has made actual symbols out of "The rest is silence," or "Ripeness is all," or "Flesh is grass," quite independent of their original contexts in *Hamlet* and *Lear* and *Isaiah*.

Let us take next what at first appears an even smaller context of effort than the repetition of words or phrases, namely the effort to make one word act like another, or several; that is, punning. Rhyme, which is the terminal form of punning, and alliteration, which is the initial form of punning, are the commonest uses of this mode of language and are of course the most effective to the widest audience, since they deal, on the surface, entirely with the sounds of the words played on: what we know without thought and cannot know better no matter how much thought we take. That rhyme and alliteration have other uses is not questioned; I merely want to emphasize how primitive and how pervasive is the pun in poetry. It is, taken in its fullest gamut as gesture (for any achieved pun is a gesture), the only direct avenue to undifferentiated sense that the poet has; it is what objectively joins the perceptions of the different senses together, heightening them into a single sensation. Not only that, but it also—and this is our chosen nexus—produces an undifferentiated gesture of meaning; under masterly hands punning is the onomatopoeia of meaning. Which is to say that the play upon words is both the most immediate and most final congeries of signs; it is the very gesture which identifies the elements of the sound with the elements of meaning.

Let us take three examples from Shakespeare, all short. The first centers in a single word spoken by Horatio to Hamlet. He says that the ghost had appeared two nights together "In the dead vast and middle of the night." *Vast* is of course the focal word, and it should be said at once that it appears in this form only in the first Quarto. In the second Quarto and the first Folio it was *wast,* and in the second, third and fourth folios it was *waste.* My contention (which I borrow in part from Empson in his *Seven Types of Ambiguity*) is that no matter which way the word is printed the effect of all three is evident and felt, with a strong possibility of a fourth sense, that of *waist,* as well. The accident of the recorded variations in printing forces the attention upon the variety of meanings bedded down to sleep in this single syllable. Let us read the line in the middle spelling: "In the dead wast and middle of the night," and do we not have all at once in the word the sense of the vast void of the night, the stretching and useless waste of the night, and the waist or middle and generative part of the night as well? And do we not have, finally, a kind of undifferentiated meaning which is a product of all three, a gesture of meaning which can only be less defined the more deeply it is experienced?

The second example is still shorter than the first and requires almost no exposition. There is a line in *Macbeth,* when murder is all acanter in the offing, which images "in his surcease, success." So far as the sound goes the words vary only enough to permit sharp play among them, but so far as the literal meaning goes there is almost direct contradiction, yet in the gesture or play which the two make together there is a new meaningfulness that could not be produced without the play. *Success* is so to speak the cadence that falls from *and* rounds out *surcease;* and with an evil omen in it unknown to the speaker.

The third example is from one of the sonnets most nearly packed with similar play of meaning ("The expense of spirit in a waste of shame"), but from which I take only the most obvious play. Speaking of lust, the poet says it is:

> Past reason hunted, and no sooner had,
> Past reason hated.

Reading these lines, the play of meaning between *hunted* and *hated* so grows upon me that I cannot help thinking somewhere between the two, as a kind of backward consequence, of the poet as past reason *haunted* as well, for that is what the whole sonnet gives as gesture out of the focus of the phrases quoted. Surely one is haunted by what one both hunts and hates.

To bring the three examples together, can we not say that the gesture of these plays upon and within words constitutes the revelation of the *sum* or *product* of all the meanings possible within the focus of the words played upon, even though we did not know what all those meanings were? Language as gesture creates meaning as conscience creates judgment, by feeling the pang, the inner bite, of things forced together.

Here is a good place to introduce, for relief from too high a tone, a conspicuous example of the superficially frivolous intellectual onomatopoeia. It is the first two lines from Wallace Stevens' poem, "Bantams in Pine-Woods," and conceals nothing which it does not also disclose.

> Chieftain Iffucan of Azcan in caftan
> Of tan with henna hackles, halt!

I should say that this was a maximum case of alliteration and rhyme taken as pun, and pun both of sound and meaning, for the sound of the lines presses into meaning and the meaning is pressed into sound. There is a kind of close roistering in the syllables, with such yelping at the heels of meaning and such a hullabaloo of meaning in the sound, which prevents one from knowing what is going on except in such a double and darting image as drunkards delight to see. More seriously we can say that these lines are an example of words which, by being momentarily deprived of their normal meanings, tend to become gesture, just as words which temporarily go beyond their nor-

mal meanings, such as the word *geo-politics* today, also tend
to become gesture. That Stevens should practice such examples,
and that we should delight in them, is altogether natural. The
whole movement in the arts known progressively as dadaism
and surrealism was devoted, in its poetry, to releasing such
gestures from language by the deliberate obliteration of the
normal modes of meaning from the context. The difference between Stevens and the surrealists is that Stevens writes his
words in such a way that they are able to resume their natural
modes so soon as the gesture is released. So with Eliot in such
lines as "I should have been a pair of ragged claws, scuttling
across the floors of silent seas," and so Shakespeare's "miching
mallecho," which the glossary says means mouching mischief,
but which means miching mallecho just the same. The Queen
was much better informed than the glossary, when she said to
Hamlet with regard to the invoked ghost:

> This is the very coinage of your brain:
> This bodiless creation ecstasy
> Is very cunning in.

The poet is likely to make his purest though not his profoundest gestures when most beside himself. If words fail they
must serve just the same. Transformed into gesture, they carry
the load, wield the load, lighten the load, and leap beyond the
load of meaning.

But in this carrying, wielding, lightening, and leaping there
are abler agents than that uncovered by the resort to nonsense;
abler because, once mastered, they are always reliable. I mean
such formal agents as plot and meter and refrain. Plot is too
large an order to discuss here, but it may be said that it is the
stress and urgency of plot that determine *what* gestures are
wanted and by its exigencies *when* they shall be released. Plot
does in a large way pretty much the same sort of thing that
meter and refrain do in the small; and if we cannot see infin-
ity in the palm of the hand and eternity in an hour, we shall
not see them at all.

Coleridge defined meter as the motion of meaning, and ac-

cepting that we must also for our present purposes turn it
around and say that motion is the meter of meaning. That is,
if meter as motion brings meaning to gesture, then motion as
meter moors gesture to meaning. There is a mutual tying-down
process, in the operation of meter, a strict and precise delivery
of detail in an order of movement, which, well used, gives a
sense of absolute speed and absolute position otherwise un-
available to the poet. Where would "Tiger tiger burning
bright/ In the forest of the night" be if its wild syllables and
wilder insights were not measured out in an expected, a con-
ventionally recognizable, order? But on the other hand where
would the speed of the meter be if it were not both initially
and finally established by the movement to and from gesture
that the words make? These are questions that could have been
asked of every quotation we have dealt with, including those
in prose, for there is a pattern to the rhythm of prose which
has much the same function as meter in verse.

Refrain, like meter, has to do with the ordering of perceptions, and in that sense we may say that refrain is a means of
emphatic ordering; but it is more than that, it modifies meaning itself by giving to gesture a conventional form. Refrain, or
nearly identical repetition, gives particular form, on a general
and dependable model, to gesture that might otherwise be
formless. Refrain is the emphatic measure of all those gestures
that have to do with the declaration of recurrence, return, re-
birth and new birth, of motion in stillness and stillness in motion, of permanence in change, and change in permanence. It
is the lyric gesture of recognition and the emphatic gesture of
identity. The ballads are full of it and the songbooks, whether
Elizabethan or cowboy or the latest collection of popular
catches. I choose as free examples, Greene's "Weep not, my
wanton, smile upon my knee," which upon its last recurrence
identifies with the substance of the poem, and Spenser's "Sweet
Thames! runne softly, till I end my Song," which makes a gesture of inclusiveness for all that mounts up to it, and Dun-
bar's "Timor mortis conturbat me," which in every repetition
makes the gesture of focus. A more deliberate example where

the refrain is used to modify the meaning backward and forward, would be Yeat's double refrain in "Crazy Jane and the Bishop." I give together the two lines that come four lines apart: "All find safety in the tomb/ The solid man and the coxcomb." Better still is the refrain in "Crazy Jane on God," for the effect of its developing action in recurrence can be briefly abstracted. The first stanza ends, "Men come, men go; *all things remain in God*," the second emphasizes the same image, and the third contrasts it. The fourth stanza reads:

> I had wild Jack for a lover;
> Though like a road
> That men pass over
> My body makes no moan
> But sings on:
> *All things remain in God.*

Thus we see by the use of refrain insight become deepening gesture.

But refrain is a mere instrument or aid to order, and will flatten a poem like a burden if it is not constantly refreshed from the common resources of language itself. Let us end, then, with brief examinations of three examples, of which the first two are determined partly by the critical words themselves and partly by the order in which they occur, and of which the third makes a pretty complete use of all the devices of lyric poetry, including all those here discussed. The first is from *Hamlet,* and is found in the dialogue between Hamlet and Horatio, just before they go in for the final duel. The passage is in prose.

> Hor.   You will lose this wager, my lord.
> Ham.   I do not think so; since he went into France,
> I have been in continual practice; I shall win
> at the odds.
> But thou wouldst not think how ill all's here
> about my heart: but it is no matter.

"But thou wouldst not think how ill all's here about my heart." Do not these words rise from what is past and fall toward what is coming, and both rise and fall as a gesture, almost his last, out of Hamlet himself? We see how order and cadence and the ear of the poet give the actor all that he has to do except that most arduous thing, put the gesture in the words into the gesture of his mere voice and body.

The second example is from *Othello*. Othello is at swords' points with himself over Desdemona's teasing request for him to make up his quarrel with Cassio, and has just dismissed her. Looking after her he exclaims:

> Excellent wretch! Perdition catch my soul,
> But I do love thee! and when I love thee not,
> Chaos is come again.

Here in the order both of the plot and of the lines, and in the fall of the plot and of the lines, too, the word *chaos* acts to pull into the context a whole realm of being not otherwise present. Shakespeare had undoubtedly re-made this line from its earlier version of *Venus and Adonis,* where "Black chaos comes again when beauty is dead," and he had probably in both instances the Graeco-Latin sense of chaos in mind; the yawning gulf or gap, the abyss of night, the original dark, as well as the sense of disorder and formlessness; both senses were Elizabethan. We have thus the gesture of invoked prophecy made actual in the gesture of a word. The mere actor can do no more than leave it alone to act itself.

Our third example does not envisage an actor and could not use one, if even the best offered, for more than its merely immediate effects; its major effects transpire only in the inward ear. It is a poem which, using alliteration and rhyme and meter and refrain, using symbol and making symbol, playing upon its words as it runs, escapes all the mere meaning in words and reaches the pure meaningfulness of gesture. You can do with it whatever you will, for with poems of this order all things are possible. It is Yeats' "I am of Ireland."

> '*I am of Ireland,*
> *And the Holy Land of Ireland,*
> *And time runs on,' cried she.*
> '*Come out of charity,*
> *Come dance with me in Ireland.*'

One man, one man alone
In that outlandish gear,
One solitary man
Of all that rambled there
Had turned his stately head.
'That is a long way off,
And time runs on,' he said,
'And the night grows rough.'

'I am of Ireland,
And the Holy Land of Ireland,
And time runs on,' cried she.
'Come out of charity
And dance with me in Ireland.'

'The fiddlers are all thumbs,
Or the fiddle-string accursed,
The drums and the kettledrums
And the trumpets all are burst,
And the trombone,' cried he,
'The trumpet and trombone,'
And cocked a malicious eye,
'But time runs on, runs on.'

'I am of Ireland,
And the Holy Land of Ireland,
And time runs on,' cried she.
'Come out of charity
And dance with me in Ireland.'

With this poem as evidence I think it may be said in conclusion that we feel almost everything that deeply stirs us as if it were a gesture, the gesture of our uncreated selves. Thus as artists we would create great gestures; and if we most often fail to do so, it is because, as Shakespeare says, "The deep of night is crept upon our talk," which is a gesture that must overwhelm us even though we realize as we consent to it, that we have made it ourselves.